RADIO FREE EUROPE

~ ~ *radio free* Europe

by ROBERT T. HOLT

UNIVERSITY OF MINNESOTA PRESS
Minneapolis

For Shirley

Acknowledgments

A GREAT number of debts have been incurred in preparing this book. My greatest debt is to the men and women of Radio Free Europe. I owe much to Joseph C. Grew, President of the Free Europe Committee, the late W. J. Convery Egan, former Director of RFE, and Richard Condon, the European Director of RFE when this study was undertaken. These men gave generously of their time and encouraged their subordinates to cooperate with me. There are a number of other people in RFE who must also be mentioned as giving me valuable aid and information. In Munich, I owe special thanks to William E. Griffith, Political Adviser, and Allan Michie, former Deputy European Director, through whom I first became acquainted with the organization. Other people in Munich who were particularly helpful include Frank Abbott, Fredrick A. Bell, Julius Firth, Talcott Hood, Jan Novak, Andre Rhoades (now with the Crusade for Freedom), Robert Sorenson, and John Wright. In the New York headquarters I spent many hours discussing the organization and its problems with John Dunning. Without his cooperation this book could never have been written. R. S. Nathan also gave freely of his time to discuss his specialty with me.

My colleagues in the psychological warfare staff, G-3, USAREUR (United States Army Europe), in 1954 and 1955, have also made a contribution to this study. I want to thank Major Harrison Youngren particularly, for helping me to make the initial contacts with RFE. Some of the ideas developed in this book were originally discussed with James B. Adler, William A. DePree, and H. W. Spanley. Mr. Adler has also read and criticized the manuscript.

Professors Harwood Childs and Harold Sprout of Princeton University and John Turner of the University of Minnesota have also read the manuscript, and its final form shows the impact of their criticism.

The Graduate School at the University of Minnesota provided a grant which enabled me to undertake the research that forms the basis for Chapter 10.

I would also like to extend my special thanks to Fräulein Gabriella Kempf, who provided much needed aid while I was in Munich; to Mrs. Mary McLaughlin, who typed one draft of the manuscript; and to Miss Lois Sovereign, who aided me with the index.

It is understood, of course, that I am solely responsible for the entire book. It is particularly important to emphasize this point in relation to the people in RFE mentioned above. Although they cooperated with this study, it is in no sense an "official" study of the organization. Indeed, some of those who discussed the organization and its problems with me might well disagree with the conclusions I have drawn.

Finally, I would like to recognize the support, both substantive and moral, that my wife has given me. The dedication of this book is only a small indication of the contribution that she has made.

Preface

At the end of the Second World War the United States confidently expected that the downfall of the Nazi tyranny in eastern Europe would give the peoples in that part of the world an opportunity to establish free and independent governments. That expectation was not fulfilled. Hard on the heels of the Nazi retreat came a new conqueror and a new oppression. The Soviet domination of eastern Europe has presented the United States with a most frustrating situation. As deeply as it was committed to the freedom of the captive peoples, there seemed little that the United States could do to relieve their plight short of an unthinkable war of liberation.

In 1949 a private organization, the Free Europe Committee, was created to do a number of things that an official governmental agency would find difficult if not impossible to undertake. This book is a study of its oldest and most important division, Radio Free Europe. It describes its organizational structure and how it operates, discusses its large-scale propaganda campaigns from 1953 until 1957, and evaluates its "unofficial" participation in the cold war. The relevant dates must be emphasized. The description of the structure and functioning of the organization applies to the years during which the propaganda campaigns discussed and analyzed were undertaken—from the Berlin riots in June 1953 through the Hungarian uprising in November 1956 and its immediate aftermath. After the manuscript was completed and I had only occasional contacts with RFE, a number of changes took place in organization and personnel. These changes should be brought to the reader's attention not because they would significantly affect the central problems discussed, but for reasons of accuracy and fairness to RFE it is necessary to point out that in several places the present tense has been used where the past would be more appropriate.

Radio Free Europe

Among the recent changes in personnel, several are significant enough to mention. In the fall of 1957 W. J. Convery Egan, who for over two years had been Director of Radio Free Europe, passed away suddenly from a heart attack. Following his untimely death, Thomas H. Brown, Jr., the Deputy Director, became Acting Director. Also in 1957 Richard Condon, who had been the European Director since the early days of RFE, left his position in Munich to join the staff of the President of the Free Europe Committee and Allan Michie resigned his position as Deputy European Director. Eric Hazelhoff succeeded Mr. Michie as Deputy European Director and as this book went to press was serving as Acting European Director.

These changes in personnel brought men with different skills into top executive positions and helped contribute to modifications in certain roles. For example, the description of the functions of the European Director on page 37 applies to Mr. Condon in that role but not to Mr. Hazelhoff. Propaganda content guidance and major matters of program guidance in the book are reported to move along a "technical chain of command" from the New York headquarters directly to the political adviser and program manager in Munich, by-passing the European Director. Mr. Hazelhoff, however, receives these communications directly and spends a considerable amount of time studying them and discussing them by teletype, telephone, and letter with New York and in frequent meetings with the top program and policy people (including the desk chiefs) in Munich. In short, he plays a central role in the policy-making process.

A number of changes have also been made in organizational structure. In 1958 a Program Analysis Unit attached directly to the Director's office was established in Munich to review certain programs at the time they are relayed from Munich to the transmitters in Lisbon and Biblis. The chief purpose of this unit is to provide for a constructive review of political programs, but it provides an additional element in the system of control discussed on pages 41–42 and 63.

There were also some significant changes made in the position of the various language desks in Munich in the latter months of 1957. The role of deputy program manager attached to the various language desks as described on page 77 no longer exists. More importantly, the desk chiefs now report directly to the European Director instead of to the program manager. Since I am unable to go to Munich to investigate just how this works out in practice, let me only remark that the organizational charts on pages 31, 34, and 36 and the discussion of them present a picture of the position of the desks in the organization which was changed in late 1957.

Other changes in organization include a modification in the position of the Central Newsroom in Munich (see pages 106–108) that facilitates more integration with the programing desks. It should also be pointed out that the increases in the personnel assigned to the Audience Analysis Section have enabled its director to apply more sophisticated techniques of research to the measurement of effectiveness than was possible for him to do with the limited resources available to him when this study was undertaken.

In addition to these changes in organization and personnel there have been some important modifications in the system of policy guidances described on pages 38–40 that should be discussed in some detail.

First, the *Policy Handbook* is being largely replaced by basic guidances which are developed individually for each of the target countries.

Second, the policy guidances that were formerly prepared following events of major importance to RFE's activities (these guidances are discussed on page 39) no longer exist in any form. They are strictly of historical interest, but it is important to point out that they were the major form of guidance employed during the campaigns discussed in this book.

Third, and most important, there is a new element in the picture. The major form of guidance since April 1957 has been a Weekly Directive. The name itself implies an important change. The "directives" have more binding force than did the "guidances." However, they are also prepared in a different manner. Guidances were usually produced by one American working largely by himself. The Weekly Directive is drafted in New York. While it is being reviewed by the executives and desk heads in New York, a draft is teletyped to Munich where the European Director, his top advisers and desk chiefs study it and propose changes if they so desire. When New York and Munich agree on the text, it is issued as a "directive" over the name of the Director of RFE.

The appearance of the Weekly Directive does not only affect the systems of policy guidance in the narrow sense, but it also modifies the nature of the relationships between the New York Headquarters and the Munich field operation as discussed on pages 38–42. Munich does not now have the autonomy that it once had, but what it has given up in autonomy it has gained in participating more directly in the development of top level, binding policy. The effect of the Weekly Directive appears to be that of bringing about more integration and coordination between New York and Munich.

One further change should be mentioned. In a number of places in the text the balloon-leaflet operations of the Free Europe Committee are referred to. In the autumn of 1956 all balloon launchings were suspended and have not been resumed to any country since that time.

Prefaces are usually the last part of a book to be written. To the reader who has struggled this far through the preface and is maybe somewhat baffled by the detailed references to passages he has not yet read, might I say that not only has this preface been written last, it should perhaps also be read last. Particularly, the reader who is interested in the organizational problems involved in conducting a large-scale international propaganda operation would benefit by reading this preface after completing the text of the book.

Minneapolis
March 10, 1958

Table of Contents

RADIO FREE EUROPE

Introduction

R ADIO Free Europe was established by a group of private citizens in December 1949, for the purpose of conducting a propaganda campaign against six Communist-dominated satellites in central and eastern Europe. It first went on the air seven months later with a small seven-and-one-half kilowatt transmitter located at Biblis, near Frankfurt, in West Germany. Its program consisted of daily half-hour broadcasts, first to Czechoslovakia and then to Hungary, Poland, Bulgaria, Rumania, and Albania. From these rather meager beginnings Radio Free Europe has grown until eight years later it operated twenty-nine powerful transmitters broadcasting a total of almost three thousand hours per week to five captive countries behind the Iron Curtain. (Albania is no longer among its target countries.) The headquarters of the organization are in New York; the site of major operations is in Munich, almost four thousand miles closer to the Iron Curtain. Its staff of about two thousand people is engaged in the business of running five semiautonomous radio stations. For in reality Radio Free Europe is a network of five stations—the Voice of Free Czechoslovakia, the Voice of Free Hungary, etc.—each with its own completely independent program schedule.

Radio Free Europe is unique in the history of foreign propaganda broadcasting. Most outstanding among its unique features is that, unlike the foreign service of the British Broadcasting Corporation (BBC) or the Voice of America (VOA), Radio Free Europe (RFE) does not speak officially in the name of a foreign government, nor does it speak officially in the name of the American people. It is the "voice of exiles" who try to provide genuinely democratic and patriotic counterparts to Radio Prague, Radio Budapest, Radio Warsaw, and other satellite stations. This means that the half-hour or hour a day that

3

the BBC or VOA broadcasts will not suffice. Radio Free Europe must be on the air to its three major target countries throughout the day. The major stations sign on about five o'clock in the morning and continue broadcasting until past midnight. And the program schedule must include something more than news and political commentary. Culture and comedy, drama and music, commentary and satire, forums and interviews are woven together to make up a broadcast week that contains something for people in all walks of life.

Radio Free Europe is an operation of considerable interest to anyone concerned with international politics. In recent years scholars have written about propaganda as one of the major instruments involved in the conduct of foreign relations.[1] These writers conceive of four major instruments of statecraft—diplomatic, economic, military, and psychological (or propaganda). Radio Free Europe provides an example par excellence of the use of propaganda against an adversary in the cold war. To be sure, RFE is a private organization. It is a division of the Free Europe Committee, which is incorporated under the laws of the state of New York. It seeks among other things a rollback of Soviet power to the historic Russian boundaries. It is a private but hardy partisan in the cold war.[2]

This study considers two general kinds of questions about RFE. The first concerns the internal operation of the organization. We shall be interested here in the process by which propaganda policy is produced and the operation of the machinery that turns propaganda policy into program content. The poverty of empirical work thus far done on this subject leaves educated guesses as about the best kind of knowledge available on the problem.

The second kind of question stems from the private nature of RFE. The organization is nongovernmental. The voices that go out over the air are the voices of exiles speaking to their fellow countrymen. But the exiles' voices would not be on the air if it were not for American support. The success of RFE is predicated on a smooth-working relationship between its exile and American employees—a relationship, except for its private nature, not unlike that which exists between the United States and the other members of the North Atlantic Treaty Organization. But from the American point of view, RFE, like NATO, is an instrument of American foreign policy—a "nonofficial" instrument, to be sure, but in terms of concentrated effort in a given area, a propaganda instrument that is unprecedented in American history. When focusing on RFE as an "officially nonofficial" instrument of statecraft, one raises the questions of advantages and possible dangers—advantages, for instance, accruing from greater freedom of action, possible dangers resulting from the lack of integration with official United States policy and perhaps from the absence of any clear-cut lines of responsibility to the people or to their elected representatives.

Aspects of both of these general problem areas will be treated in this study. A significant part of the technical question will be dealt with in an empirical analysis of the operation of RFE. The basic policy of the organization is, by and large, developed in the New York headquarters, while about 85 per cent of the programs are done in Munich. We shall focus our attention on the machinery involved in developing policy, in turning policy into programs, and on how this machinery operates. Davison and George have used the term "communications behavior" to refer to a part of this problem.

Once communication policy is decided, specialists in the use of international communications take this policy and transform it into action . . . This transformation process we refer to as "communications behavior". Study of communications behavior includes consideration of the machinery by which communication policy is transformed into communication content, and also study of the personnel who operate this machinery and the techniques they use.[3]

Scholars in the field of propaganda research have suggested that the study of a propaganda agency and its activities be carried on in the perspective of the formula: *Who* says *what* to *whom, how, why,* and with *what effect?* [4]

However, this formula cannot be used as a basis for organization for this study. It has two weaknesses. First, it stakes out too large a research area. An adequate consideration of "what" would demand a detailed content analysis.[5] The problem involved would be immense. Jahoda and Klapper have reported on some of these problems, as they encountered them, in a content analysis of VOA scripts.[6] Their experiences with these problems—many of which were not successfully solved by a staff of qualified experts—would suggest that it would be a brave man indeed who would attempt alone a content analysis of RFE's voluminous output as a study in itself and a foolhardy one who would attempt it as a first part of a study.

The second weakness of the formula is that it tells us nothing at all about the possible interrelationships among the variables identified. It serves adequately as a checklist for the description of a propaganda operation, but leads to dangerous oversimplification if used as the basis for analysis.

In the parts of this study dealing with "communications behavior" we shall be largely describing the organization and operation of RFE. Chapter 2 will present the basic policies of the organization. Chapter 3 will deal with organization, setting, and personnel; Chapter 4 with the programing and policy development; Chapter 5 with the language desks (the various stations that make up RFE); Chapter 6 with the news and information services; and Chapter 7 with problems of transmission. Chapters 9 and 10 treat the development and execution of a propaganda campaign.

With those among the readers who had anticipated a more systematic and analytical study the author can sympathize, but feels it essential to point out that such a study would have to be based on a rigorous conceptualization of the communication process and of the process involved in "communications behavior." No such conceptualizations exist, and their development lies far beyond the scope of this study. Even in matters of domestic communication our knowledge—both empirical and conceptual—is so limited that it is adequate only for the analysis of limited problems in specific situations. Davison and George have stated the problems encountered when one moves on into the international field:

The study of communication is sufficiently complicated if we confine it to the domestic scene. When we turn our attention to international political communication, where the "who" is a complicated propaganda apparatus in one culture, the "whom" is an amorphous audience in another culture, and the purposes and circumstances are bound up with all the intricacies of international relations, then it is clear that we are not yet qualified to undertake a *systematic* study of international communication. All we can hope to do is to illuminate certain aspects of the process, and perhaps help to pave the way for more systematic study at a later date.[7]

We can only add a most deferential concurrence and hope that this study will "illuminate certain aspects of the process, and perhaps help pave the way for a more systematic study at a later date."

Chapter 11 will be devoted to an evaluation of RFE as a nonofficial instrument of American foreign policy. Some people might object to referring to RFE as a "private" or "nonofficial" undertaking because it is commonly believed that it has received funds from the United States government. Obviously any financial relationships that might exist between Washington and RFE cannot be discussed in this volume. However, the matter of financing is peripheral to the issues under consideration. The important point is that the United States government emphasizes the private status of RFE. The official position was clearly stated in replies to Czechoslovak and Hungarian protest notes to the State Department asking that the radio and balloon-leaflet operations sponsored by the Free Europe Committee be halted. The reply to the Czechoslovak government read in part as follows:

The Crusade for Freedom, an organization of private citizens, is supported by millions of Americans and expresses the aspirations of the American people for the freedom of all peoples. . . . The [radio and balloon-leaflet] operation was undertaken by this private organization and neither the U.S. Government nor the U.S. authorities in Germany were involved. The U.S. Government rejects the protest of the Czechoslovak Government which is without foundation.[8]

The American Legation in Budapest replied in essentially the same manner to Hungarian protests by pointing out that "the activity in question was undertaken by the Crusade for Freedom and Radio Free Europe on *their own initiative and responsibility*. These are *private organizations* established and supported by private American citizens."[9]

Statements such as these lead us to refer to RFE as an "officially nonofficial" instrument of American foreign policy. The advantages and disadvantages of this status will be discussed in Chapter 11.

A word should also be said about the methods used in this study. Most of the material was gathered during a four-month period when the author carefully analyzed the inner workings of RFE-Munich. He attended meetings, read interoffice memos, interviewed personnel at all levels, and generally observed the operation. This approach is an ideal method of learning about the organization, but it makes the problem of documentation difficult. Over one hundred different meetings were attended. These meetings are very informal. Although they are important in developing day-to-day tactics, no minutes are kept, and often the significance of remarks may not become clear until days or even weeks later. Comments on the role these meetings play in the process of propaganda production are very difficult to document, for they are based upon the author's impressions gained over several months. Also, a number of important insights as well as valuable information were often obtained in a casual conversation over a cup of coffee. These conversations could hardly be called "interviews," and yet it would not be quite proper for a footnote to read, "Mr. X in conversation over a cup of coffee, January 26, 1956." If therefore, documentation in certain parts of the study appears somewhat thin, it is due to the manner in which the material was collected.

The material on RFE's treatment of the Hungarian and Polish uprisings in the fall of 1956 was gathered in New York and included a careful reading of policy guidances, scripts, teletype communications between New York and Munich, and long interviews with key personnel.

⌒1

The Origins of Radio Free Europe

T HE public received its first indication that an enterprise like Radio Free Europe might be formed when on June 2, 1949, the *New York Times* carried an announcement that an organization called the *National Committee for Free Europe* [1] had been incorporated under the laws of the state of New York. Joseph C. Grew, former ambassador to Japan, was chairman of the board; DeWitt C. Poole was executive secretary.

It is a relatively simple task to trace the immediate origins of Radio Free Europe and of its parent organization, the Free Europe Committee. There is no great tradition to identify, no succession of predecessors on whose foundations it was established. If one follows the newspaper accounts, one gets the impression that suddenly, almost out of nowhere, there appeared a Free Europe Committee. Actually, the planning goes back only a few months from the June announcement.

In the early months of 1949 a number of exiles and refugees from the captive countries behind the Iron Curtain were paying frequent visits to the State Department. Many of these people were well-known and respected in their own country (outside official government circles) and abroad. Some of them were in dire economic straits, but what they wanted most was sympathy—sympathy and encouragement not only for themselves and other refugees, but also for their fellow countrymen suffering under the heel of Soviet oppression. As much as men in the State Department appreciated their feelings, it was difficult to extend to them what many officials felt were their just deserts while maintaining formal diplomatic ties with the governments the exiles were dedicated to overthrow. A former State Department official put it in words to this effect: "It was embarrassing to have two gentlemen waiting in your anteroom—one an official representative of a country behind the Iron Curtain; the other a persecuted ex-government official from that country. Although some of us objected to the policy of formal recognition of these regimes in 1945 and 1946, once the action had been taken, there were certain rules of the diplomatic game that had to be followed."

A number of people both in and out of government met under the informal leadership of George Kennan and discussed the problem. They came to the conclusion that the proper place for help and comfort lay not in the official chambers of the United States government, but in the hearts of the American people. The propriety of official action was at the best questionable, but a nonofficial response could be diplomatically justified and would be congruent with the best of the American tradition. As early as February 1949, Mr. Kennan sat down with Joseph C. Grew to discuss the problem.[2] Mr. Grew, with over forty years' experience in the Foreign Service, could understand and appreciate the problem faced by the Department. And with all his formal affiliation with the government a part of the past, he could take the kind of nonofficial action Mr. Kennan and his associates felt was the most appropriate.

About the same time Mr. Kennan passed on the essence of his thoughts to Dean Acheson, then Secretary of State.[3] Mr. Acheson was apparently in agreement with the diagnosis of the situation that had been made, for shortly after this Mr. Grew received a message from the Secretary asking him if he would establish a private group to help deal with certain aspects of the refugee problem.[4] Mr. Grew's first action was to call his old friend and former Foreign Service colleague, DeWitt C. Poole. The two of them met in the library of the Grew residence in May 1949, to discuss implementation of the idea. They agreed that the first step would be the formation of a committee of not more than fifty members that would be broadly representative of the major religious, economic, and political groups of American society.[5] It was further decided that the purpose of the group would not be to extend charity to the refugees, some of whom were unemployed and others performing the most menial of tasks. The purpose would be to find or provide them with suitable employment—employment that bore some relationship to their training and abilities. But these two elderly gentlemen were thinking of more than this. Some of the perspective of history had been built into their lives as a result of their long careers. They had through the years watched governments come and go and looked forward to the day when the Soviet grasp on eastern Europe would weaken. It could take five years; it could take fifty. But part of their faith was that some day it must come.[6] And when it did there would be a period of chaos and social confusion. Mr. Poole had been chargé d'affaires in Moscow in 1917. He knew from firsthand experience the advantages that accrued to an organized elite in a period of social disintegration. In addition to finding some kind of suitable employment for the refugees, then, one of the ideas at the very beginning was to develop and maintain a genuinely democratic leadership in exile, in preparation for the day when the Iron Curtain disintegrated.[7]

As a result of this meeting invitations were sent out to men from all walks of American life—men like Frank Altschul, New York banker; Adolf A. Berle, Jr., lawyer, scholar, and former Assistant Secretary of State; James B. Carey, labor leader; Dwight D. Eisenhower, retired general; and Charles P. Taft, businessman and well-known church layman—inviting them to join in the founding of the Free Europe Committee.[8]

On June 1, 1949, just four short months after discussions began, the Free Europe Committee was incorporated. At this time Mr. Grew held a press conference at which he introduced to the American people the Committee, the reasons for its foundation, and its purposes. He began by telling his audience that in one sense the new undertaking stemmed directly from Yalta. At that conference in 1945 the Soviet Union joined with the United Kingdom and the United States to promise national independence and the fundamental democratic freedoms to the peoples of eastern Europe, liberated from the Nazi tyranny. But that promise was not kept. A new tyranny had risen, and from that tyranny many of the democratic leaders from the countries of eastern Europe had escaped to the West as refugees and exiles.

Mr. Grew went on to say that the program of the new Committee "begins with the tangible fact of the presence [in the United States] of these exiles and refugees." The program he proposed had four major goals:

As item no. 1 in our immediate program we propose—have in fact already begun—to find suitable occupations for these democratic exiles who have come to us from Eastern Europe.[9]

This was not looked upon as a philanthropic undertaking, for Mr. Grew went on to talk about the day when the Communist oppression in eastern Europe would collapse or be destroyed:

When that time comes, there will be something close to social chaos and political vacuum, for the first effort of totalitarian regimes is to destroy all constructive elements which might build anything different from themselves. Looking forward to that historic and critical time we have in mind that, if meanwhile democratic leaders have been helped to keep alive and in vigor in the democratic havens to which they have been driven, we can hope that, returning, they can have parts in a democratic reconstruction.[10]

In discussing the second goal Mr. Grew indicated that an organization like Radio Free Europe was in the offing:

Our second purpose will be to put the voices of these exiled leaders on the air, addressed to their own peoples back in Europe, in their own languages, in the familiar tones. We shall help them also, if we can, to get their messages back by printed word.[11]

A third aim in the program was to enable these exiled political leaders to experience a broad contact with American life on the assumption that one factor in their continuing devotion to democracy would be their observation and understanding of the success of the democratic process in America. This would have the further effect of providing themes for their messages to their homelands:

If their impressions are on balance favorable, these exiles and refugees will become independent witnesses to the worth of our American endeavor. Then, if we enable them to communicate by radio or printed word with their peoples in the East European homelands, their messages will not be formed of theory and hypothesis but living substances. They can testify to what the trial of freedom and democracy in the United States has brought.[12]

The growth of the Free Europe Commitee was rapid. Organizations and programs were within a matter of months developed to implement the goals that Mr. Grew had so eloquently projected. And with the growth of the organization came a change in emphasis—new goals were developed, new operating principles devised. These changes will be discussed in later chapters. But while there has been a change in focus over the years, the basic concept behind the organization has remained the same. Mr. Grew stated that concept in these terms:

There goes on in the world these days a struggle to determine the future of our civilization. How our children are going to live depends upon the outcome.

Three types of defense are at hand. First, there is military preparation. On that we are spending billions. Military safeguard is indispensable certainly, but it is a safeguard only for the time being. Even if we win a war, we are still defeated by the social destitution and chaos which must ensue.

In the economic field we support the Marshall Plan, very wisely. The Marshall Plan promises enduring results. Our military and economic efforts are superb, but there remains the field of ideas.

Only in the field of the contest of ideas can we hope to achieve a victory which will last. The Committee's basic purpose, which we shall implement in every way which we find to be feasible as we go along, is to contribute to that lasting victory.[13]

By 1957 the Committee was working for the achievement of these purposes through three instrumentalities:

1. *Free Europe Press*—engages in carrying the printed word behind the Iron Curtain by means of balloons. It also publishes the journal *East Europe* (formerly called *News from behind the Iron Curtain*) and various works dealing with eastern Europe.

2. *Free Europe Exile Relations*—maintains contact with and supports various exile political and professional organizations, among which are the Council of Free Czechoslovakia (and similar groups from the other captive countries), the International Peasant Union, the Assembly of Captive European Nations, and the Union of Bulgarian Jurists. It encourages these groups to cooperate with one another in the common cause of freedom and helps them carry the lessons they have learned as victims of Soviet imperialism to peoples threatened by that same imperialism or wavering before the sophistic enticements of the Soviet Union.

3. *Radio Free Europe*—the oldest and most important of these organizations, and about which more shall follow.[14]

In July of 1949, hardly a month after the founding of the Free Europe Committee, a Radio Committee was set up to explore ways and means of putting the voices of exiles on the air to their own countries. It was headed by Frank Altschul, with Robert E. Lang as general director. In December of the same year the Radio Committee became Radio Free Europe, a division of the Free Europe Committee. In July of 1950 it first went on the air with a 7.5-kilowatt short-wave transmitter located near Frankfurt on the Main in West Germany.

By the end of the year it was broadcasting one and a half hours a day to the people of Poland, Czechoslovakia, Albania, Hungary, Rumania, and Bulgaria. Programs were prepared on tape in New York and flown to Germany for transmission.

By the end of 1951, the year of adolescent growth for RFE, a 135-kilowatt medium-wave transmitter equipped with a special directional antenna was broadcasting a full day's schedule to Czechoslovakia. Two 50,000-watt and one 10,000-watt short-wave transmitters with curtain antennas were completed at Biblis and were broadcasting to Poland, Hungary, and Czechoslovakia. Negotiations were concluded with the Portuguese government, which gave RFE the right to build a relay station on Portuguese territory, and the original 7.5-kilowatt transmitter was moved to Portugal to supplement a new 50,000-watt short-wave transmitter that had been built there. Wings 1 and 2 of the studio and office building were completed in Munich, which enabled RFE to take the first steps in overcoming the weakness inherent in preparing all programs in New York. By December, total broadcast time had increased to sixty-eight hours a day.

But growth was not the only change in RFE in its first two years. In June of 1949 the establishment of an exile radio seemed more closely related to the problem of employing exiles and to maintaining a democratic political leadership in exile that would be known and respected in the satellites than to contributing directly either to limiting the usefulness of the satellites to the Soviet Union or, eventually, to their liberation. But when it went on the air just one year later, RFE had for a goal the liberation of the captive nations.[15] It was explicitly engaged in a campaign of "psychological warfare." From the very beginning, then, new personalities and a new world situation caused RFE to be cast in a mold different from that which the founders of the Free Europe Committee had earlier envisioned.

By July of 1950, just one year after Mr. Grew announced that an attempt would be made to put the voices of exiles on the air, the cold war had become a hot war in Korea. The true nature of the adversary was imprinted with force upon the minds of the American people. And the men who both officially and nonofficially were concerned with active measures to combat Soviet imperialism were forced to think of new measures that would be commensurate with the threat. Mr. Lang, first director of RFE, had had OSS experience during World War II, and it is likely that this affected his approach to the problems facing the organization. The president of the Free Europe Committee in 1951 was C. D. Jackson, well-known member of SHAPE's Psychological Warfare Staff in World War II. Another important figure on the scene in 1950 was General Lucius Clay, who had retired from the army and returned to the United States. He says of his decision to join the Free Europe Committee:

When I left Germany, I came home with a very firm conviction that we needed in addition to the Voice of America a different, broader voice—a voice of the free people—a radio which would speak to each country behind the Iron Curtain in its own language, and from the throats of its own leaders who fled for their lives because of their beliefs in freedom. I returned home determined to develop such a voice, and I found that one was already getting under way in the National Committee for a Free Europe—known as Radio Free Europe.[16]

General Clay's interest in an undertaking similar to RFE probably stemmed from his knowledge of the success of RIAS (Radio in the American Sector). He was thinking of a private RIAS on a grander scale.[17]

The physical growth that had been so rapid in 1951 continued through the year 1952. Total broadcast time rose from sixty-eight hours per day in December 1951 to 218 hours a day one year later. Nine new transmitters were put into service broadcasting directly to the target countries while the number of relay transmitters sending programs from Munich to Lisbon was increased from two to six. Four more wings of the Munich office and studio building were completed (making a total of six), which provided 70,000 square feet of office and studio floor space. Twenty-two studios in all were in operation in Munich by the end of the year.[18]

But more important than the growth in technical facilities was the improvement in the methods and techniques used to conduct the campaign of "psychological warfare." Greater emphasis was placed on the systematic analysis of the target countries and in the planning of programs and program schedules that would better implement the basic policies of the organization. This was the year that RFE became cognizant of the long-term nature of its campaign and started developing the organization and techniques that would be effective over the long haul.[19]

Modifications in planning and new program techniques developed even more rapidly in 1953, for 1953 was a year of crisis in the Communist world. In March the man who for twenty-five years had been the political and spiritual leader of Communists all over the world, died. Demonstrations occurred in Czechoslovakia. Rioting broke out in East Germany. The purge of Beria suggested the beginnings of a power struggle that might shake the Soviet regime from top to bottom. News and commentaries on these happenings and on events in the West were broadcast to the captive peoples. Much of this information might not have been available in these nations if it were not for RFE. And the knowledge of the importance of the operation was a challenge to improve techniques further and to expand facilities. On the night of Stalin's death "saturation broadcasting" was begun. All available transmitters were turned alternately for half-hour periods on Poland, Czechoslovakia, and Hungary. The power was so great and so many frequencies were employed that jamming was impossible. Saturation broadcasting is now used at the end of every daily broadcast schedule for a review of the highlights of the day.

By 1955 twenty-nine transmitters were in operation. Total broadcasting hours were up to 2,800 per week. At this time the Free Europe Committee described RFE's distinguishing characteristics as follows:

It is a private, not a governmental station. It does not broadcast to the Soviet Union or East Germany, but only to the five Iron Curtain countries named above [Poland, Czechoslovakia, Hungary, Rumania, and Bulgaria]. To three of these countries—Poland, Czechoslovakia and Hungary—it delivers a full radio service of approximately eighteen to twenty hours a day, including programs of culture and entertainment as well as news, editorial matter, anti-communist polemics, and demonstrations of the ethics and institutions of true democracy. Its five "voices" are national voices—Poles speaking to Poles, Hungarians to Hungarians, etc., in their own name, not in the name of the U.S. Government or of the American people. Its chief center of operations is in and around Munich [Germany], broadcasts prepared in its New York studios cover some fifteen per cent of daily total airtime. It maintains a relay service in Portugal, with headquarters in Lisbon.[20]

In the barest terms, this is a description of the organization that is the subject of this work.

Basic Purposes and Policies

Immediately upon seizing power in a country, the Communists do four things: They abolish all opposing political parties and establish a one-party dictatorship; they create a secret police; they establish a ministry of propaganda to tell people what they shall know and how they shall think; and, finally, they surround the whole system with an Iron Curtain.[1] It is moot to ask which comes first. They are interdependent; take away one and the entire structure is threatened. They are the four walls of the Communist house.

With the establishment of these four institutions, the process of sovietization has already begun. The building of the new society is carried on by two kinds of active instruments—instruments of coercion and terror and instruments of propaganda.[2] If instruments of coercion and terror are to be effective, there must be no possibility of escape for anyone except by complete submission to the regime, and even then security is not guaranteed. If propaganda is to be effective, it must be monopolistic. Every bit of information that passes into the hands of the people must be controlled by the proper authorities. Newspapers, schools, radio stations, books—in short, everything that affects what people know and think—is harnessed by the state for the building of the socialist society. Radio Free Europe sets out to break this monopoly on information that the satellite regimes feel is so essential to their success. And by breaking this monopoly it hopes to contribute to the eventual rollback of Soviet power to the historic Russian boundaries.

It is difficult to write a simple and yet meaningful statement on the policies of RFE.[3] For its goals and, perhaps more important, the strategies employed to reach them are meaningful only in terms of the world situation in a given period of time. The world situation on both sides

17

of the Iron Curtain remained relatively constant from the middle of 1948 until the death of Stalin in 1953. It was a pattern of continuing Communist expansive pressure—Berlin, Korea, Indochina—and the increasingly determined defensive response of the West. Although even in this period RFE's major goal was the eventual liberation of the captive peoples in eastern Europe, its policy posture—after its original enthusiastic and naive optimism had declined—tended to be rather defensive. The *President's Report for the Year 1954*, for instance, described the Free Europe Committee as a "political warfare operation engaged in a struggle against Soviet Russian colonialism behind the Iron Curtain and communist influence on this side of the curtain."

But even as this statement was written, RFE was developing strategies that were something more than defensive. For since Stalin's death there has been a crescendo of change throughout the Soviet bloc—the Berlin riots, the rise and fall of Malenkov, the purge of Beria, the *rapprochement* with Tito, "de-Stalinization," Poznan, the uprisings in Poland and Hungary. Each of these happenings was greeted with surprise if not amazement in the West. Most of them meant change for RFE. In two later chapters we will discuss how RFE's strategies evolved in response to the changes that were taking place in the Soviet orbit. In this chapter we will look briefly at RFE's basic goal of "peaceful liberation," at the basic operating principles that have been developed to guide the organization, and at the general limits within which it operates.

This last point will be taken up first. Radio Free Europe is not an American *voice*, but it is the American management of five European exile voices. The essential responsibility of RFE is described in the organization's official *Policy Handbook* as follows:

As a non-governmental station responsible to the millions of American citizens who support it, RFE cannot take a line contrary to United States Government policy or to the beliefs of the people of the United States and American institutions. It holds itself free, however, to express independent views concerning the omission of the U.S. government to act in respect to the countries to which its broadcasts are addressed, as well as views concerning the timing of acts and pronouncements.[4]

The official position of the United States on the "peaceful liberation" of the captive nations has been defined many times, and RFE's position is congruent with official policy. Secretary Dulles outlined it clearly and forcefully before the House Committee on the Baltic Countries on November 30, 1953. "The captive peoples should know that they are not forgotten and that we are not reconciled to their fate; and above all that we are not prepared to seek illusory safety for ourselves by a bargain with their masters which would confirm their captivity." It was restated in unequivocal terms in President Eisenhower's reply to Khrushchev's attack on his 1955 Christmas message to the captive peoples. In words that could not be misunderstood the President said, "The peaceful liberation of the captive countries has been, is, and until success is achieved, will continue to be a major goal of United States foreign policy." The Republican party's platform in 1956 stated that "We are going to continue our efforts to liberate the captive countries" and the Democrats essentially agreed, saying, "The United States under Democratic leaders has never . . . condoned the extension of the Kremlin's tyranny over Poland, Bulgaria, Rumania, Czechoslovakia, Hungary, Albania, and other countries. We look forward to the day when the liberties of all captive nations will be restored to them and they can again take their rightful place in the community of free nations."

On November 15, 1956, after the brutal Soviet suppression of the Hungarian uprising, President Eisenhower was asked in a press conference, "In view of the latest developments, could you explain, sir, what the liberation position of the Administration is?" He replied, "I think it's been perfectly clear from way back in 1950, as far as I'm concerned, and I didn't happen to head the Administration when I was then in NATO. I believe it would be the most terrible mistake for the free world ever to accept the enslavement of the Eastern European tier of nations as a part of the future world of which we approve. . . . I do say the policy is correct in that we simply insist upon the right of all people to be free to live under governments of their own choosing." And if American foreign policy ever recognized the Soviet domination of eastern Europe as legitimate, RFE would either suspend operation or the character of the organization would be vastly changed.

But the question remains: "How does one accomplish 'peaceful liberation'?" United States foreign policy is clear on liberation as a goal, but the strategies to be employed to reach this goal—i.e., the combination of the instruments of statecraft and the methods of employing them—have never been clearly worked out. Certainly, liberation cannot be accomplished solely through the use of propaganda, nor by any other single instrument of statecraft. The policy advisers of RFE feel that a plan for the use of the propaganda instrument can be effective only if it is based on a profound appreciation of the social and historical forces at work and is part of an integrated strategy employing all instruments of statecraft. There is no official strategy that meets these two criteria. Through the years RFE has been working on a plan conceived to meet the latter criterion and suggest the general role of other instruments of statecraft. The process involved in its development will be treated in detail in Chapters 9 and 10. The major outlines will be presented here.

The policy advisers of RFE feel that there are three forces working for the liberation of the satellite states—*internal, orbital,* and *external.* The external force derives from the western "situations of strength" at crucial points along the periphery of the Soviet orbit. The positions of strength serve two functions. First, they contain the physical expansion of the Soviet Union. Second, they provide the physical support necessary for successful diplomatic negotiation. Specifically, in the case in which we are interested, they provide the "hardware" or material confirmation of the determination of the United States to refuse to accept a *status quo* in eastern Europe in exchange for a promise of "peaceful coexistence." American policy is to continue to increase the pressure through such actions as the rearming of West Germany within NATO, consolidating the "Northern Tier" through support of the Baghdad Pact, and increasing the armed power of the SEATO alliance. It is believed that the more the external force is increased, the greater will be the willingness of the Soviet Union to withdraw within its own boundaries. Radio Free Europe has little to do with the external force except to send reports of western strength and determination through the Iron Curtain.

The orbital pressures first became manifest when the Yugoslavs broke with the Cominform. This split, the violent polemic battle that ensued and the subsequent purges in the satellite states in which "Titoism" was an important charge, indicated that even within the "monolithic" Communist parties there were pressures to break away from the Kremlin. The United States responded to these developments (although not necessarily on the basis of an explicit identification of orbital pressures as one of the forces that could contribute to the liberation of the captive countries) by sending military and economic aid to Tito and by encouraging the Turk, Greek, Yugoslav Pact.

The orbital force did not have a particular significance for RFE's programing until after Bulganin and Khrushchev went to Belgrade to mend the break with Tito. In the Belgrade declaration signed on June 2, 1955, by Bulganin and Tito, the Soviet leaders recognized that each country has the right to its own "internal organization, and . . . different forms of Socialist development." Radio Free Europe knew that a number of Communist leaders in the satellites would like to have more freedom from Moscow, and the Belgrade declaration gave these leaders a pretext for action. The centrifuge began to spin with vigor following the Twentieth Party Congress in early 1956. The measure of freedom obtained by Gomulka and his followers for Poland later that same year indicated the potential strength and limitations of the orbital force. Radio Free Europe's policy as it developed during this period will be discussed in Chapter 10.

Finally, there are the internal pressures working toward liberation—the internal resistance of the people themselves to the Communist takeover and attempts to build the new society. The captive nations have a long history of subjugation. Some have struggled for centuries against foreign oppression and have known only short interludes of independence. Their struggle against oppression and exploitation—material and spiritual—must be looked upon within this context. However, the oppressor of the twentieth century is different from his historical predecessor. Modern techniques of social control have been highly refined by Nazis and Communists alike. Open resistance is usually suicidal.

Radio Free Europe works for the liberation of the satellites by trying to maintain and enhance the peoples' nonviolent resistance to the Soviets. Early in 1957 the Director said in an official memorandum that this internal force was at that time the most important of the three working for liberation.

The captive peoples are the prime movers in any progress towards their own liberation, under present circumstances. No Khrushchev, no Tito, no local Communist figure, wants true, steadily increasing liberalization. The West has little practical opportunity to advance the course of liberalization except on the small scale of economic aid or person-to-person contacts if and when opportunities make themselves. Only alert, cool-headed successive moves by the peoples themselves, armed with understanding of their situation and a clear sense of what they want, promise any real fruits.[5]

The *Policy Handbook*, written in 1950 and 1951, lists four ways that RFE might use to sustain the morale of the captive peoples and stimulate them in a spirit of noncooperation:

(a) by reminding [the] listeners constantly that they are governed by agents of a foreign power whose purpose is not to further the national interest but to carry out the imperialistic aims of the rulers of Soviet Russia; (b) by displaying the moral and spiritual emptiness of communism as an ideology and the material incapacity of communism, as an economic system, to provide an acceptable standard of living for the working class; (c) by inculcating hope of eventual liberation through a convincing display of the superiority of the skill, resources, and military strength of the West, and through reiteration of the promise that the West intends that [the] listeners shall be free; (d) by sowing dissension in each regime through exposing the ineptitude of its officials, and sowing fear among the officials by denouncing confirmed acts of oppression and cruelty, and threatening retribution.[6]

In January 1957, six years after the above policy was put in writing, a report issued following a top-level staff conference further clarified RFE's role as follows:

RFE's broad role would appear to be to keep alive the pressure for freedom among our peoples, supplying them with the facts, the comprehension of free democratic methods, and the inspiration of free-world achievement which will enable them to chart effectively their own courses towards freedom.[7]

Three points should be made in regard to this basic approach that RFE has outlined for itself. First, RFE does not feel that it can legitimately assume a directing role in the struggle for liberation. It does not manipulate the behavior of people in accordance with some master plot; it does not advise the listening audiences as to what actions they should take. Rather, RFE tries to carefully inform the captive peoples of events and situations in their homelands and in the world at large, and to interpret these events in such a way that they will accept coolly, and deal realistically with, the practical opportunities of the moment. Furthermore, in its interpretations attention is also focused on the long-range perspective and the potentialities and limitations of the future.

As a second point, planning the course leading to liberation and providing the blueprint for the new world remain the privilege and responsibility of the captive peoples. Radio Free Europe is fully aware that they have their own vision of the future:

The captive peoples want a new world. Their concept of their future is a revolutionary one: with few exceptions they no more want to return to a warmed-over version of the 1930's than they want to remain Communist. They do not object to everything that Communism has introduced in the fields of educational facilities, social protection, and abolition of privilege, nor do they automatically accept as applicable the economic, political, and social patterns of the West.[8]

Radio Free Europe has only one requirement for the future: basic democratic institutions must be given an opportunity to operate. It does hope that while it participates in the struggle for liberation it can help build the foundations for a polity that will destroy the conditions that historically have led to conquest, tyranny, and a low standard of living in eastern Europe. After liberation RFE would like to see the creation of a democratic united Europe which would include all the satellite states. It is not that RFE has any grand design for a united Europe, nor that it lends its support to any of the plans and proposals discussed since the end of World War II. It does not regard unity as a panacea for the multitudinous ills that have plagued eastern (and western) Europe for centuries. But RFE does feel that its audiences should be informed that

. . . the West is not concerned merely with bringing about a withdrawal of the Soviet tide from their countries, but is seeking in anticipation of their liberation to lay the foundation of a Europe in which all people will be able to live in peace because they live fraternally, in prosperity because their combined resources will be rationally employed, in freedom because the human personality will be respected, in security because in union there is strength.[9]

A third point that should be emphasized is that RFE's approach is a peaceful approach. It rejects the idea that liberation can come through war or violent revolution. Acts of terror on the part of the captive peoples are not conceived to be useful in the long run. Therefore, RFE's basic policy documents state explicitly that no program should stimulate or encourage action that might bring severe reprisals either by inflammatory incitement or by promising or implying that action would be supported by armed intervention from the West. A clear statement of this policy appears in the "Special Guidance for Broadcasts on Liberation" which was written during the presidential campaign of 1952 when debate raged on the issue of "containment" versus "liberation."

We of RFE . . . cannot comment upon these statements [on liberation by General Eisenhower and Mr. Dulles] with unqualified optimism, for to do so would be to deceive our listeners by inspiring in them exaggerated hope of Western intervention. . . . not one word in these statements (on liberation) can be used to encourage militant anti-communists to go over from passive to active resistance in the expectation that such resistance will be supported by Western elements.[10]

Basic Operating Principles

In the first five years of operation, a number of "operating principles" were developed which guide the organization in the use of its instruments of propaganda for the attainment of its goals. Some of these principles were a part of the thinking at the very outset—others developed out of the experience gained after RFE began to function. The five listed below have become a permanent part of the operating code of the organization.

The Strategy of Objective Truth. From the very beginning of the operation it has been a basic rule in RFE to report the world of events accurately and to comment on it honestly. Behind this rule there is both strategy and belief. One dogma probably accepted by successful propagandists throughout the world is that "credibility is a condition of persuasion." The broadcasting of falsehoods that can be proved false by the audience destroys credibility, not only in the single instance but reflects disadvantageously on the whole operation. Radio Free Europe is not the only western station broadcasting to the captive nations. Its news and commentary can be compared with those of the BBC, VOA, and others. To achieve credibility over the long run, RFE must gain a reputation for trustworthiness and reliability. Accuracy and honesty are felt to be the key to credibility.

But in addition to this strategy of truth there is a belief in truth. Behind the completely cynical propagandist who reports accurately only when his audience has an opportunity to check up on him lies a contempt for mankind—a rejection of democratic principles. Observers have often commented on the moral orientation of American foreign policy in general, and it does not take many weeks in the organization to discover that this quality also permeates RFE and influences its day-to-day operations. Its dedication to the democratic proposition is explicitly stated in one of the policy guidances as the basic reason for its rule of honesty and accuracy:

It is because we believe in democracy as an ethic, and application to politics and to society of the religious principle that "all men are created equal and are endowed by their creator with certain inalienable rights," that it is impossible for us to adopt and hold to the "big lie" as a guiding principle in propaganda. We might believe intellectually that this was indeed the best propaganda line, but it is not in our nature to pursue such a line. Our hearts would not be in what we wrote, and we should soon find ourselves straying instinctively from such a line if we started it.[11]

But this dedication to accuracy in reporting and honesty in commentating does not take the form of "the truth, the whole truth, and nothing but the truth." Sometimes in a propaganda operation, the middle requirement is not observed. One of the reasons for this is credibility itself—there are times when the whole truth is simply too incredible to be believed. For example, during World War II Allied propaganda to German troops telling them that prisoners of war received eggs for breakfast was used by the Germans as evidence that Allied propaganda consisted of lies. In actuality the statement was not false, but to the German *Ländser* it represented a completely unbelievable standard.[12] Accurate reporting of American war production apparently had the same effect on some foreign audiences. Thus, as a precaution in the interests of credibility, the whole truth is sometimes withheld.

There are many cases in which simply the accurate reporting of facts may actually lead to misunderstanding and confusion. For example, the detailed, accurate reporting of charges and countercharges made during American presidential campaigns might leave a foreign audience unschooled in American politics with the impression that no matter which man wins, the United States government will be led by either a fool or a rogue. Thus statements or events that are likely to be badly misinterpreted are either played down or withheld from broadcast. An example of the latter was reported above (see p. 24), where one of RFE's policy guidances was quoted which placed restrictions on broadcasting statements about the "liberation policy" out of fear that they might be interpreted as an encouragement to a possibly suicidal action by some of the more militant anti-Communists.

A "Home Service" Radio. In the ideal totalitarian state "everything that is not compulsory is forbidden." The function of the propaganda machine is to inform the people what they must do and what they must not do. But more than that, it must so shape their "world of meaning" that they know of no alternatives to the bidding of the regime. It is monopolistic, overwhelming, all-prevailing. It touches every aspect of human existence. If RFE is to be successful in combating this instrument, it cannot rely upon several hours of news and political commentary a day; it must join the contest day and night, not only with "propaganda" but with a program schedule that supplies information and entertainment for people in all walks of life. The ideal is to provide the captive peoples with something comparable to the "home service" of the BBC. In other words, RFE tries to be what Radio Warsaw or Radio Budapest would be if Poland and Hungary were free and independent countries. Music, comedy, sports, and education have their place along with news and political commentary. And in providing a type of "home service," it must be aware of the different tastes and listening habits of the peoples in the various target countries. For instance, one finds more political commentary in the Voice of Free Czechoslovakia and more satire in the Voice of Free Hungary. The style of newscasts and commentary and the type of continuity also differ considerably among the five stations.

If the "home service" type of program schedule is to be attractive, the programs must originate as nearly "inside" the target countries as possible. Radio Free Europe's stations must respond quickly and decisively to events in terms that are meaningful to the audiences. Thus editors and writers have to know what their audiences are thinking about, how they react to local and international events, and how they feel about the issues that are important in their everyday lives. This requires close physical proximity to the audiences—close enough to receive newspapers and other publications before they are hopelessly out of date; close enough to monitor medium-wave broadcasts; close enough to facilitate quick access to refugees who have escaped through the Iron Curtain. But physical proximity is not enough. The exiles who operate the stations must be able to "empathize" with the people in their native lands. The exiles must live two lives: a physical one in Munich and an imaginative one behind the Iron Curtain. A psychological environment must be developed which, in effect, creates a "little Czechoslovakia," a "little Poland," a "little Hungary" in the middle of Munich.[13]

The "home service" idea also has some limitations. The broadcasters must always bear in mind that they are not behind the Iron Curtain. No matter how close they feel to their countrymen, there is always that difference. There are certain things that RFE cannot say precisely because it is not behind the Iron Curtain. The exiles should sympathize, they should "empathize," but they should never say anything that would cause their listeners to retort, "It's all right for you to say that, sitting in comfort in Munich, but come over here and see what you'll say!"

A "Tactical" Operation. In addition to being attractive because it is a "home service," RFE tries to win listeners by being fresh and timely. One way to compete effectively with the all-pervasive Communist propaganda apparatus is to "beat it to the punch"—to provide important news before the regime radio does and therefore gain a reputation in the captive countries for speed as well as accuracy. "If one wants the *latest* news, listen to RFE." And some notable successes have been scored in this regard: RFE "scooped" the satellite stations in the first announcement of Stalin's illness by three to nine hours. The first satellite announcement of Malenkov's demotion came from Hungarian Radio Kossuth at 2:10 P.M. But the Hungarian listening to RFE had already heard the news at 11:39 A.M. The equivalent of the American "We interrupt this broadcast to bring you a special bulletin" is not unknown in eastern Europe. And such diligence and alertness are not reserved only for reporting political events. The Olympic games at Cortina d'Ampezzo were given full coverage and the Czechs, for instance, could hear about the fate of their famous hockey team on RFE before they could get it from Radio Prague.

Autonomous Station Operation. Success in providing a tactical "home service" demands autonomy—autonomy from New York for the entire Munich operation; autonomy for each of the five stations to enable the exile staffs to make full use of the intuitive knowledge of their homelands that no American can acquire and present a convincing picture of a genuinely patriotic endeavor. In the next chapter we will see the nature of the relationship between Munich and the

New York headquarters and the latitude of freedom that Munich has in dealing with events. A word is now in order about the autonomy of the various stations.

Radio Free Europe was established to enable exiles to broadcast to their homelands. Its success is predicated on the listeners' believing that this is a genuinely patriotic group of stations. The aura of patriotism cannot be convincingly simulated; it can only be achieved if the exile staffs genuinely feel that they are working for the good of their own countries and are not the lap dogs of a foreign power. This requires at the outset that a great deal of autonomy must be granted the exile desk chiefs. It means, furthermore, that American control of what is in the last analysis an instrument of American foreign policy must be effective, but so subtle as to be almost imperceptible. Scripts are prepared only by the exile staffs and are rarely read before production. American control is exercised only at the very top (through the desk chiefs) and largely assumes the form of suggestion and advice. Initiative in day-to-day operation and in the selection of targets rests with each desk chief. Policy "directives" are almost unknown. Policy "guidances" providing analyses of situations, followed by a discussion of the proper propaganda treatment, take their place. And people on the desks feel free to criticize the guidances and their arguments are listened to. As the writer of one type of guidance remarked, "If the propaganda line I lay out does not convince the exiles on our staff, then perhaps it has little chance of succeeding with the audience for whom it was designed." [14]

The achievement of necessary autonomy without jeopardizing legitimate American control is based on two ingredients: (1) skilled and trustworthy desk chiefs who appreciate the nature of the gift that has been given them, who are aware of their responsibilities both to Americans and their own people in administering it, and who are so attuned to the policies and goals of the organization that constant consultation is not necessary; (2) American administrators who have the rare ability to maintain authority and control without giving the impression of exercising either.

No Exile Politics. Radio Free Europe is a platform from which exiles speak to their homelands; it is not a stadium in which the bickering and sterile game of exile politics is played. Exile politicians from ancient Greece to the present time have been notable for their quarrelsomeness. Their energies have frequently been consumed in internecine strife; few have produced constructive ideas and programs for dealing with the ills of their homelands. From the beginning RFE has not wanted to become involved in this aspect of exile affairs. Its exile staffs have been chosen for reasons of professional competence. And although pains are taken to see that all shades of democratic political thinking are represented, internal politics are excluded from their radio work. Radio Free Europe may not be used to advance the interests of any particular exile faction. Attacks of one exile leader on another are not reported; exile politicians who appear as guest speakers are instructed to forget about internal rivalries and intrigues while using RFE's facilities.

Organization, Personnel, and Setting

Most organizations have some kind of official organizational chart. Its use may vary from playing an important role in re-establishing lines of authority after an administrative reorganization to covering up a spot on the wall where eggnog was spilled at the Christmas party. But whatever function it may perform for an organization, such a chart is useful to an observer studying that organization. It is not that he can fully rely upon the chart for a complete and accurate picture of lines of authority, responsibility, and communication. Organizational charts are notorious for their inability to give an accurate representation of how an organization functions. But for the observer they do provide a useful point of departure, offering a theoretical scheme—a kind of "ideal"—against which the observed operations may be compared.

Unfortunately, RFE has no official organizational chart. And after a few hours are spent trying to draw one, the reasons for its absence become obvious. There are two fundamental aspects of the organization that are very difficult to portray accurately on paper. One is the relationship between New York and Munich; the other, the position of the five independent stations in the total organization. Although a chart showing these two aspects is very complex, it is easier to discuss the organization on the basis of a graphic portrayal.

The Organization and Operation of RFE-New York

There are two separate and distinct functions performed in the New York office. (See Figure 1.) It is the headquarters of the organization and it contains five "desks" that produce programs. The headquarters, of course, is superior to Munich, but as a rule the desks are subordinate to the desk chiefs in Munich. They operate as New York bureaus,

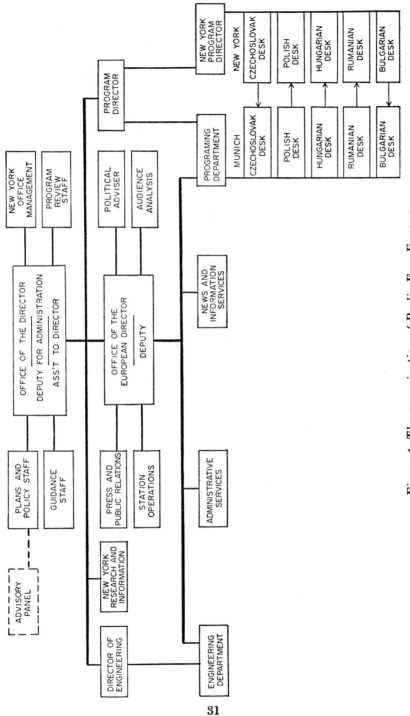

Figure 1. The organization of Radio Free Europe

31

doing the programs that are directly related to the American scene plus most of the international commentaries.

In the headquarters of RFE we find the Office of the Director with four staff units and three operating divisions. Three of the staff units are of particular interest to this study, the Plans and Policy Staff, the Guidance Staff and the Program Review Staff.

The staff director of the plans and policy unit is assigned the job of working primarily on long-range plans. He writes few program guidances, but concerns himself with such problems as developing research projects to gather information useful in developing broadcast strategies and programs. Such problems as keeping informed on the changing wage-price structure in the satellites, on developments of and reactions to Communist ideology, and gauging their impact on RFE's plans and programs fall under his jurisdiction. In this role he supervises the activities of a section of the Research and Information Division in New York. Outside the formal RFE organization he has two important contacts. One is with an advisory board consisting of a number of men who have had considerable experience in international propaganda. This board was set up in 1956 to provide a panel of experts with whom RFE could consult when it so desired. It is entirely advisory in its functions. The other important contact is with the various American universities currently undertaking important Soviet or satellite research programs.

Whereas the Plans and Policy Staff can be looked upon as the adviser on "strategic" matters to the Director of RFE, the Guidance Staff consists of the expert tacticians. The two major functions of this staff are to prepare a daily guidance for distribution both in New York and Munich and to consult at a daily meeting with the major scriptwriters in New York. Both of these functions will be examined in detail below.

The other staff unit of interest in this study is the Program Review Staff. Its primary function is to examine the scripts produced both in New York and Munich to see whether policy guidances are being implemented in programs. The problem of control is one of the most difficult problems faced by RFE and the development and operation of this staff will be dealt with later in this chapter. The fourth staff unit, Office Management, is confined to a purely administrative function.

Of the operating divisions, only one, the Office of the Program Director, is of major interest. Half of the next chapter will be devoted to a discussion of its operation. However, at this stage it is important to point out that the Program Director of RFE has, in effect, two deputies, the program director in New York and the program manager in Munich. It can be seen from Figure 1 that this arrangement makes the program manager in Munich responsible to two superiors—the Program Director of RFE and the European Director of RFE. This complex relationship is further complicated at the echelon just below the New York program director and Munich program manager. These gentlemen have the formal responsibility for the operation of the five independent stations that RFE comprises. But whereas the New York program director and Munich program manager occupy parallel positions in the administrative structure, the New York desks that are supervised by the New York program director are also subordinate (in most cases) to the desk chiefs in Munich.

The Engineering Department in RFE is almost as complex as the Programing Department. The engineering director in New York has a subordinate both in Munich and at the relay station in Lisbon, but the chief engineer in Munich is also responsible to the European Director.

The Organization of RFE-Munich

The Munich operation of RFE is headed by the European Director (see Figure 2). The Office of the Director has four staff units attached to it (the Political Adviser's Office, Audience Analysis, Station Operations, and Press and Public Relations) and directs the activities of four operating units (Administrative Services, the Engineering Department, News and Information Services, and the Programing Department). In this study we shall be primarily concerned with the functions of the Programing Department, the Political Adviser's Office, the News and Information Services, Audience Analysis, and to a lesser degree with the Engineering Department. In the Programing Department one finds the stations that make up RFE—The Voice of Free Czechoslovakia and comparable stations for the other captive nations. The political adviser is the chief policy man in Munich and can be looked upon as a sort of "chief propagandist." The News and Information Services are concerned with collecting the vast amount of ma-

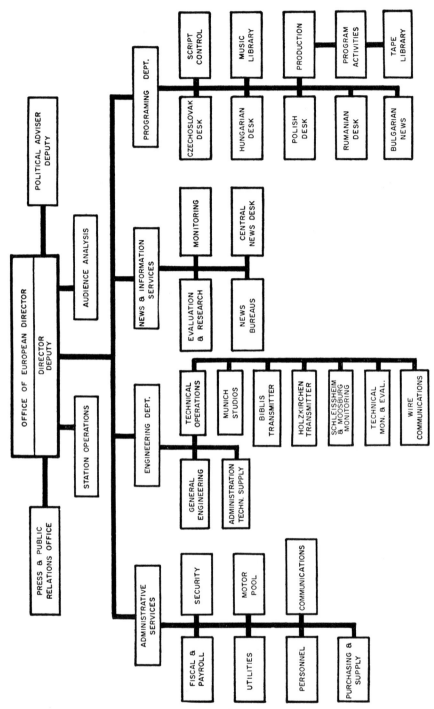

Figure 2. The organization of Radio Free Europe, European Division

terial necessary to keep four stations plus a news desk broadcasting about five hundred hours a week. The Engineering Department is responsible for delivering the programs to the people behind the Iron Curtain while Audience Analysis has the task of assessing the effectiveness of the operation.

The official chart of the Munich organization (Figure 2) gives one an idea of the structure of administrative responsibility in RFE-Munich, but it may lead to some distorted views on how the organization functions. Even the casual observer might be somewhat surprised to see that the Voice of Free Czechoslovakia and the other semiautonomous stations (desks) occupy a position on the chart comparable to that of the Motor Pool. It does not take many weeks in the organization before one discovers that the chart is misleading in other ways. Perhaps the most important source of misconceptions is the portrayal of the Political Adviser's Office, which is attached as a staff unit to the Office of the European Director in a manner similar to that in which the two policy staffs (Plans and Policy, and Guidance) are attached to the Office of the Director in New York. But unlike the situation in New York, where the staffs function by and large as staffs (performing a staff function rather than a line function), the policy adviser in Munich does not operate as a member of the Director's staff in performing his major functions. For example, in *advising* the desks on day-to-day political propaganda tactics and *checking* to see that policy is implemented, he works directly with the desks as if he had a line relationship with them in regard to these matters. Indeed, his position vis-à-vis the European Director on the one hand and the desks on the other, on matters of propaganda content, advice, and control, is very similar to that of the Munich program manager's line relationship in regard to programing policy. This observation and our dissatisfaction with the position of the desks on the official chart led to the development of a "logistical support chart" which indicates more clearly both the function of various units in RFE and their interrelationships. It also makes it possible to describe more clearly the complex relationship between the New York headquarters and the field operations in Munich (see Figure 3).

This chart will also undoubtedly raise some questions in the mind of the reader. What is the nature of the relationship between the program manager in Munich and the political adviser? Is their dual au-

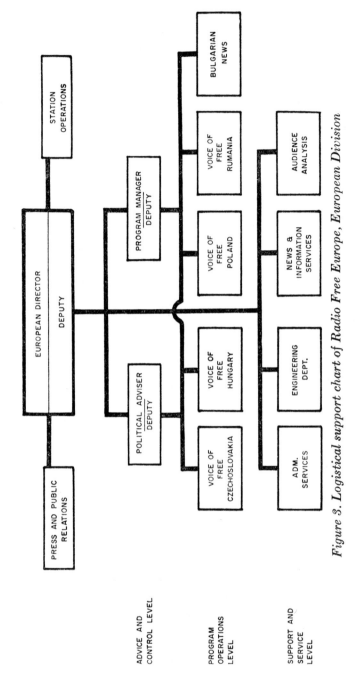

STATION OPERATIONS

PRESS AND PUBLIC RELATIONS

EUROPEAN DIRECTOR

DEPUTY

PROGRAM MANAGER
DEPUTY

POLITICAL ADVISER
DEPUTY

VOICE OF FREE CZECHOSLOVAKIA

VOICE OF FREE HUNGARY

VOICE OF FREE POLAND

VOICE OF FREE RUMANIA

BULGARIAN NEWS

ADM. SERVICES

ENGINEERING DEPT.

NEWS & INFORMATION SERVICES

AUDIENCE ANALYSIS

ADVICE AND CONTROL LEVEL

PROGRAM OPERATIONS LEVEL

SUPPORT AND SERVICE LEVEL

Figure 3. Logistical support chart of Radio Free Europe, European Division

thority a possible source of friction? Is a desk chief placed in the unenviable position of a man with two masters? Why are the duties of the policy man in Munich not performed in a manner similar to that in New York? The answer to this last question lies in the different skills and interests of the top executive in New York and Munich and the differing administrative load. Ideally, the top executive position in RFE both in New York and Munich calls for a man who in addition to the necessary administrative skills has a thorough knowledge of eastern European history, culture, and politics. He should also be a skilled political propagandist, thoroughly familiar with radio programing and production, and able to function well in RFE's multinational environment. Such a person would be rare indeed, if not altogether mythical. In the beginning the problem was solved both in New York and in Munich by splitting the function and having one man responsible for the radio and administrative aspects and another for political propaganda content, advice, and control. This solution could be tolerable only if three conditions were met: (1) there must be a clear-cut line of demarcation between the authority of the political adviser and the Munich program manager in relation to the activities of the desks; (2) the two men must be personally compatible and recognize each other's authority and competence; (3) both men must be responsible to the same superior who has authority to resolve any conflicts that might arise.

For about the first five years of RFE, the Directors both in New York and Munich delegated much authority in policy and program matters and performed the superior role mentioned in the third point above. When a new Director came to New York in 1955 he was a man with much experience in international propaganda and began to take an active policy role, using his policy staffs as staffs. The Director in Munich is an engineer by training and still prefers to delegate much authority in program and policy matters. However, it should also be pointed out that the purely administrative responsibilities in Munich are in a sense greater than they are in New York. About three times as many people are employed, and they form a small community which is dependent on RFE for housing and other logistical support. Thus RFE-Munich gets involved in a greater number of personal problems and conflicts. Much of the European Director's time is consumed in dealing with these problems. Indeed, in some respects, his tasks resemble those of a governor as much as those of an administrator.

It is also possible to relieve the European Director of active participation in programing and propaganda operations because his subordinates in these areas are in many ways responsible to New York through what might be called a "technical" chain of command.

On the "logistical support chart" (Figure 3), the program manager and the political adviser are placed at the "advice and control level." Directly subordinate to them at the "operational level" are the four language desks and the Bulgarian news desk. It is at this level that all scripts are written and all programs produced. Finally, a "service and support level" is shown, consisting of Administration, Audience Analysis, News and Information Services, and Engineering.

The Relationship between New York and Munich

There are two principal functions performed by the New York headquarters—that of *direction* (forming and transmitting the basic policy and principles of strategy) and that of *control* (checking to see that the policy is being implemented and the strategy followed). From the point of view of *direction* there are two points of contact between the Office of the Director in New York and the Munich operation that are pertinent to this study. First, there is the formal chain of command between the Director in New York and the Director in Munich. This is the formal route for propaganda content guidances, but as it works out in practice, guidances go directly from the Office of the Director in New York to the policy adviser in Munich.[1] Secondly, policy relating to programing goes directly from the Program Director of RFE in New York to the program manager in Munich.

Policy Direction. There are three major instruments through which New York exercises policy control over Munich: the *Policy Handbook*, the policy guidances, and the daily guidances. The *Policy Handbook* was written in 1950 and 1951. It lays out the policy objectives of RFE and contains sections on how certain subjects (such as Titoism, Communism, anti-Semitism, etc.) will be dealt with and the basic principles that will be observed in broadcasting to certain groups (workers, youth, women, intellectuals, etc.). It is a form of "standing directive." However, it has not been revised for some time and is becoming more and more of purely historical interest.

More important than the *Policy Handbook* are the policy guidances produced in New York in the form of analyses of important situations and events that have particular significance for RFE, followed by a propaganda line. They range anywhere from one to twenty-five pages in length and are so varied in the kind of subjects they treat that it is difficult to typify them. Sometimes they apply to a single country (for instance, after a major purge has occurred); more often they deal with major world events as they affect all the target nations. For instance, following each of the Geneva conferences in 1955, a policy guidance was issued which contained a thorough analysis of and commentary on the world situation, particularly as it affected the captive nations. The general international situation following the conferences was discussed, and specific problems such as German reunification and the Belgrade agreements between Tito and the Russian leaders were put into the context of world events. The propaganda guidance follows directly from the analysis and commentary. It is of more than psychological significance that these guidances are not called "policy directives." Part of their importance comes from their authority; a great deal arises from the penetrating logic of the analysis and the cogency of the critique. They are as much a form of persuasion as of command.

However, in the middle of 1956, policy guidances, particularly at very crucial moments, began to become more authoritative. One gets the impression that the guidance dealing with the treatment of the Poznan riot and its aftermath did not leave Munich as much freedom as the earlier guidances did.

Several policy guidances are written each year, but every day Munich receives from New York by teletype a daily tactical guidance dealing largely with international events. The purpose is to shape the treatment of current developments in the news broadcasts and political commentaries in such a way that it will be consistent with and effective in achieving RFE's objectives. However, the daily guidance is deceptive in form. It appears to present only the events of the day, but in reality it discusses these events in a way which develops and presents a definite propaganda line. It resembles somewhat a broad-gauge international commentary.

The daily guidance reflects its originators' dissatisfaction with the OWI-type directive, which told writers what they could or could not say. It is based on the recognition that good script-writers are, by and large, an independent lot and resist directives of the dogmatic type. They are "directed" much more effectively by a rational approach which indicates reasons why things should be considered in a certain light rather than by directives that rigidly impose specific treatments.[2]

In Munich the daily guidance does not have the authority of the policy guidance. The political adviser at his discretion may modify it, although this is seldom done. The impact of the daily guidance, even more than that of the policy guidance, is a result of the cogency of the propaganda line suggested.

In addition to these formal "instruments" of policy control, of course, New York remains in almost constant teletype contact with the political adviser in Munich. Furthermore, there are rather frequent trips across the Atlantic for key personnel.

Programing Direction. Direction concerned with the technical aspects of programing—format, scheduling, and the like—involves problems entirely different from those inherent to the direction governing program content. The content of RFE's political commentaries must be acutely attuned to the events of the day, and when events (such as the Berlin riots in 1953 or the Geneva conferences in 1955) demand rapid changes in propaganda lines, the necessary changes can be made quickly because they do not involve any great technical and administrative difficulties. Such is not the case in regard to programing. Except for periods of acute crisis when the number of commentaries may be increased, there is no demand for sudden changes. And luckily so, because it is a far more difficult problem to develop a new program or series of programs than it is to change a propaganda line.

Thus there is not such a heavy demand for constant teletype communication between the program directors in New York and Munich as there is between the policy advisers. But changes in the program schedule require much more planning in administrative, technical, and personnel matters. Since these kinds of problems cannot be dealt with adequately at long distances, the Program Director of RFE spends from four to five months a year in Munich. In fact, the program manager in Munich is a deputy who acts with the full authority of the Program Director of RFE while the latter is in New York.

The Problem of Control. Any headquarters is going to be interested in how its policies are implemented. On administrative and programing matters this, of course, is no problem in RFE. Evidence is obvious and easily obtainable. But the question of policy implementation in program content is rather complex both because of the prodigious number of scripts involved and because of legitimate questions of what constitutes implementation of a policy in a script (except for the extreme case). The changes that have occurred in the methods of dealing with this problem suggest that RFE has not yet discovered an altogether acceptable means of coping with it. By 1956 a new system was in operation to regularize procedures, but in order to understand how this is expected to work, it is necessary to look briefly at the previous attempts.

The original script review section operated as an integral part of the policy setup. A regular group of trained readers went over the political commentaries continuously, and other types of scripts sporadically, to test not merely the subject matter and phrasing, but also the "feel" of the script, that is, whether it conveyed hope, enthusiasm, determination, indignation, or whatever was called for.

This system died a natural, quiet death in late 1953, under a certain amount of criticism. Some people felt that because it was tied to policy-making, the readers repeatedly succumbed to the temptation to judge scripts from a partisan viewpoint. At times they tried to make up for the shortcomings of the original policy formulation by blaming the script-writers for not guessing what the policy writer had meant but did not quite say; at other times they objected because a commentator had found it impossible to discuss for five minutes what the guidance had said in one sentence without stepping out of bounds or playing uncalled for variations on the originally prescribed theme.

Another weakness was purely mechanical. Because scripts were mailed back from Munich the flow was uneven and the reviews were always several weeks behind events. Consequently they were often little more than post-mortems, of historical interest mainly.

Perhaps the most important reason for the process being unsatisfactory was that the organization and working methods of the Programing Department and the desks were not geared, administratively or psychologically, to making effective use of script review findings. Some of the writers on the desks looked on them as an unwarranted intrusion of American management, and the Programing Department

41

did not have the time (or perhaps the inclination) to use the findings in a sit-down-around-the-table community effort at constructive self-analysis.

The present program review section is set up as a staff unit in the Office of the Director of RFE and is independent from the units concerned directly with policy. This new unit has two functions: (1) The easier, more obvious, but less fundamentally important function is that of keeping a running check and record on how RFE is handling the issues of the day and projecting ideas. This answers the question, "What is being done?" and gives executives who must discuss problems and represent RFE to the public an idea of program content. It will also locate weak spots in the output and point the way to thorough investigation. (2) The more fundamental purpose is to do detached studies of individual types of output, concertedly, one at a time, to measure just how good they are and where they fall down. This may be a policy check as to over-all effectiveness of the implementation of certain themes, or a technique check as to the skill of writing or effective use of sources, or a general check as to whether in the broadest terms a certain type of script really achieves anything, or a cross check of similar programs among the desks to see whether one might not learn something from another.

Every week the chief of the Program Review Staff sends an eight to ten page memorandum to the Director of RFE, containing a summary (sometimes with comments) on the political commentaries broadcast during the previous week. This is the basic document used for checking on policy implementation.

General Comments on Organization

The above discussion and all that follows on organization in succeeding chapters must be interpreted in the light of two important facts. First, no preliminary blueprint or comprehensive design for the organization of RFE was ever projected. The favorite analogy among "old timers" in the organization is that with *Topsy*—it just grew. New functions were created and old ones revised to meet situations as they were confronted. The approach has since continued to be experimental; pragmatic criteria predominate. Secondly, there are over 3,000 miles between the headquarters and the site of major operations. These two facts are responsible for many of the organizational characteristics of

RFE. Five of these characteristics are important for the understanding of the organization:

1. The process of "bureaucratization" has not gone very far. This is not meant to be a value judgment. By bureaucratization is meant the process "whereby more of the rules, precedents and methods of operation . . . are no longer easily subjected to challenge." [3]

2. In many important positions personality is more important than role in determining function. This means that changes in personnel are extremely important insofar as the functions of a given office are concerned, and that positions that are more or less parallel in Munich and New York may be filled by individuals who perform quite different roles.

3. Changes in organizational structure are frequent. Indeed, one of the difficult aspects of carrying out this study was the continuing process of organizational change during the eighteen months in which RFE was under observation.

4. A great deal of authoritative communication is informal—much of it oral.

5. Within the broad limits set by New York, Munich enjoys a considerable degree of operational autonomy in both policy formation and implementation matters. Although in late 1956 and early 1957 there seemed to be a trend toward firmer New York control, Munich remains in important respects a highly autonomous organization.

Personnel

From one point of view Radio Free Europe can be looked upon as a partnership between the Americans and the exiles, each with something unique and exclusive to contribute. In the beginning RFE operated on the basis of an assumption that a genuinely patriotic radio-in-exile would have a listener appeal in the captive countries beyond that of an official western station. Although there has been some recent evidence that this factor is not as important to RFE's listeners as it once might have been, the official broadcasting character of RFE is still that of the "Voice of the Exiles." This means, of course, that exiles must be employed and also that they be given more independence than they would have in an official foreign radio operation like the foreign service of the British Broadcasting Corporation.

In RFE the most important position held by an exile is that of desk chief. The desk chief's role includes authority and responsibility for much of the program, policy, and administrative direction in the various independent stations that make up RFE. Almost all the personnel on the various desks, including writers, editors, directors, producers, and clerical personnel are exiles. Exiles also perform important duties in such divisions as News and Information and Audience Analysis.

The Americans occupy the top executive, consultative, and administrative positions that have functions applicable to all the desks. In the following chapters a more complete description of the Americans and the exiles will be undertaken. Here we will be concerned with two aspects of the personnel problem, recruitment and morale.

RECRUITMENT

Finding adequate personnel is one of the most difficult problems faced by RFE. As was pointed out above, each of the desks is headed by an exile desk chief. The editors, writers, producers, actors, and narrators on the desks are all exiles. But only an insignificant percentage of the emigrations from RFE's target countries had any prior radio experience. More had journalistic experience. Radio Free Europe's task from the beginning has been to train a staff to operate five radio stations. The first step was to find people who, if they had no experience, had some potential talent. For the Poles and the Czechs this was not an overly difficult problem because of the size of the emigration. For the Bulgarians and Rumanians it was far more difficult. But even those with potential talents are not always potential employees. Many emigrees do not want to work for RFE. They are interested in becoming assimilated into their new-found homes in the West. For some the security problem also raises its ugly head; a number of people with talent and promise just cannot meet the rigid security standards that RFE must set for itself.

Personnel problems also arise in regard to Americans. In the preceding section we commented on the combination of skills and talents that would be desirable in certain top positions and on the near impossibility of ever realizing this ideal.

Generally speaking, there are five professional groups represented among the Americans in RFE-Munich. The largest is made up of professional journalists. In Munich the Deputy Director, the acting head of News and Information, the heads of Monitoring and the Central Newsroom are all former foreign correspondents. And the younger Americans in these sections are mostly aspiring young journalists or writers. In addition most of the Field Offices (see below, p. 103) employ American journalists.

The second largest group of professionals we might label "academic" because of their advanced university training. These are men who, if they were not in RFE, would perhaps be either in a university or in government service. The political advisers and the Americans in Audience Analysis would fit into this category. These men with special abilities have usually been employed directly upon completion of their university work.

Another group, important because of the positions they hold rather than because of their numbers, includes people who have had years of experience in official governmental foreign propaganda operations. The Director of RFE, his staff assistant and the man in charge of the daily guidance would fit into this category.

Next come the professional radio men. Most of the Americans in the Programing Department and the head of Public Relations in Munich are men with considerable experience in radio in the United States. Finally, there are a few American engineers in the top positions in the Engineering Department.

Thus RFE is competing with a number of other potential employers when trying to fill its positions that call for Americans. And RFE is not in the best competitive position. A radio station needs qualified radio men, and RFE is faced with unusual problems when it tries to hire suitable executive personnel with radio experience. It cannot hope to compete financially with the major radio networks for executive personnel. But even for the person who has no pressing pecuniary motivation, there is another serious question that looms in his mind when considering a job with RFE. Where is this going to lead? A three-year assignment in Munich will mean three years of more or less isolation from his profession, during which time he will be developing skills not necessarily related to anything he might want to do later in the United States. The Munich program manager who has simultaneously directed the activities of five different stations without understanding a single word that has gone out over the air may be a man who has acquired a rare talent, but it is difficult to see where he could market it outside of RFE.

Even the man who can do as well if not better financially in RFE than in another place of employment, and who may be acquiring skills that are of use in other organizations, has some questions. Radio Free Europe offers no pensions or retirement plans. Furthermore, the life expectancy of the organization is so closely tied up with the imponderables of world politics that it is difficult to predict how long it may last. In other words, it is hardly an organization that provides a great deal of long-term security, and the person who demands that would not look favorably on employment with RFE.

Who, then, works for RFE? We have gathered together a few short biographical sketches on a number of the top personnel, both exile and American, which may begin to suggest an answer.

Fredrick A. Bell, Program Manager.[4] I started in radio on station KGW, Portland, Oregon, in 1927, handling all the usual starting assignments in an announcing capacity and with some continuity writing on the side. Inasmuch as my great interest was the acting or announcing field, I pursued this line which included theater, motion pictures, summer stock, and moved from small station experience up to regional network experience. In 1935 I was in New York as a free-lance performer and writer. I remained a free-lancer until 1940, when I was offered a job with the Compton Advertising Agency on a permanent basis. From 1940 until 1953 I worked at Compton with approximately a three-year interim period in the army. I started as an assistant production man on the daytime serial shows (soap operas) doing occasional writing, producing, directing, and being in charge of the casting and network contact. Some of these shows were "Life Can Be Beautiful," "Ma Perkins," "The Goldbergs," "Road of Life," "The Right to Happiness," "Vic and Sade," and "Against the Storm." A year or two after I had been with the agency I was assigned to nighttime operations with all sorts of news and dramatic shows. My particular phase of operations was the "Truth or Consequences" show with which I was associated, for two years prior to my going into the army, as an advance man and contact man for the various federal agencies with whom we were cooperating.

We toured the United States twice during this period, working for the Treasury Department, Labor Department, Army, Navy, etc. At the time I was drafted into the U.S. Army I was a full-fledged producer and when I returned, I reassumed practically the same duties with, however, some additional shows and experimental television. I took a leave of absence for six months and worked with a friend who had a series called "Studio 13" on the Columbia Broadcasting System. Here I learned the trade of floor manager, dolly man, technical director, and was thoroughly briefed in every phase of the television industry which was so soon to come to great promise.

From 1948 until 1953 I was the Executive Producer and Assistant to the Vice President in charge of Radio and Television and was involved in all phases of radio and television production. I have given lectures on these subjects at CCNY, Hunter College, and many other universities and high schools in the general area of New York City. I developed local television shows for the Socony Vacuum Company throughout all of the Midwestern and eastern United States. The main part of my job was to devise, create, and set up new programs and new program ideas, participate in the presentation to clients, get them started on the air, and then assign one of my assistants to take over the operation on an everyday basis while I stood by for more new assignments and the necessary trouble-shooting on the old ones.

In 1953, on passing my fortieth birthday, I became a little dissatisfied with myself and the whole commercial approach that I necessarily felt toward the industry. My choice was either to continue on up the ladder to both financial and social success, or to break away from it once and for all and do the kind of show that gave me a deeper, personal satisfaction. After a month's relaxation in the Maine woods with my wife, I came to the decision that I would leave the agency where I had spent so many years, and enter what I choose to call the "service field" of radio and television. While I was being contacted by such organizations as Ford Foundation, the Protestant Radio and Television Commission, I heard of Radio Free Europe. The opportunity to work with such a project and to have experience in Europe for both me and my family seemed like a step in the direction that I was looking for.

I came to Europe for Radio Free Europe in September 1953 as the Deputy Program Manager for the Voice of Free Hungary and assumed the responsibilities of the Program Manager for all five stations of Radio Free Europe in July 1954.

W. J. Convery Egan, Director. The Director of Radio Free Europe first joined the organization in May 1954, and less than a year later was raised to the position of Director and made a vice-president of the Free Europe Committee. Mr. Egan came to Radio Free Europe after completing twelve years of government service. He entered government service in 1942 in the Rockefeller Office of Inter-American Affairs. Later service with the Department of State and the United States Information Agency included assignments as Chief of the Information Division under the United States High Commissioner in Germany; Chief of the Public Affairs Division in Berlin under HICOG, Public Affairs Officer at the American Embassy in the Hague, and principal Public Affairs Specialist at the American Embassy in Brazil, where he was stationed from 1944 through 1948. Immediately prior to his joining RFE he was Western European Public Affairs Officer representing the United States Information Service on the staff of the American Ambassador to NATO and other European regional organizations.

In the German headquarters of the High Commissioner, Mr. Egan was responsible for supervising the German language daily newspaper, *Die Neue Zeitung*, two monthly magazines, a fortnightly pictorial publication, the United States radio station in Berlin (RIAS), and other information media including a nationally distributed weekly newsreel and documentary film production. During his Berlin assignment, he was also in charge of American propaganda activities in that enclave.

Prior to his entry into government service, Mr. Egan was a newspaper man. After spending seven years with the *Trenton Times* following graduation from high school in 1930, he began working for the Associated Press in 1937. During the thirties he studied at night at the University of Pennsylvania.

Allan A. Michie, Deputy European Director.[5] Mr. Allan A. Michie was born in Aberdeen, Scotland, on July 4, 1915. His family emigrated to the United States at the end of 1925 and settled in Menasha, Wisconsin, where he went to public schools and high school.

Mr. Michie attended Ripon College, Ripon, Wisconsin, from which he graduated with a B.A. in 1936, majoring in history, economics, and English. He specialized in debate and public speaking, taking part in national tournaments. He also managed the college dance band, and after graduation in 1936 took a small dance band to Europe that played its way across. While touring Europe he was granted a scholarship to the University of Chicago Law School, which he entered at the end of 1936.

In 1937 Mr. Michie gave up his scholarship and went into journalism, aiming at foreign affairs. He began as a member of the foreign affairs staff of *Time* in July 1937, moved up to be Assistant Foreign Editor and then left *Time* early in 1939 to write a book in Washington. He set sail for Europe in August 1939, arrived in Britain on September 3, 1939, the day of the outbreak of World War II, and rejoined the staff of *Time* in London a few days later. He remained in Britain as a war correspondent for *Time*, a writer for *Fortune* and news editor for *Life* until early in 1941; then went to the Middle East, India, the Far East (and around the world) as a war correspondent for *Time* and *Life*. Returning to the United States after Pearl Harbor, he joined the *Reader's Digest* as a roving editor and returned to Britain, where he served as a war correspondent until the end of the war, covering mainly the air offensive against Germany, D-Day (attached to General Eisenhower's headquarters), the "liberation"—occupation of Belgium, Holland and, finally, Germany and Denmark.

He remained in Europe as roving editor of the *Reader's Digest*, based in London, until the end of 1949, when, after a lecture tour of the United States, he parted company with the *Reader's Digest* and joined *Collier's* as an associate editor, based in Britain. At the end of 1950 he parted with *Collier's* and remained in England to work on a book on the British monarchy.

Mr. Michie joined RFE on November 1, 1952, as London bureau chief, became acting Director of the News and Information Service during March 1953 (in Leland Stowe's absence) and was moved up to be Deputy European Director on RFE on April 16, 1953.

Jan Novak, Chief, The Voice of Free Poland. Mr. Novak was born on May 15, 1913, in Warsaw, entered the University of Poznan in 1932, and received a Master's degree in economics and political science in 1938. From 1936 to 1939 he was senior assistant to Professor Taylor who held the Chair of Economic Theory at the University of Poznan.

The coming of World War II interrupted his academic career. In the early years of the resistance he worked on an underground newspaper designed to spread defeatist and subversive propaganda among the Germans. This, of course, meant that the paper had to be distributed in Germany, and Mr. Novak organized an underground distribution network. He himself crossed the German-Polish border many times. In 1943 he was sent as a courier from Poland to Stockholm and after returning was sent to London with important dispatches for American and British authorities. The British parachuted him back into Poland in 1944 and during the Warsaw uprising he was one of those responsible for the operation of the underground radio "Blyskawica" (Lightning). Shortly before the capitulation of Warsaw in October, General Bor Komorowski dispatched Mr. Novak to London with reports and documents. He crossed Germany and was the first man to arrive in London with an eyewitness account of the Warsaw uprising.

In 1945 and 1946 he was assigned to Polish Headquarters in London. After the war he worked for the Polish Radio in London and when recognition was withdrawn from the Polish government abroad, joined the BBC. In 1950 he was the first Pole to be employed by RFE. He has been chief of the Polish desk since its beginning.

Ferdinand Peroutka, Chief, The Voice of Free Czechoslovakia. The history of Ferdinand Peroutka's career as a Czechoslovak journalist parallels the history of Czechoslovak democracy. He began writing in 1919, and the ten books and thousands of articles he has produced indicate his conviction in the Masaryk-Beneš type of western democracy. Shortly after the Nazis took over Czechoslovakia in 1939, Peroutka was arrested and imprisoned for six years in the notorious Buchenwald concentration camp. When he was liberated by the Americans in 1945, he returned to Prague to become editor of the leading Czechoslovak newspaper, *Svobodne Noviny (The Free World)*. On the very first day of the Communist coup in 1948, Peroutka's newspaper was seized, he was removed from his position as editor, and his books and plays were banned.

In April 1948, he escaped from Czechoslovakia in the face of impending imprisonment and death, and gained admittance to the United States. Shortly after his arrival he was designated Chief of the Czechoslovak Desk of RFE, and has held that position ever since.

MORALE

One might imagine that morale could present a considerable problem in Radio Free Europe. The exile is a man adrift. It is perhaps impossible for one who has not gone through the experience to really appreciate the fears and aspirations of the exile and to understand the pressure to which he is subjected. In some ways, perhaps, this life presents the ultimate in insecurity and transitory existence. Many of the exiles in RFE have made a remarkable adjustment to their difficult position and it would be quite inappropriate to speak of them as retaining an "exile mentality." Others have not done as well. But for both types, changes in the international scene might have a great impact on their morale. The advent of German sovereignty was a real blow to some. Rumors were rampant that RFE was going out of business. For the Americans this would mean looking for a new job; for the exile it could mean the end of any suitable employment. The first Geneva conference in 1955 and Eisenhower's handclasp with a smiling Bulganin was an indication that the cold war was over and the United States would accept the position of the Soviet Union in eastern Europe. This would mean the end of a dream for which some exiles had been fighting for over a decade. It is small wonder that morale might be mercurial.

The morale problem is complicated by still another difficulty. In any organization in which some positions are reserved specifically for "us" and others occupied solely by "them," one might expect the development of a "we/they mentality" which could have severe implications for morale. This is not a serious problem for RFE, but on the one hand—in the view of this observer—it leads to a certain amount of evasion of supervision and control solely for the sake of evasion. On the other hand, it may also partially account for a certain tendency on the part of RFE's American administration to be somewhat arbitrary and picayune at times.

Some of the "we/they mentality" may be related to a naïveté that originally marked relations between the Americans and the exiles. At the outset a number of Americans considered their role to be solely that of providing the physical plant. Of course, this would be an impossible arrangement, and if it ever existed it was only for a short time. However, for some exiles American policy direction has always been interpreted as a violation of an original "agreement," and has been a cause for resentment. Several years ago an unfortunate phrase, "illusion of freedom," was coined in Munich and was used to characterize the role of the various stations. As will be pointed out below, this phrase hardly does justice to the role of the exile. Indeed, were it accurate, a number of exiles would terminate their relationship with RFE. But the whispered use of the phrase indicates the existence of a certain "we/they mentality."

But considering all the problems involved, the morale at RFE is high. Particularly the staff at Munich has some of the spirit of the fighter on the front lines who prides himself that he is in the thick of the fight. And the trend seems to be in the direction of more of a joint exile-American endeavor. This should help destroy the "we/they mentality" and build more solid foundations for morale.

The Setting

Although a private organization, RFE seeks to support American foreign policy. Thus it must be aware of the official governmental position on the issues and events it treats in its news and commentaries. However, RFE has no formal relationship with the State Department or other governmental agency. It follows American foreign-policy developments by the use of three techniques: First, and by far the most important, the *New York Times* is carefully read and digested. American policy is followed as it is revealed in that newspaper. Secondly, RFE receives the basic news service of the Voice of America and thus is aware in advance of how the official Information Agency is treating events of the day. Finally, a number of RFE officials have personal friends in the State Department or in the Information Agency whom they can contact if necessary. Furthermore, it should be pointed out that the policy guidances are sent to the State Department so that it may keep abreast of RFE's strategy.

Radio Free Europe also maintains an informal contact with the various exile groups from the countries to which it broadcasts. It keeps posted on the activities of such groups as the Polish Council of National Unity, the Hungarian National Council, and the Assembly of Captive European Nations. Although relations are informal—mostly personal—the Free Europe Committee's Division of Exile Relations has more formal contacts which RFE may use if it will.

An organization that is supported by public contributions must be aware of its public relations. The major portion of the public relations function is handled through the Crusade for Freedom, which since 1950 has maintained an almost continuous publicity campaign. By and large the American reaction to RFE has been friendly, as indicated by the considerable number of favorable articles that have appeared in newspapers and magazines and the contributions that are made to keep RFE in business. Most of the attacks on the organization come from either the extreme right or left. The journals with an extremely conservative orientation have been most bitter in their comment. In February 1953, the *National Republic* carried an article by Kurt Glasser. The title of the article, "The 'Russia First' Boys in Radio Free Europe," suggests the nature of its criticism. A similar position, but with more sweeping charges, was assumed in *Facts Forum News* three years later. This article advances the position that the center of the Communist world conspiracy apparently has been removed from Moscow and is situated "in the West, in all these radio stations as the Voice of America [and] Radio Free Europe, in the American Intelligences services . . . in the Western Cryto-Communist press and radio, in the Crusade for Freedom and Free Europe." [6]

The criticism from the non-Communist left has not been as acrimonious as that from the right. It revolves around two main issues: that RFE is run by "reactionary" exiles who have lost touch with developments in the homelands; that RFE is "irresponsible" and broadcasts incitements to action. These criticisms will be dealt with in more detail below.

The European setting of RFE is in many ways more complex than its American setting. There were a number of reasons that led RFE to decide on Munich as its site of major operations. If it was going to be successful in providing a genuine "home service" for the people of the captive nations, it would be necessary to be close enough to the Iron Curtain to receive newspapers and periodicals before they were out of date and to monitor medium-wave broadcasts. Physical proximity was also a necessity were there to be any medium-wave transmitters. From the geographical point of view, then, Munich was ideal. The fact that in 1950 Germany was still an occupied country and Munich was in the American zone of occupation made it possible for RFE to begin operations there. Negotiations were handled through the Allied Military Government rather than through the government of an independent state. The advantages are obvious.

When West Germany regained its sovereignty, the Free Europe Committee obtained a license to continue operations. The following six conditions were established:

1. The radio installations may only be opened for the purposes of the Free Europe Committee; they may not be used for purposes of third parties unless prior written consent is obtained from the German government.

2. RFE is not allowed to change the technical specifications of its transmitting installations or to put in additional radio transmitting installations without prior written consent from the *Bundesminister für das Post- und Fermmeldewesen.*

3. Duly accredited representatives of the German government shall be given free access to all technical installations during or after office hours (the latter only upon prior notification).

4. Recordings will be made of all broadcasts and kept for at least 30 days. They will be made available at the request of the German government.

5. The license is not transferable; it can be revoked at any time without notice if one of the conditions should be violated and such violation should continue despite request to desist.

6. The license is valid for a period of five years and can be extended unless three months prior to its expiration date either the Free Europe Committee should renounce its rights or the German government announce its intentions not to renew the license.

Although Munich was an ideal location for technical and, at the beginning, political reasons, there are certain disadvantages of being located in Germany. One of the favorite Communist characterizations of RFE is that it is the voice of the neo-Nazis who want to re-establish the German domination of eastern Europe. This theme is used with particular intensity in Czechoslovakia and Poland. The fact that RFE is located in Munich is used as "concrete" evidence of German domination. The Communists ask the people, Would the Germans allow any station on their soil which did not advance German interests?

But no matter what the Communists say, Germany is not a particularly hospitable home for RFE. Indeed, German expellees from territories now controlled by Czechoslovakia or Poland are extremely hostile. One tenth of the German population of Bavaria is made up of refugees from the East, most of them *Sudetendeutsch.* The percentage is higher in Munich. The head of the *Sudetendeutsche Landsmannschaft,* Lodgman von Auen, is a pre-1914 pan-German who gives little indication that he has learned anything from two wars in the twentieth century. If today he should object to the Hitler solution to the *Sudetendeutsch* problem, it would probably be on the grounds that it was not enduring. His vision of a Czechoslovakia without the Russians differs diametrically from that of RFE. Hardly an issue of his newspaper, *Die Sudetendeutsche Zeitung*, is published without a diatribe against the Czechoslovak desk at RFE. In addition to attacking its policy, he attacks its personnel and continually accuses them of pro-Communist leanings.[7]

These attacks, if confined solely to the politics of the expellees, would be harassing but not overly serious. However, some of them are picked up and reprinted in the regular German press and thus gain a much wider audience. And a part of the German press feels that the expellees are doing a real service to Germany by bringing the "facts" to the attention of the German people. For example, *Welt Am Sonntag* published a story on RFE in which it said:

The German public knows only very little about this establishment [RFE] which employs over 1200 people. One would know still less if one would not hear from time to time sharp criticism of its broadcasting policy. Violent attacks against the work of this station are made by the Central Association of Expelled Germans, the Union of Expatriates and member of the Federal Parliament, Wehner (SDP). They even demanded the withdrawal of Radio Free Europe from the Federal Republic. What is the matter?[8]

The article went on to decry the facts that the emigrees from eastern Europe were "writing the actual programs"; that there was nobody present at the time the organization was created to represent German interests; that the political adviser, Mr. Griffith (mistakenly referred to as the "American head of the broadcasting station"), was the former Chief of Denazification in Bavaria; and that the station looked "for support rather to the Military Government than to the Federal Republic."

This caused the German interests and feelings to be constantly injured, not only regarding the question of the *Sudetendeutsch* or the Oder-Neise line but also in the general attitude towards Germany. For instance, the Soviet-directed wave of anti-Semitism in East Germany was described as a "Russian effort to win the Neo-fascist groups growing especially in the Federal Republic."

The question whether Radio Free Europe is abusing the right of hospitality is therefore completely justified.[9]

55

In addition to these people who are concerned that RFE may be harmful to German interests in eastern Europe, there are those who are afraid that some day the Russians may retaliate against the Germans for allowing RFE to broadcast from German soil. For example, a deputy said on the floor of the Bavarian *Landtag*, "If . . . the first atom bomb should fall on Munich, we would have RFE to thank for this." [10]

For about two years preceding the Hungarian revolution in October 1956, German attacks on RFE (outside of those in the expellee press) subsided somewhat. This is perhaps attributable to the fact that RFE had been paying more attention to its public relations in Germany. Another factor is also probably involved. Thinking Germans realized that if RFE should be pushed out of Germany, it would set up business in some other country and that it is a greater advantage to have it on German soil where it may be watched and partially controlled than to have it operating where the German would have even less influence than he has now. The article from *Welt Am Sonntag* quoted above ended with this paragraph:

The refusal to extend the validity of its license in the future would only considerably sharpen the opposition and change nothing in fact, because the station would be moved most probably to the Saarland or Portugal. It would be therefore advisable to extend hospitality and to demand at the same time that the representatives of the expatriate groups be granted the right of exercising a certain amount of influence. It should be even considered whether or not there is a possibility to extend its broadcasts to East Germany, to the Germans living in today's Poland and to the 400,000 Germans who remained in the Sudetenland. "Free Europe" is really reaching the ears and hearts behind the iron curtain. [11]

However, following the brutal Russian intervention in the Hungarian revolution, the West German press launched a bitter attack on RFE, accusing it of being (in the words of one paper) an "accessory to the crime." This attack led to a formal investigation by the German government which cleared RFE of the charges made. In the spring of 1957 the press comments were neither as frequent nor as bitter as they previously had been, but RFE had not regained the position it had held prior to October 1956. Details of this German reaction will be discussed in the last chapter.

Policy Formulation and Programing

R ADIO propaganda has two aspects—the vessel and the content. The vessel is the program schedule. In Radio Free Europe the major responsibility for providing an attractive vessel—a proper mixture of news, music, drama, and commentary—rests primarily on the shoulders of the program directors and managers. It is their job to see that the dials of the radio audiences behind the Iron Curtain are tuned to RFE. Responsibility for the content of political programs, however, is less concentrated in the hands of an individual or a department. The Director of RFE takes an active part in developing policy for political commentary. In New York he is aided by his staff assistant and by the Plans and Policy Staff, while delegating much authority for the development of daily tactics to the Guidance Staff. The political adviser in Munich and his assistants play the role of policy-makers in Munich. These men devise the recipes for the liquor that fills the vessel.

Policy-Making and Policy-Makers

Although it is possible to discuss the Programing Department and the duties of the program directors in New York and Munich together, the organizational setup for developing propaganda policy and the manner in which it operates in New York and Munich are so different that they must be discussed separately. There are two important reasons for this difference. We pointed out in the last chapter that the man who became Director of RFE in 1955 had already acquired a great deal of experience in propaganda operations, and began to draw directly into his hands the propaganda policy-making power which under his predecessor had been delegated. In Munich, however, the political adviser, and not the European Director, is the effective maker of tactical propaganda policy. Also, the policy function in New York differs from the policy function in Munich. Munich is primarily concerned with day-by-day tactics, and tactical policy is the forte of the political adviser. New York is largely responsible for long-range strategy. This requires a different set of talents and also is an operation in which the Director can engage at first hand without completely disrupting his other duties. In New York the authority for tactical policy is delegated almost completely to the Guidance Staff and in this regard is similar to Munich.

POLICY-MAKING IN NEW YORK

Although the difference between strategy and tactics could hardly be called spurious, there are situations in which it is difficult to distinguish meaningfully between the two. Tactics are concerned with the short-range and the immediate. In a propaganda operation, tactics largely involve the treatment of daily events in such a way that an agreed-upon strategy will be implemented. Strategies are concerned with developing a plan of action which will lead to the achievement of basic objectives. In periods of crisis, however, objectives may suddenly be changed and old strategies scrapped. In these situations decisions about basic objectives and the strategies developed to achieve them must be done rapidly. Tactics and strategy may for a short time become indistinguishable. The first crucial days of the Polish "revolution" in October 1956 were a time when this situation prevailed. Radio Free Europe's goals in Poland changed rapidly, and as new strategies were developed to achieve these goals, they were conerned with day-to-day if not hour-to-hour events.

Strategic Guidance. From the early days of RFE until about June of 1956 the responsibility for developing long-range guidance was largely in the hands of a man who acted as a counselor for the president of the Free Europe Committee. These guidances were not done on any regular basis, but were produced when changes in the international situation or in the Soviet bloc called for a change in RFE's strategies. Thus guidances of this kind were produced following the Geneva conferences in 1955 and the Twentieth Congress of the Communist Party of the Soviet Union in February 1956. These guidances applied both to RFE and the Free Europe Press.

Following the guidances produced on the Twentieth Party Congress, however, the counselor began to assume more the responsibilities of personal adviser to the president of the Free Europe Committee, and the policy-making function in RFE was performed more directly by the Director of Radio Free Europe. The manner in which this role is played changes, of course, with each new development in the situation facing RFE. When Khrushchev and his colleagues arrived in Warsaw on Friday, October 19, 1956, to challenge the actions of the Polish Central Committee in restoring Gomulka to a position of power, the situation was in such a state of flux that at any moment the basic assumptions on which RFE's policy rested could change. On Saturday, October 20, the Director of RFE in New York, his staff assistant, the Program Director, and the Chief of Plans and Policies waited eagerly in the New York offices for the reports and analysis of the situation in Poland that were coming in on the teletype from Munich. As the reports began to form a pattern of what was happening in Poland, policy statements were issued. Of course, in a tense and fast-moving situation like this the policy relationship between New York and Munich is reciprocal. Munich is directly on the firing line. At the first reports of the momentous events taking place in Warsaw, the Voice of Free Poland was on the air with news reports and commentaries. Summaries of these commentaries were sent to New York along with factual reports and analyses of events. In developing policy in New York it was necessary to pay close attention not only to Munich's analysis of developments in Poland but also to the stand that had been taken in the scripts.

In tense situations like the one described above, there is no time for formal policy guidances. The only guidances are teletype messages. Furthermore, decisions must be made rapidly. In other circumstances there is much more time, and RFE's policy-making structure responds much differently. In stark contrast to the necessarily quick reaction of RFE described above was its reassessment of the whole operation, in late December 1956, following the "victory" in Poland and the bloody defeat in Hungary. There was no need for a sudden decision, however. The desk chiefs from Munich were called back to New York, and for three days in the quiet, unrushed atmosphere of Princeton, New Jersey, the top policy men from RFE-New York, the desk chiefs, and the newly created Advisory Board sat down to analyze carefully the situation in the satellites and lay the foundations for a new strategy for RFE. From these meetings came a number of decisions that affected RFE's later procedures and organization.

Tactical Guidance. The development of strategy can be rather sporadic. When conditions are relatively stable in the world a given policy guidance may remain in effect for some time. However, every day there must be a tactical guidance to indicate how the events of the day should be treated in order to implement the long-range strategies. In New York this task is handled by the Guidance Staff. Every morning this staff carefully combs newspapers like the *New York Times* and the *Christian Science Monitor* and reports coming into the Newsroom from wire services. The daily guidance, discussed in the last chapter, is produced with this material as background. Late in the morning the chief of the Guidance Staff attends the meeting called by the New York program director and attended by key political writers at all desks. At this meeting the chief of the Guidance Staff is the dominant figure. He goes over the news of the day, presenting his interpretation of events and his ideas on how RFE should shape its commentary. This meeting is informal and amounts to a kind of round-table discussion on news events and the requisite propaganda line for the day.

POLICY-MAKING IN MUNICH

When discussing the organization for policy development in New York, it is necessary to bring in several individual positions that belong to separate staff units. In Munich responsibility for policy rests in the Office of the Political Adviser. This office is made up of the political adviser and his deputy, assistant advisers for each of the desks (one assistant deals with the two minor desks), a chief of Soviet Affairs, and a German Press Review Section. In addition to the major responsibility for advising the desks on political propaganda output, the office has four major duties: to check on the program output to see that policy limits are not trespassed and that an agreed-upon policy line is implemented; to report to New York daily on developments in the target countries and on the propaganda line pursued in relation to them; to make available to the desks specialized information, particularly on the Soviet Union; and to keep abreast of developments in exile politics in Europe.

Advice. There are two ways in which the political adviser plays his role. The first is largely routine: his office serves as the relay point between New York and the desks for the passage of the policy guidances. The second is creative: the political adviser, in consultation with the various desk chiefs, develops the propaganda response to events in the world on both sides of the Iron Curtain. He is the "chief tactician" in RFE-Munich. The terrain on which he operates is the day-to-day events and happenings in the world that are significant to the target audiences. It is a shifting terrain—somewhat different today from what it was yesterday, somewhat different again tomorrow. Success is dependent on the utmost alertness and flexibility; it is predicated on the availability of reliable, up-to-the-minute knowledge of events on both sides of the Curtain, knowledge that is shared and appreciated by all editors and writers so that the operation can be integrated and purposeful.

The discussion of events and happenings and the propaganda response that RFE will make takes place at a series of morning meetings. Every day, beginning at 10 A.M. with the Poles, the political adviser meets with the chief personnel from each of the desks for one half-hour. The morning meetings might be called a *dialogue with audience participation.* The principals of the dialogue are the political adviser and the desk chief; the audience consists usually of the key political editor-writers and the news chiefs from the desks, the assistant political adviser for that particular desk with his language expert, the program manager and/or his deputy and the deputy program manager for that particular desk, and representatives from the Newsroom, Evaluation, Research, Monitoring, and Audience Analysis. Prior to the morning meeting the desk chief has already met with his key political editor-writers to discuss the events of the last twenty-four hours and plan topics for the programs of the day. At the morning meeting he reviews for the political adviser the important contents of the local press, monitoring reports and other source materials in the homeland language which would not be immediately available to the political adviser. The contents of the day's programs are then discussed with the political adviser. The political adviser for his part may call the desk's attention to an important newspaper article in the western papers and comment on the important items in the news budget from the point of view of RFE's news coverage for the day. He also may have comments to make on the various programs for the day. If he objects to any of the topics or the way in which they will be handled, he may intervene at this point to state his position and discuss his objection with the desk chief and the respective editor. But in the two and one-half months during which this author attended almost every morning meeting, not one program was rejected by the political adviser.

The "audience participation" at these meetings may come about in several ways. The political adviser might ask the representative from the Newsroom about a certain item in the news budget, or request that the chief of the Newsroom secure some special information on a given topic. One of the editor-writers may volunteer or be asked for comments about a subject on which he has special information. The representative from evaluation may be asked about a particular information item.

The morning meetings also offer an occasion for discussing the New York daily guidances.

It is difficult to comment on a "typical" morning meeting. They differ from desk to desk and also according to whether the political adviser, his deputy, or one of the assistants conducts the meeting, and according to the events of the day. But all the meetings are very informal. No minutes are kept. They are a kind of forum in which an interpretation of the happenings of the day is developed jointly by the Americans and the exiles. Their frequency is one of the factors that minimizes the possibilities of great differences of interpretation arising between the Americans and the exiles.

The morning meetings are the key to the success of the tactical orientation of RFE. They occur often enough to keep abreast of events. The whole approach to developing a propaganda line is highly empirical. Events are reviewed first, after which the Americans and the exiles jointly discuss the day's tactics for dealing with them.

In addition to the morning meetings the Political Adviser's Office sponsors an afternoon news meeting. This is usually conducted by an assistant political adviser, and is attended by all the news chiefs and a representative from the Newsroom. This is a forum devoted exclusively to how RFE's various stations will "play" the news of the day. Questions of priority and emphasis are discussed. These meetings also give added assurance that RFE's stations will be covering all the important news of the day in its hourly newscasts.

The advisory function of the political adviser does not stop with these meetings. There are also many informal meetings with the desk chiefs. Lunches together, afternoon discussions, and interoffice memos all play a part. Furthermore, the Political Adviser's Office discusses with the desk any target papers which may be developed on the desk and occasionally issues a target paper of its own. For instance, the guidance on how to deal with the Beria downfall was produced by the Political Adviser's Office in Munich.

Control. The advising function of the Political Adviser's Office is rather highly centralized. Most of it is assumed directly by the political adviser himself or his deputy. Rarely, for instance, are the morning meetings conducted by one of the assistants. However, the opposite is true of the control function. Most of the routine work involved is done by the assistant political advisers; in fact, this can be looked upon as their primary function. We saw in Chapter 3 that American control (distinguishing control from direction or advice) is a post-factum control. Few scripts are read in advance by Americans. But the Political Adviser's Office does keep a close watch on content, particularly of the political programs. A number of the important political commentaries from each desk are translated each day and read by the assistant political advisers and sometimes by the political adviser himself. In addition, each assistant political adviser has in turn an assistant who is fluent in the language of the desk. This language assistant can listen to the programs as they come on the air, and keep an eye out for any possible deviations from RFE's basic policy. Although most of the work involved in examining the control function is done by the assistants, important differences between the desks and the political adviser are settled directly between the desk chief and the political adviser.

The political adviser also exercises a more direct control over program content—more direct, but more subtle. It amounts essentially to controlling output by controlling input. Some items in the news budget are released on a "not for broadcast" basis by order of the Political Adviser's Office. Such items are usually those of doubtful accuracy, or they may be insignificant but provocative enough to engage RFE in a tedious and futile exchange of polemics with the regime and therefore should be played down. As will be pointed out below, the Political Adviser's Office also makes available to the desk a great deal of information about events and trends in the Soviet Union, which helps to determine the content of programs about the Soviet Union.

Reporting. On a regular basis, usually every day, the Political Adviser's Office reports via teletype to New York on the important developments in the satellites and the manner in which they were treated in the day's programs. This is most essential for the coordination of activities between New York and Munich. There are instances, for example, when the international commentary done in New York will touch on issues that may also be the subject of another political commentary done in Munich. It is therefore necessary for the writers in New York to know how these subjects have already been treated.

Reporting is also important for the coordination of the planning effort. We have pointed out above that Munich has complete autonomy in dealing tactically with the events of the moment, while the long-range planning is done in New York. But long-term policy guidances would not be very meaningful unless they were based on an awareness of how Munich had been treating the major events of the past six months or year. The daily reporting of the Political Adviser's Office in Munich keeps the policy advisers in New York informed of its day-to-day treatment of events.

Providing Specialized Information on the Soviet Union. One of the most impressive things to the outsider about the Political Adviser's Office is the amount of information on the Soviet Union that it makes available to the desks and other interested persons through the efforts of the chief of Soviet Affairs. Events in the Soviet Union very often presage events in the satellites. The fall of Beria set off repercussions that were felt throughout the captive countries. The denunciation of Stalin had implications for all the little Stalins. Changes in agricultural policy in the Soviet Union, for example, may indicate that similar changes are due in the satellites. In any case RFE must keep a close eye on events in the Soviet Union.

Several times a week the political adviser distributes at the morning meetings short papers prepared by the chief of Soviet Affairs or one of his small staff. The operation of this small group is illustrated by its activities during the Twentieth Congress of the Communist Party of the Soviet Union. In the weeks preceding its assembly, a number of papers were written on topics related to the Congress. For instance, there was an analysis of the leadership change in the MVD (the removal of S. N. Kruglov and his replacement by N. P. Dudorow), a paper called "Party and State," one on Khrushchev and the Ukrainian apparatus, another on the possible rehabilitation of Voznesensky, and one on Soviet marshals.

When the Congress actually got underway, the chief of Soviet Affairs began holding a series of noon meetings mostly for the desk chiefs and key editor-writers who would be preparing scripts on the Congress. At these meetings, which lasted about an hour, the events of the Congress were scrutinized and interpreted. The audience had an opportunity to ask questions and discuss events. For several days during the Congress Professor Franz Borkenau, well-known historian of the Comintern, was at RFE and gave several lectures on his interpretation of the Congress, in addition to making a contribution at the noon meetings.

These meetings were supplemented by a continuing stream of background and interpretative papers. An eleven-page analysis of Khrushchev's speech came out as soon as the chief of Soviet Affairs had read the TASS text, which came in through monitoring. There was also a detailed analysis of the composition of the Central Committee. A number of items that could be of direct use for program purposes were put into the news budget by the chief of Soviet Affairs. However, most of his work is concerned with the analysis of trends and developments and not with the "output" intelligence that provides direct support for the preparation of programs.

Keeping Abreast of Exile Politics in Europe and Informed of the German Press Comment on RFE. These two duties of the Political Adviser's Office are both peripheral and routine. Radio Free Europe feels that it is necessary to keep informed about developments in exile politics because of the import they may have for its own employees. It is also necessary to be aware of the attitudes of the German press toward its operations. There is no special unit set up to collect information on exile politics. This function falls on the political adviser, his deputy, or one of the assistants. However, there is a special German Press Review Section that turns out a five-to-fifteen-page weekly review of German press comments on the various Free Europe Committee operations in Europe.

GENERAL COMMENTS ON POLICY-MAKERS IN RFE

The role of policy-maker in a propaganda operation like Radio Free Europe calls for an unusual combination of talents. It calls for men

65

with an encyclopedic knowledge of eastern Europe—of history, politics, and economics, of personalities, trends, and potential for change. It needs men with acute and fast-moving analytical minds who can quickly, dispassionately, and accurately analyze the reams of material that pour into RFE each day. Combined with the dispassionate and analytical capacity must be a proper amount of enthusiasm, and more important, the ability to create enthusiasm in other people. But since the roles of Director in New York and political adviser in Munich also include the responsibility for seeing that policy limits are abided by and agreed-upon policies implemented, they call for men who can enforce discipline and, as mentioned above, who have the rare quality of being able to exercise authority and control without creating resentment. Finally, men are needed who can work in cooperation with many nationalities and who respect their subordinates for their talents and appreciate the difficult circumstances in which some of them live. In short, effective policy-makers in this kind of organization are highly prized for their unique abilities.

The Programing Department

The previous chapter began with a comment about the complexity of the relationship between RFE-New York and RFE-Munich. It is most intricate in regard to the relations among the various program directors and managers and the desks in Munich and New York. The Program Director of RFE has two deputies, the program director in New York and the program manager in Munich. The program manager in Munich in turn has his deputy. This group, with help from the deputy program managers attached to each of the desks in Munich, has the responsibility for providing a program schedule that will attract listeners in the captive countries and provide the best possible vessel for carrying RFE's policy.

Although little direct evidence is available, one could build a convincing case for the proposition that a number of *regular* listeners is a *sine qua non* for any successful radio propaganda operation. There is some difference of opinion in RFE about the best manner to attract and hold a regular listening audience. Some people feel that the captive peoples are so starved for objective news about events in both their own countries and in the rest of the world that RFE can maintain a large audience if it concentrates on objective, reliable news.

Others argue that the percentage of any population with enough political interest and awareness to become regular listeners to news broadcasts is small and that, by and large, the factors that would give RFE a good "Hooper rating" among its audiences are the same as those that make for a good "Hooper rating" in the United States: it must be *good* radio, providing both news and entertainment. With RFE's full broadcast day it is possible to make both kinds of appeal. Ten minutes of news are provided every hour, while the other fifty minutes are absorbed largely by nonpolitical programs. The problem is to achieve a proper balance, and it is the primary function of the program directors to provide an attractive, balanced program schedule that can compete successfully with the regime radios in spite of jamming and official *encouragement* to local populations not to listen to western stations.

Part of this function is performed by the program directors and managers in their roles as executives. They can see that the various stations are maintaining a proper program balance. They can bring writers and producers from the five desks together for play-back sessions in order to promote the cross-fertilization of ideas; they can see that good scripts and programs from one desk are brought to the attention of the others. But, by and large, their role at RFE is not executive; it is pedagogical. One cannot *direct* people to write and produce good shows. It is possible, where there is a large reserve of talented personnel, to hire and fire, promote and demote, and through what are largely executive techniques build up a good programing department. But at RFE there is no reserve of talent. Very few of the exiles in the western world have had radio experience. If it were possible to hire more, RFE probably would. But where the available personnel have had almost no previous training in radio, the program director must be more of a mentor than a director. He cannot tell people to produce good shows; he must teach them how. And the task is not an easy one. His students are working in five different tongues. They are writing and producing for an audience that they know with an intimacy that an American could never achieve. The program directors are always faced with the problem of determining which of the techniques of good radio they learned in America are applicable only to the *homo sapiens americanus,* and which ones are more universal. They are always confronted with the argument: "but in Poland it is done like this," or "but the Czechs object to continuity slogans." Are these kinds of objections valid or are they merely related to the fact the people in these countries have never known anything else? This is a question that the program directors must struggle with day after day.

In the beginning some of the situations were incredible. Former journalists, for instance, would write political commentaries as if they were writing for a newspaper. This kind of situation could be overcome, but the task of providing an attractive schedule becomes more subtle and more difficult as the years go by. The regime radios, perhaps partly under the pressure of RFE competition, have improved their notoriously dull program schedules. For example, jazz music now has great popularity among the younger people in the satellites and was formerly available only on western radios. This gave the West a running start in the competition for youthful listeners. But by 1955 jazz had the acquiescence if not the enthusiastic support of officials behind the Iron Curtain. And the person who has a choice of jazz on the medium band of a local station or on the jammed short-wave band of RFE is likely to choose the former. Thus by 1956 RFE was confronted with an entirely new situation. The local radio backed by a puppet regime had little appeal. But a local radio of a partially independent Communist regime was something worth listening to. Some of the programing techniques RFE has developed to deal with new situations will be discussed later in this chapter.

The program directors and managers (including the language-desk deputy managers) have another job related to increasing the attractiveness of RFE. A minor radio station cannot hold a large audience over a long period of time. A small operation is not likely to have many listeners, nor is it likely to be accepted as an authority. If RFE is going to try, in effect, to be a Radio Prague or a Radio Warsaw or a Radio Budapest, it must be a major radio network and give this impression to its audiences. Events which are of interest to RFE's audiences must be covered, no matter where they may take place. Minor events may be covered by the various RFE correspondents and stringers. But major political events, such as the two Geneva conferences in 1955, require special coverage. Although the political adviser may attend events like the Geneva conferences, the prime responsibility for complete coverage is in the hands of the program manager. And many nonpolitical events also require special on-the-spot coverage. It may be winter sports at Cortina D'Ampezzo, or a special wedding in Monaco, but the job of clearing the project with the European Director and perhaps with the political adviser, the job of getting the engineers together with the people from the desks who are doing the actual covering is the responsibility of the program manager. Most of the technical work on events in Europe outside of Munich which are being covered by more than one station is supervised by Central Production, a section in the Programing Department at Munich. This involves supervising the coordination of the engineers with the commentators from the various desks as well as acting as the responsible head of the RFE "delegation" to these events.[1]

In New York the Newsroom is a part of the Programing Department. It is not only a switchboard operation which receives news from the outside world and routes it to the proper desk in RFE. When events of importance are happening in the satellites, for instance, the riots of Poznan, the Newsroom (under the general supervision of the program director) generates newsworthy copy by such devices as requesting statements from prominent Americans.

Only about half of the program managers' time is spent on matters directly relating to programing problems. The rest is spent on administrative and personnel problems. One must remember that RFE is more than just a corporation or a radio network. Particularly in Munich, it is a small community. For instance, it controls assignments to the apartments where most of the American and exile personnel live.[2] This puts RFE officially right in the middle of a large number of personal and community problems. If a man wants a larger apartment or is having trouble with his neighbors and feels that his requests or complaints do not receive proper consideration by Administration, he goes to his American superior and asks him to intervene. Since the Programing Department is the largest, the program manager and the American deputies on the various desks have a large number of such problems to deal with.

In Chapter 3 we pointed out that in RFE personality and personal skills are sometimes more important than role in determining function. Although the New York program director and the Munich program manager occupy parallel positions, and their job descriptions are quite similar in regard to programs and program content, they function quite differently. The program manager in Munich is an old radio and TV showman and executive. His interests are centered on seeing that good program schedules and good shows are produced. He feels he has little competence in political matters. He attends the morning meeting at which the propaganda line for the day is planned, but the meeting is conducted by the political adviser. The program manager takes no active role. In fact, because the political adviser in Munich has such sweeping competence in regard to the content of political commentaries, the "logistical support chart" (Figure 3) places him in a line position sharing authority with the program manager and actively supervising the desks on policy matters.

The New York program director is a former Washington newspaper correspondent and has an acute interest in political affairs. The morning meeting in New York to work out the propaganda line for the day is presided over by the program director, and although he immediately turns it over to the chief of the Guidance Staff, he is the man in charge. He also takes an interest in interpreting American politics to his script-writers, some of whom because of inadequate training in American history, politics, and culture need his expert advice. As most of the work on program schedules is done in Munich, he is less active in this regard than his opposite number in Munich.

THE BASIC PROGRAMING CONCEPT AT RFE

The basic programing concept at RFE is influenced by five factors that differentiate it from the programing concept in a normal commercial radio network.

1. A commercial network is interested in its audience largely from the point of view of size. If a program has a good "Hooper rating," it can be sold. How the audience responds to the advertising that is tacked onto the show is not the network's concern. Radio Free Europe, on the other hand, is interested not only in getting people to listen to its broadcasts; it is also concerned with getting people to adopt or maintain certain attitudes and to engage in certain activities.

2. Radio Free Europe is broadcasting to people whose governments go to great length to keep them from listening. Although breaking through jamming is primarily a problem for the engineers, the fact of jamming (and other measures to keep people from listening) also has its effect on the basic programing concept.

3. Radio Free Europe has no facilities for audience research comparable to the kind depended upon by commercial networks. We will

see in Chapter 8 the efforts that RFE makes in order to provide some substitute for "Hooper," but the fact remains that as successful as these efforts are in the light of the problems confronted, the output is not real audience research.

4. We have had occasion to mention above that RFE's talent reserve is somewhat limited. An adequate number of competent editors, writers, actors, and producers is hard to find among the exile populations in the West. Yet a *home service* radio on the air about nineteen hours every day has a tremendous appetite for radio talent.

5. Radio Free Europe is broadcasting to tremendously diversified audiences. Each target country has its own culture, values, social structure, language, and institutions. Men like Joseph Harsh and Alistair Cooke, who write and broadcast for both English and American audiences, have commented on the significant differences in the style of their output for the two countries—differences that are so great that it is most unwise to try to use the same script for the two different audiences. But the differences among RFE's audiences are much greater than those between the United States and Great Britain.

Radio Free Europe has developed two major techniques for dealing with these five problems. The first is organizational. In the United States a radio network is a group of stations, located in different parts of the country, which use a number of the same programs. Radio Free Europe is not a network in that sense. It is a group of five stations which share some of the same technical, research, information, and consultative facilities, but whose programing schedules are completely independent. This is how RFE copes with the problem of its diversified audiences.

The second technique used to deal with these problems is the programing concept itself. Although RFE is on the air to its major target countries about nineteen hours daily, it presents only seven or eight hours of original programs. Every hour on the hour there is an original ten-minute newscast. Most of the other programs are repeated three times. Thus almost any program can be heard at four different times during a twenty-four hour period. Generally speaking, the day's block of original programs begins at 1100 hours and lasts until 1500. This block is repeated twice on the same day and once the following morning. Of course, a few original programs, usually those of highly topical interest, are introduced at various times during the day.

This system of block programing has several advantages. First, it enables RFE to get maximum mileage out of its small staff. Second, it enables the listener to adjust his listening habits to the hours of best reception. Third, the listener can adjust his listening to work schedules. Some people would argue that block programing also makes it possible for word to spread on good programs so that, for instance, a person who listens to one of the early performances can encourage his friends and neighbors to listen in the next time around. However, this is a two-edged sword that could cut in either direction.

THE NEED FOR NEW PROGRAMING CONCEPTS AND TECHNIQUES

By 1957 RFE's position vis-à-vis its audience had changed considerably from that of seven years before, when it first went on the air. At that time it could count on listeners (a) because of the sheer novelty of the operation; (b) because the hope for liberation was still high and it indicated that perhaps the West was willing to take more aggressive steps in that direction; (c) because of the relief it offered from the dreadful monotony of the regime radio. All these conditions have since changed, and the novelty has certainly worn off. While the hope of liberation persists, that goal is now viewed in a new and entirely different perspective. Finally, the notoriously dull routine of the Communist radio has been shaken up. For instance, Radio Warsaw has been known to play popular American songs from music flown from New York. The domestic radio in the satellites is becoming more attractive by the introduction of more music, more "nonpropagandistic" programs, and by the use of better radio techniques. And while the competition is becoming stiffer, RFE's small staff is beginning to wear thin. Some writers have produced more than a thousand scripts on the same general subject.

The Programing Department is responding to the challenge by trying to develop new techniques and programing concepts in order to increase the attractiveness of RFE. The most radical suggestion has been made by John Wright, deputy program manager in Munich (and acting deputy program manager for the Polish desk).[3] Mr. Wright feels that the great failing of RFE's programing is the "system of slots." The backbone of the program schedule is the ten minutes of news every hour. Between newscasts there is a fifty-minute segment that is divided up into "slots" of five, ten, and fifteen minutes. Each "slot" calls for a specific program on a specific day. But why should any writer be required to produce exactly fifteen minutes on the same subject every day? Some days the subject may require five minutes, another twenty-five, perhaps on certain days nothing at all. Yet under the demands of the "system of slots," the program goes on the air every day whether or not there is something to be said. Under the new system proposed, the fifty minutes between news would be handled in a different way. First, each newscast would be preceded by fifteen minutes of music. That leaves thirty-five minutes. Instead of breaking down this interval into "slots" for specific programs, it would be assigned to a key editor aided by two assistants. These men would have a specific theme to develop in line with existing guidances and targets. Every day there would be four of these thirty-five-minute segments in the original block that, as in the present system, would be repeated four times.[4]

Assume for the moment that the theme assigned to a given team on a given day is "Document and dramatize some of the reasons why, contrary to the thesis promulgated by regime radio and press, the Cold War is far from being ended." After a short discussion the key editor would take one aspect of the subject for himself and delegate others to his two assistants. He does not tell them how much time to devote to their problem; he asks only for good radio treatment of the subject in a script of not more than ten minutes. When the assistants have completed their work, they turn it over to the segment editor who edits, prunes, sharpens the idea, and weaves the scripts together with his own narration and background. The result may, for instance, only take up twenty-one minutes, leaving fourteen minutes of the original thirty-five blank. This could be filled by one of the "regular" non-topical programs prepared well in advance. Another possibility would be to recruit one of the "specialists" on the desk to do a special program. Any few odd minutes left in the thirty-five could be filled up by music.[5]

This new programing concept has one more important feature—that of a radio "front page." The last thirty-five-minute segment belongs to the editor-in-chief. To him belongs the power of requisition. He can choose the best scripts of the day and use them in whatever way he sees fit to fill out his own segment, which is supposed to be the highlight of the daily schedule and is presented every evening from 2000 to 2100 hours.[6]

The concept is more refined than this brief presentation would indicate. Only the general outline is presented here, but it indicates one of the possibilities which RFE is exploring, even though personnel and technical problems make it difficult to implement. Less ambitious and more feasible is a program developed early in 1956 by the Hungarian desk. The desk chief recognized that although RFE's articulate and detailed political commentaries provided a good exposition of the important political events and trends, they were scattered throughout the broadcast day in such a way that any listener would have to devote several concentrated hours at his radio in order to get more than just a fragment of the total picture being presented. Although they are on the air only a fraction of the time RFE is, the BBC and VOA have a certain advantage because they have to concentrate what they have to say in short broadcasts.

The remedy was to develop a fifty-minute program that presents excerpts from and condensations of the main political commentaries for broadcast every evening. This new program (called the "Daily Mirror") begins with a ten-minute review of the news. With this as background, a narrator introduces excerpts of the important commentaries of the day. In less than an hour the core of RFE's political commentaries for the day has been presented. The Voice of Free Poland is also experimenting with a similar program called "The Magazine of the Air," which combines news, music, and commentary (both political and nonpolitical) in a one-hour program.

The Voices of Radio Free Europe

AT THIS point we come to the production "heart" of RFE—the people who write and produce the programs that go out across the Iron Curtain. It is impossible in a study dealing with all aspects of RFE to do justice to the individual desks. Each of the major desks deserves a book in itself—or two—for in addition to the unique lessons in propaganda broadcasting that one could learn from a detailed study of each, there is enough drama in the lives and struggles of the persons involved to produce several novels with all the tragedy and pathos— and one can also say hope—that is the history of the middle decades of twentieth-century Europe. In this study we are forced to treat the desks more or less together. By doing this we are emphasizing similarities while gliding over differences. Some of these differences are great, reflecting the variety in culture, history, and language among the Czechs, Slovaks, Hungarians, Poles, Rumanians, and Bulgarians. They also reflect the diversified range of temperaments and training among the personnel. But in this study consideration of these differences must be sacrificed to the end of presenting an over-all picture of RFE.

The Organization and Functioning of the Desks

The organization of each of the five desks more or less follows a a single pattern. Each is headed by a desk chief and is divided into a program and production department. The program section is made up of the editors, writers, and news chiefs who prepare programs, while the production section contains the producers, actors, and announcers.[1] Furthermore, each desk is divided between New York and Munich. The Hungarian, Polish, and Rumanian desks have their headquarters and desk chiefs in Munich. The chief of the Czechoslovak desk and the entire Bulgarian desk—except the news operation—were located in

New York until 1957, when they were moved to Munich. But even for the Czechoslovak desk when its chief was in New York, the vast majority of the programs originated in Munich. The New York sections of each desk have been referred to as New York "bureaus"; they are responsible for covering the American scene, the United Nations, and international events that can better be covered from New York than from Munich.

The desk chief occupies one of the most crucial positions in the organization of RFE. He not only holds the highest ranking position open to an exile, but he comes as close to being a "station manager" as one finds in RFE. He has responsibility for policy, programing, and administration. As far as policy goes, he has two kinds of duties. The first is to see that his station implements the policy guidances and operates within the basic policy limits of RFE. Secondly, where the desk has the policy initiative, he must be the driving force. On matters of long-range strategy this latter function involves presenting the view of the desk to the political advisers and taking a leading role in the development of desk target papers or their equivalent. Tactically, the assignment of topics for the various topical commentaries is made by the desk chief each day in consultation with his senior political writers.

However, the desk chief is not altogether master in his own house. The top administration of the desk involves one of those administrative anomalies not uncommon in RFE. We have seen that each language desk has an American deputy program manager who can be looked upon as an agent of the program manager. The desk chief shares with him some of his programing and administrative responsibility, and so, in some ways, it is useful to think of the desk being run administratively as a sort of partnership. In fact, Radio Free Europe, as a partnership between Americans and exiles is typified by the relationship between the deputy program managers on the desks and the desk chief. They must work together hand in hand, each contributing his own peculiar talents to the success of the enterprise.

The importance of the deputy program managers on the various desks should not be underestimated. In fact, the role calls for such a wide range of duties and responsibilities that it is difficult to imagine how any one human being could perform them all. As it works out in practice each deputy does the jobs for which he feels he has some competence and the workday is over before he could possibly attempt the others. Only one of these men understood the language of the desk to which he was assigned, and he spent his time auditioning programs and helping to train the exiles in radio technique. On the other desks the deputies lent assistance to programing, but spent most of their time dealing with administrative matters as well as performing an extremely important function in maintaining good personnel relations. These deputies serve as the liaison between the exiles and the American management on both official and personal or "community" problems. In the deputy program manager on each desk the exiles have an American who will sympathetically understand their point of view and, at their request, will present this point of view to the top management.

Both the desk chief and the deputy program manager are directly subordinate to the program manager in Munich. But it is hardly accurate to consider the desk chief as being subordinate to the deputy program manager. "Partnership" comes as close as any word to describing their relationship.

In the program section directly under the desk chief are from five to ten senior editor-writers.[2] Senior editor-writers are usually responsible for several programs apiece, dealing with subjects related to their specific competence. They write some of these programs themselves and delegate others to writers who work with them. One of the senior editor-writers on the Polish desk, for example, specializes in economic subjects and also writes some political commentaries. In all, he is responsible for seventeen weekly programs—including "From Our Point of View," "Reflector," and the "Economics of Common Sense"—and is also in charge of the economic round-table discussions that occur about once a month. "From Our Point of View" and "Reflector" are five-minute expository (as distinguished from polemical) political commentaries designed for a general audience. The first deals with some important event in the Soviet Union or in the satellites; the second "puts the spotlight" on some specific happening or situation in Poland and discusses it. The "Economics of Common Sense" analyzes the economic situation in Poland, the Soviet Union, or in the West. It is designed for an audience who knows something about economic thought.

Before the editor-writer on a specialized group subject can be a writer, he must be a researcher. A tremendous amount of information comes into RFE daily through the News and Information Services. Although individual items are evaluated as to accuracy, by and large, they are not compiled and analyzed for trends and developments. The senior editor-writer on labor or on economic affairs must take the vast quantity of isolated bits of information that comes across his desk and construct a picture of things in his country. The labor editor-writer, for example, is faced with the problem of taking hundreds of isolated comments about working conditions and developing a general picture of the working conditions in the country with which he is dealing. Economic editors use the reports that come in on retail prices to develop cost-of-living indices, which are absolutely necessary if editor-writers are to comment accurately about the effect of price reductions and currency reforms. Finally, editor-writers in charge of the polemic programs must keep abreast of the Communist propaganda in their countries in order to answer it quickly and decisively, exposing its inconsistencies and falsehoods.

Programs and the Program Schedules

One of the basic objectives of RFE is to provide a complete "home service" radio for the peoples of the captive nations. Table 1 shows the number of original minutes allotted to programs of various categories prepared in Munich and New York for the major stations.

This program analysis indicates the rich variety of programs that RFE makes available to its audiences. Less than 20 per cent of total broadcast time is devoted to political commentary, or what would be called "propaganda" by most people. About 15 per cent consists of news programs; the rest of the broadcast week is consumed by what is from the point of view of content "nonpolitical." However, in this study major interest is focused on the newscasts and the political commentaries.

NEWS BROADCASTS

The hourly newscasts are the backbone of the RFE program schedule. One of the major purposes of RFE from the beginning has been to provide the audiences in eastern Europe with an objective, non-Communist source of information about happenings in their own country and in the world. RFE feels that a significant proportion of its listening audience is attracted to RFE because of a hunger for infor-

Table 1. Program Schedule Analysis, Showing Number of Original Minutes of Programs per Week

Category	The Voice of Free Hungary			The Voice of Free Czechoslovakia			The Voice of Free Poland		
	Munich	New York	Total	Munich*	New York	Total	Munich*	New York	Total
News	947	...	947	1375	35	1410	1016	...	1016
Political commentary (specialized)	245	10	255	456.5	98.5	555	130	10	140
Political commentary (general)	715	40	755	440	260	700	292.5	202.5	495
Cultural and educational .	475	25	500	202.5	117.5	320	297.5	97.5	395
Entertainment (general) .	45	...	45	30	75	105	110	...	110
Entertainment (music) ..	640	...	640	345	100	445	375	...	380
Religious	110	40	150	122.5	62.5	185	150	10	160
Other	320	...	320	260	45	305	285	10	295
Total	3,497	115	3,612	3,231.5	793.5	4,025	2,656	335	2,991

* Includes some programs prepared in London and Paris.

mation that does not originate in the Communist regimes in the captive countries. In order to satisfy this need RFE concentrates on making its news broadcasts accurate and objective as well as interesting and topical. The advisers and desk chiefs know that the listener has opportunities to compare the news offered by RFE with that disseminated by other western broadcasters and will choose the program from which he gets the most information and which he has learned to trust.

Over the years a number of principles have been developed concerning the newscasts. The most important is that only information and facts may be presented. All editorial comment is reserved for the political commentaries, which are distinct and separate programs. When opinions of important personalities are quoted, care is taken to make clear the source of the opinion.

Another principle is that the selections of items, the order in which they are broadcast, and the length of each item must be related to the hierarchy of interests of the listening audiences in the target countries.

A third principle is that all important events of the day must be covered, including those that may be unfavorable from the point of view of the listening audiences or of certain segments among them.

The news chiefs on each of the desks are responsible for seeing that these principles are followed. They have a staff of editors and writers working under them, preparing the hourly newscasts from the news items that are carried to them from the Central Newsroom several times each hour.[3] Unfortunately, news broadcasts are rarely translated, and so an analysis of content is impossible in this study.

POLITICAL COMMENTARIES

Of more interest to this study than the newscasts are the political commentaries, which take up from 15 to 20 per cent of the broadcast week. In the program schedule analysis shown in Table 1, the political commentaries are divided into two kinds—specialized and general. Specialized commentaries are those designed for a specific audience— workers, farmers, youth, etc., while the general commentaries are not written for any specific group within the target country. Tables 2 and 3 show a list of the political commentaries broadcast weekly by the Voice of Free Czechoslovakia.

What makes up a day of political commentary on a major desk?

Table 2. Specialized Political Commentaries, Voice of Free Czechoslovakia

Program	Minutes per Week		
	Munich	New York	Total
Calling the Communist Party			
Current Events	30		30
Kaleidoscope of Paradoxes	10		10
History of Communism		10	10
Letter to a Friend		10	10
Farmers' Programs			
Behind the Iron Curtain	10		10
Agriculture in the West	10	10	20
Having a Look at Our Villages	10		10
Talk by Farmer Konopa	10		10
Sunday Forum	15		15
Farmer Klas Speaks	10		10
Labor Programs			
Workers in Opposition	10		10
Discussion after Work	15		15
Commentary by Kelansky	10		10
Commentary by Baraba	10		10
Labor Forum	15		15
Trade Union News	10	10	20
Women's Programs			
Commentary by Chaloupeck	15		15
Talk with Parents	7.5	7.5	15
Literary Review	7.5	7.5	15
Horacka and Novacka	15		15
News of Women's Life	7.5	7.5	15
Women and Politics	7.5	7.5	15
Youth Programs			
Do You Speak English?	20		20
Youth Group I	30		30
Youth Group II	30		30
Youth Group III	30		30
Youth Program	15		15
Student Program	15	15	30
Miscellaneous			
To the Army	15	10	25
Europe without the Iron Curtain	30		30
New World in the Making	15		15
Programs of economic commentary	30		30
Programs for civil servants	6.5	3.5	10

Source: Program schedule in effect from June 1955 to June 1956. The Czechoslovak desk broadcasts many more political commentaries than the other desks.

Table 3. General Political Commentaries, Voice of Free Czechoslovakia

Munich Programs	Minutes Per Week	New York Programs	Minutes Per Week
Best Article	60	From Official Soviet Sources	15
Iron Curtain News	15	How It Really Happened	15
Local Commentary	70	Inside USA	15
Messages	90	International Commentary	70
Night Commentary	40	Medical Messages	15
Other Side of the Coin	90	New York Correspondent	60
Round-table Discussion	10	Carpatho Ruthenian Report	5
Spotlight	35	Night Commentary	10
Voice of the Opposition	30	Our First Republic	15
	—	Peroutka Talk	15
Total	440	Round-table Discussion	10
		Who Is Who?	15
			—
		Total	260

Source: Program schedule in effect from June 1955 to June 1956.

Before one can get an idea of the significance and objectives of the commentaries, it is necessary to be reminded of the important events of the moment and the issues then commanding the attention of the peoples of the world on both sides of the Iron Curtain. We shall look at a day in the last week of April 1956. By that time the repercussions of the denunciation of Stalin at the Twentieth Party Congress were being felt around the world. Khrushchev's "secret speech" had been leaked to the press over a month before. That there was confusion among the leaders in the satellites was becoming apparent. The process of rehabilitation of some of the previously purged traitors, started during the Party Congress, was continuing. There was a degree of liberalization manifested in both the domestic and foreign policies of the Soviet nations. Concessions were being made to workers in Poland. There was talk of a new era of "popular fronts" in the West.

On Monday, April 23, Khrushchev and Bulganin were in Britain. It was not one of Khrushchev's best days. In the afternoon he delivered a speech at the British Industries' Fair in Birmingham, in which he attacked the West for its embargoes on the shipment of strategic goods to the Soviet Union. He went on to boast, in a manner interpreted as threatening, that the Soviet Union would soon have a guided missile capable of delivering an H-bomb to any corner of the globe. In the evening he and Bulganin were entertained at a dinner given by British Labour party leaders. Khrushchev exchanged some rather sharp words with Gaitskell over the matter of imprisoned socialists.

In the United States, Secretary Dulles delivered a speech in which he stressed the need for greater efforts to unite the West politically and economically without at the same time neglecting its defensive potential. He also stressed that the West must be on its guard lest it be caught napping by the new Soviet tactical offensive, especially in Asia and the Middle East.

In Geneva, the U.N. Economic Committee for Europe terminated its meetings and prepared to submit its report to the U.N. The Consultative Assembly of the Council of Europe prepared a draft resolution calling upon Russia and all the satellites to release all political prisoners immediately.

On April 24, 1956, the Voice of Free Hungary broadcast the following political commentaries:

1. *Local Commentary*

SUBJECT: Bulganin and Khrushchev at the dinner given by British Labour party leaders.

PRECIS: The banquet and the reception of Bulganin and Khrushchev are not more than acts of courtesy, and certainly in no way imply that any kind of collaboration is developing between the Communists and the British Labour party. The true opinion of the British Labour party concerning Communist-Socialist cooperation is best expressed by the article just published in the Labour party organ. This paper— of which Gaitskell is one of the staff members—points out that there can be no cooperation between the Communists and Democratic Socialists. There could be a similarity in the principles only until the Communists triumphed in Russia. Since then, it has been proven that (1) the Communists do not ensure the workers' rights, nor do they safeguard their interests; the workers are not given any role in directing their own fate, and (2) there is no hope of making the Communists see reason, for they still refuse to deviate from their basic tenets. The Communists feel that whatever means they use to achieve their ends, history will always justify their actions.

2. *Workers' Program*

SUBJECT: The working class and criticism "in the party spirit."

PRECIS: In a recent speech, Lajos Acs (Communist official in Hungary) admits that the party and the regime are out of contact with the working masses. The Communists are trying to win the workers' sympathy and cooperation by permitting criticism "in the party spirit," thereby trying to give the impression that the workers will in the future have their say in deciding their own fate. Such criticism "in accordance with the party spirit" means only criticism that is allowed by the party. No criticism may be voiced, for instance, against Rakosi or the party resolutions, nor may any social measures of the party be criticized. This kind of "concession" is only a subterfuge to make the workers feel that their opinions and feelings are being taken into consideration in forming policy. But it is just a sham concession that means nothing.

3. *Calling the Communist Party*

SUBJECT: Rakosi and Co. and party democracy.

PRECIS: Since the Twentieth Party Congress in Moscow, Budapest leaders have constantly emphasized that "the Leninist principle of party democracy be restored and put into effect." But what is "the Leninist principle of party democracy?" What is "criticism in accordance with the party line?" Why are the practical meanings of these expressions not clarified? Rosa Luxembourg in her essay, "The Russian Revolution" (1918), says that party democracy was not put into effect even during Lenin's lifetime. "A few dozen leaders always practiced dictatorship within the Party." If Rakosi and Co. were to take party democracy seriously, they would have to call a party congress and there freely debate the new Moscow-dictated line.

4. *Home Commentary*

SUBJECT: Public opinion and the Yugoslav financial negotiations.

PRECIS: Following the Twentieth Party Congress, the process of liquidating the Stalinist past has started in the Peoples' Democracies. In certain countries this had led to some benefits for the people, but not in Hungary. There has been neither an increase in wages nor a reduction in prices, nor has there been any let-up in applying the methods of the Stalinist class struggle. It is characteristic that, although the Congress paved the way for criticism and for greater consideration of public sentiment on issues, public opinion is completely neglected in Hungary. The Yugoslav-Hungarian financial negotiations now underway are a case in point. The public was not informed on the subjects to be discussed in Belgrade. How much money is involved? What are the true reasons for the negotiations being dragged out? Who are the members of the Hungarian delegation other than Minister of Finance Karoly Olt? The secrecy, however, does not cover up the fact that Yugoslav demands are particularly heavy because of the presence of Rakosi and Co. An agreement must, sooner or later, be reached—yet no matter what the details of such an agreement, it will be far less advantageous than if the Hungarian nation had been represented by a capable government which considered the true interests of the Hungarian people.

5. *Reflector*

SUBJECT: An Answer to Lajos Acs.

PRECIS: "Before the law, every Hungarian is equal!" This statement was made by Lajos Acs in his speech at the Opera House. What is the situation in reality? Radio Budapest today announces that suspicion and differentiation is to a certain extent justified in the cases of persons of kulak families, of "poor political family background." It further discloses that a kulak is recognized not only by his financial status, but by studying the data produced by personal investigation. The radio further mentions that those dismissed are unable to find other jobs, since inquiries are inevitably made at their former place of work, where the answer is "he had some disagreeable affairs here." This is an obvious reference to political unreliability. In his speech Lajos Acs emphasized that criticism reflecting disadvantageously upon the party is not permissible. Thus, should anyone make any statement disadvantageous to the present regime, he will again be put on the black list and will be referred to as "having had disagreeable affairs." All this proves that, basically, nothing has changed in Hungary. The police state remains. Only the means of execution are different. Hungarian society still continues to wear prison clothes—it is merely the shape of the clothes which has changed. And it is of this society that the speakers at the Lenin festivities declared that there are no classes, that everyone is equal before the law.

6. *Economic Commentary*

SUBJECT: The Five-Year Plan in Hungary.

PRECIS: Typical of the deep-rooted contrasts within the Communist party is the fact that the authorities are faced with the problems of preparing the new Five-Year Plan for the second year. It might be assumed that Rakosi and Hegedus have suggested such a ruthless plan that the majority of the Budapest Politbureau could not even accept it. They are now trying a new method. They are trying to mobilize the factory workers and give them the impression that they are preparing the new plan. We remind the workers that their present mobilization is meant to result in still further exploitation. The plan cannot be decided upon in the factories, for the main questions will have been answered long before any workers are consulted. The regime knows that the workers would not produce a plan in which the Moscow-dictated requirements for heavy industry are met. The workers want an increase in real wages and an improvement in living conditions. But the Five-Year Plan will have to concentrate on the development of heavy industry and thus the workers cannot be given a chance to express their own interests.

7. *International Commentary* (prepared in New York)[4]

SUBJECT: A review of Dulles' speech of the day before.

The following political commentaries were broadcast by the Voice of Free Poland:

1. *On Your Neighbor's Farm*

SUBJECT: The role of the free peasants in Poland.

PRECIS: Communist propaganda claims that agriculture in Poland lags behind industry and that the free peasants must be blamed for this. To remedy this state of affairs it is suggested that agriculture should be completely collectivized. Mr. Wencel, a recent escapee from Poland, puts on record the Polish peasants' view on that question. The towns owe their supplies of foodstuffs mainly to independent peasants who, although they have no help whatsoever from the state, have better results than *kolkhosi*. The fact is that independent peasants, though severely handicapped by lack of help from the state and industry, and enjoying none of the aid given to inefficient *kolkhosi*, still feed the nation with their produce.

2. *No Curtain Shall Divide Us*

SUBJECT: Pay Increases.

PRECIS: Pay increases are so widely recognized as essential to good labor relations throughout the world, and workers' resistance to the regime in Poland has become so stern, that the Communists in Poland have decided to make a gesture which would show that they, too, have a concern for labor's well-being. But as usual their gesture amounts to no more than a niggardly dole. Although recent pay increases in Poland must be welcome if only for the reason that any alleviation of the workers' plight is a positive development, an analysis of how these pay increases affect the workers' situation leads to the following conclusions. The pay increase recently decreed is unsatisfactory. The working class demands a bigger share in the rising national income, pay increases for all categories of workers and not only for those least paid, and the fixing of the minimum wage at a level guaranteeing decent existence. Furthermore, pay increases should be supplemented by price cuts.

3. *From Our Point of View*

SUBJECT: The New Soviet Tactics.

PRECIS: On the international scene the object of new Soviet tactics is (a) to secure the acceptance by the West of the principle of coexistence, which is tantamount to approval of the Soviet position in eastern Europe; and (b) to pave the way for the establishment of popular fronts. The idea of popular fronts, however, has been firmly rejected by the Socialist International. The meeting between Khrushchev and British Socialists ended in an atmosphere of tension. In his speech Eisenhower stressed that eastern Europe remained under Soviet dominion and in this way he put an end to Soviet Russia's hope that her conquests might be recognized by the West. To achieve her two objectives Soviet Russia made a great effort and many sacrifices, but all in vain. No wonder that the irritated Khrushchev, speaking in Birmingham, threatened the West with a hydrogen bomb.

4. *Reflector*

SUBJECT: The denunciation of Stalin and the ZMP (Polish Communist Youth Organization).

PRECIS: The fall in the party's prestige, after the demolition of the Stalin myth, has also seriously affected the ZMP. The ZMP is getting sicker and sicker. First and foremost, there is the constant hostility of young people to the organization through which the regime tries to regiment them. Recently the ZMP expelled thousands of recalcitrant members. Secondly, the end of the Stalin legend has created an atmosphere of confusion and uncertainty in the ZMP leadership. There have been some purges. Alarmed by the decay of the ZMP its leaders speak of reforms. But nothing can stop the growing gulf between the Communist-dominated ZMP and Polish youth.

5. *The Other Side of the Coin*

SUBJECT: The continued domination of Moscow.

PRECIS: The revival of the faked Seym is part of the present Communist effort to build up the appearances of democracy in Poland. Delivering a speech in the Seym, Cyrankiewicz was at pains to suggest that the new line had not come from Moscow, but had been a spontaneous development in Poland. Explaining the recent events, Cyrankiewicz said that the party had recently discovered some new truths while the Polish people had been slowly learning the democratic ways and graduated into democracy. Whatever Cyrankiewicz argues, what happens in Poland has nothing to do with democracy and he is not a democratic leader. He is no more and no less than an obedient executor of Moscow's policy. He took his orders from Stalin; now he takes his orders from Khrushchev. Never does he go beyond what is sanctioned by Moscow. He confesses to have followed wrong policies but nevertheless he stays in office. Can such things happen in any democratic system? Is not this the best proof that the Polish nation is enslaved?

6. *You and Your Neighbor*

SUBJECT: The reaction of the French Socialists to the new appeal for "popular fronts."

PRECIS: The organ of the French Socialist party, *Le Populaire*, in a series of articles explained why western Socialists will not cooperate with Communists. The stand taken by *Le Populaire* is particularly interesting in view of the fact that it was in France that the Communists much hoped to enter into a common front with the Socialists. *Le Populaire* rejects the Communist contention that the end of the Stalin legend has brought any fundamental changes in Soviet Russia. Tactics have changed but aims have remained unaltered. Notably there has been no democratization of political life in Russia. *Le Populaire* states that Socialists could start negotiations with Communists only if the latter first fulfilled a number of conditions. Among these conditions, one of the most significant is the restoration of freedom to East European countries.

7. *West European Press Review*

SUBJECT: Western European comment on the Soviet leaders' visit to England.

PRECIS: The *Times* and *Daily Mail* report that the British people are maintaining their reserve. The *Manchester Guardian* attacks Soviet jamming of the BBC. The *Daily Telegraph* comments on the fact that after the dissolution of the Cominform the WFTU continues the diversionary tasks previously carried out by the Cominform. The *Times* and *Daily Herald* emphasize the close links between Britain and the United States. The *Neue Zuricher Zeitung* is confident that the British leaders are unlikely to be fooled by Soviet perfidy. *Le Monde* feels that British leaders must show great skill not to be on the losing side of a meeting they initiated.

The topics for these commentaries are chosen by the editor-writers in consultation with the desk chiefs and reviewed by the political adviser. In the previous chapter the daily morning meetings were discussed. Prior to this meeting the desk chiefs (or their deputies) meet with the senior political editor-writers. Each of the editors is responsible for coming to this meeting with a knowledge of the material currently available from one of the important sources of daily information (monitoring, news budget, press, etc.). At the meeting they discuss events and developments in their particular countries and throughout the world. Subjects for the various topical programs for that day are decided upon and the writers for the various programs chosen. The political adviser is advised on these decisions at the morning meetings. However, the scripts themselves are rarely reviewed by any American before broadcasting.

Of course, topics for commentaries and their content are developed in the light of the guidances from New York. For instance, the program summarized above, dealing with the denunciation of Stalin, was related to Special Guidance No. 25. However, the desks also have a role in formulating general propaganda goals and lines. Two and three years ago it was common practice for the desks to produce "target papers" that usually spelled out in detail how a New York policy guidance would be implemented on that particular desk or treated a problem that was more or less unique to one country. On the Hungarian and Czechoslovak desks these "target papers" are no longer considered necessary. Their function is now performed in a less formal manner through discussions or short memos. The practice, however, continues on the Polish desk. One of these papers is worth reviewing in detail because it indicates the area in which the desks have the policy initiative.

"Polish Target No. 9, Progressive Catholics" was completed in August 1955.

The introduction to the paper identifies the "Progressive Catholics" and states the aims of the propaganda campaign.

The "Progressive Catholics" acts [sic] as a non-Communist group which has ostensibly set as its main goal the defense of the Church and of the Catholic religion in Poland. The chief task of our campaign will be to demonstrate the falsehood of this thesis and to prove to the broad masses of our listeners that the "Progressive Catholics" are but a tool of Soviet policy in Poland and that they work for the destruction and not the defense of the Faith and the Church.[5]

The first sections of the paper deal with an analysis of the situation that begins with a discussion of Soviet theory and practice in the struggle against religion. In Communist theory, of course, religion is viewed as a mere artifact of the economic organization of society and must, therefore, disappear when this organization is transformed. Lenin, however, recognized that although it merely reflected economic organization, the organized church could become a bulwark of that organization. Its destruction could not be left solely to the workings of the automatic laws of history. An active campaign was necessary. But at the same time, he recognized that the campaign would be of a long-term nature and that it must be conducted in a manner that would not conflict with the more immediate task of the Communist party.[6]

As for the tactics pursued in the struggle against the church, the Soviets are looked upon as having learned much from their experiences in the Soviet Union. In the period from 1917 to 1941 the party waged unceasing war against religion by subverting the church organization, fostering internal splits, closing down churches and arresting, imprisoning, and deporting churchmen. This policy, however, was not noted for its success and, following 1941, the direct attack against the church was abandoned and attempts were made to capture the church organization and use it as a tool of the party. This has proved more successful, and the organized church in the Soviet Union today has the following characteristics:

(1)It is exclusively made up of men who are supported by the state and who carry out obediently any instructions issued by the Soviet authorities; (2)the Church is confined to the performance of rites such as the celebration of the Mass, the administration of the Sacraments, etc. It is unable to counteract anti-religious teaching and propaganda. Preaching from the pulpit must be limited in contents to matters which conform to the current interests and needs of the Communist state.[7]

The "Progressive Catholic" movement is looked upon as an attempt to create a church in Poland with these characteristics.

The theology of the "Progressive Catholic" movement in its most general and abbreviated form can be stated as follows:

God is Lord of the universe as (1) *Creator* and (2) *Redeemer.* Hitherto, Catholic teaching has placed all emphasis on the Redemption and has clearly ignored the Creation. This emphasis should be reversed. The continuation of the Act of Creation consists in "transforming and perfecting the world," i.e., in service to progress. The Communist system represents and realizes this progress.[8]

Thus the Christian duty of every Catholic is to support "progress," i.e., to support the Communist party in its efforts to build the new society. The dictates of the Gospel must be interpreted in such a way that they provide support for the policies of the regime. The leader of the "Progressive Catholics" states it this way:

An interpretation of the commandment to love one's neighbor which, avoiding the performance of civic duties, redeems itself by the performance of some so-called "good-deed," must disappear from the Catholic way of thinking. . . . Such a concept of the love of one's neighbor should be propagated as will be manifested in the day-to-day work of building the common prosperity of the entire nation.[9]

An understanding of the sociopolitical genealogy of the "Progressive Catholic" movement is important to any propaganda campaign designed to combat it. Boleslaw Piasecki, the leader, and most of his closest collaborators were notorious in the prewar "Falanga"—a thoroughly fascist organization. However, early in the Nazi occupation period he was arrested but later released after Mussolini himself intervened. During the war he directed a clandestine organization known as the "National Confederation," guerilla detachments of which fought both Germans and Russians in eastern Poland. In 1944 he and some of his associates were captured by the NKVD. Although most of his collaborators were shot, Piasecki himself was given a prison term. After seven months' confinement he was released and, following a series of talks with a colonel in the Russian security forces, was allowed to organize his followers into a group called "Progressive Catholics."

Today the group has at its disposal five periodicals, a publishing house, considerable financial support, and a nationwide organization called the "Committee of Lay Clerical Catholic Activists Attached to the National Front." The priests who associate themselves with the movement are able to celebrate Mass, administer the sacraments, etc., but the price they pay for these rights is complete subservience to the regime and support of its attempts to use the church to speed the process of transformation to the new society. Of course, the "Progressive Catholics" depreciate the role of the Holy See. They ostensibly recognize its supremacy in matters of faith and morals, but reserve for themselves the right to define the limits of the Pope's competence and take a major role in setting the lines of "political" action in which the church may (and should) engage.[10]

Although the people at the top of the organization are undoubtedly completely cynical, a considerable number of people apparently have either been completely duped as to the ultimate purpose of the movement or feel that it can serve a positive role by actually influencing the regime itself.

Directly from this analysis followed the *program guidance*—a statement of the approach and some of the themes that would be used by the Voice of Free Poland in attempting to undermine the "Progressive Catholic" movement. The most important technique used was that of dispassionate, factual reporting. The history of the movement and its leaders was presented in detail to the Polish people on the assumption that the tarnished reputation of its leaders, if known, would help contaminate the whole movement.

Programs also directly attacked the leaders of the movement, since it was believed that many of the followers were acting in good faith. It was demonstrated that since the "Progressive Catholic" movement was being used as a weapon to destroy the Roman Catholic Church in Poland, the "Progressive Catholics" would be destroyed as soon as this objective was achieved. Therefore, "Progressive Catholics" were men working for their own destruction.

This review of the target papers on "Progressive Catholics" indicates the kind of problems on which the desks have some policy initiative. (This function is performed, of course, in connection with the Political Adviser's Office.) It also indicates another of the duties of the desk chiefs and the senior editor-writers who are responsible for these papers or their equivalent.

NONPOLITICAL PROGRAMS

There are differing ideas in RFE on the functions of the nonpolitical programs—or at least differences in emphasis. Some feel that these programs are the strongest attraction in winning and holding the audience to RFE. The hope is that people who have tuned in for a drama, music, or comedy show will not turn the dial when a political commentary comes on. But it can be argued that the nonpolitical programs play a more direct role toward achieving the goals of RFE. One of RFE's objectives is to support the morale of the captive peoples. This can be done as much, if not more, through nonpolitical as through political programs. Music that is on the regimes' black lists, and plays and stories by native authors who are in disrepute behind the Iron Curtain but are popular with the people, help to achieve RFE's goals. The recognition of this fact is affecting RFE's basic approach to its problems. In the spring of 1956 this author noticed a trend (which had probably been going on for some time) away from the hard-hitting, polemical broadcasts. The phrase "propaganda through information, education, and entertainment" was repeated more than once by a number of different people at RFE. Time and effort were being devoted to developing programs or blocks of programs which combined the political message with good entertainment.

Important as they are, it is impossible to present a detailed analysis of RFE's nonpolitical programs. There are too many of them, and scripts are rarely translated. Furthermore, their impact is gained as much through the manner of presentation as through pure content. An adequate evaluation could only be made after actually listening to the programs as they are broadcast. Unfortunately, this author understands no Polish, Czech, Slovak, or Hungarian. However, three nonpolitical programs—one from each of the major desks—will be reviewed briefly to suggest to the reader the way in which they are related to RFE's basic objectives.

The Hungarian Desk's Coverage of the Celebration at Mariazell on June 10, 1956. On June 10, 1956, Hungarian emigrees in Austria and Hungarians of Burgenland celebrated at Mariazell the five-hundredth anniversary of the victory of Nandorfehervar (over the Turks). Mariazell is an old Hungarian place of pilgrimage in Austria. It is full of Hungarian memories, and the victory of Nandorfehervar is an event famous in Hungarian history. In the past, many thousands of Hungarians used to visit Mariazell. The inhabitants of the frontier villages usually made the journey on foot. Today the Iron Curtain prevents the Hungarians from visiting this beloved shrine.

But Radio Free Europe covered the event. Engineers went to the famous shrine and set up their equipment to broadcast the ringing of the noonday bells and the festive High Mass said by the Archbishop of Salzburg. Narrators described the scene and commented on the famous victory that was being celebrated that day.

All of this was broadcast to the Hungarians who had to stay at home and whose regime ignored the celebration at Mariazell. One can only guess whether or not the listeners related the historic victory over the ancient oppressor from the East, who for so many years had seemed invincible, to their plight today. One can only guess whether or not it helped people to believe that "this too shall pass away." For this was a program aimed at reinforcing a hopeful spirit, indicating to the listeners that there were people in the West who were interested in their fate and dedicated to their eventual freedom.

The Czechoslovak Desk's Coverage of Kubelik's Appearance in the Berlin Sportpalast. On March 15, 1956, Rafael Kubelik, famous exiled Czech conductor, appeared with the Vienna Philharmonic Orchestra at the Berlin *Sportpalast* and directed the orchestra in a performance of Smetana's "Ma Vlast" (My Homeland) and Dvořák's "Slavonic Dances." To an American this date, this place, and this music have little special significance. But to a Czech or Slovak they are pregnant with meaning. March 15, 1956, was the seventeenth anniversary of the German take-over of Czechoslovakia, the *Sportpalast* was built by Hitler and was one of his favorite places for addressing his followers. Smetana and Dvořák are two of the great Czech composers. The Czechslovak desk recorded the concert and broadcast it to the homeland, preceded by a short interview with Kubelik.

The introductory comments were not hard-hitting or polemic. No mention was made of Hitler's name or of the German armies. But Kubelik's voice was filled with emotion when he said to the RFE interviewer, "You certainly know the feelings we had many years ago these days of March . . ." The interviewer knew and, undoubtedly, so did many in the listening audience. Again, one can only guess what it meant to a listener in Czechoslovakia to hear a Czech conductor playing music from his native land to an enthusiastic audience of eight thousand Germans on March 15. But many who heard the program probably thought back on March 15, 1939, and perhaps derived a quiet satisfaction from the drama that was being enacted in Berlin seventeen years later. Perhaps in some it instilled a new hope that one day the present tyrant would also be destroyed.

The Polish "Radio Tea Party." Both of the programs reviewed above were special broadcasts; the Polish *Radio Tea Party*, however, is a regular Sunday feature of the Voice of Free Poland. The *Tea Party* is a variety show whose lineage goes back to prewar times. The Polish radio before the war carried each Sunday, at teatime, a program of music and entertainment broadcast from various *cafés* in Polish cities. The custom was not taken up by the Communist radio after the war, but when the Voice of Free Poland was first established, the radio tea party idea was revived. Of course, it is no longer possible to broadcast from a *café*, but Poles living in and around Munich are brought into an RFE studio to provide the audience that is so necessary for the success of such a show.

This author attended the recording of the two-hundredth performance of the *Radio Tea Party*. There was singing—both original songs written for the show and currently popular numbers—sketches, and monologues.

One of the features of the program is an original song, dedicated to a Polish city. On this particular program the song was dedicated to the city of Cracow. One of the distinctive features of Cracow is the playing of a bugle from the high tower of St. Mary's Church every hour. There is a legend that during a Tartar invasion of Poland in the thirteenth century a defender of the city climbed high up into a tower to sound the alarm on his bugle. But before he was finished a Tartar arrow pierced his throat. Today when the hourly call is played in Cracow it ends abruptly on the unfinished and plaintive note of the medieval bugle call, played to warn the residents of an invasion seven hundred years ago. The song in the *Tea Party* was dedicated to the man who has played the bugle for the last thirty years. It sent him greetings and wished him a long life in his unusual profession.

Another regular feature is a sketch called "A Conversation between Two Portraits." In one of the episodes, the portraits of Bierut and Rokossovsky chat back and forth. As the discussion continues, a growing uneasiness becomes apparent, culminating in a foreboding that, in the near future, they might be removed from the wall and replaced by something more "collective." They visualize in their places pictures depicting the familiar Russian countryside—pictures of the Lubianka prison or the forced-labor camps of Vorkuta and Svierdlovask.

News, Information, and Research

Program schedules such as those discussed above require tremendous amounts of news and information if they are to be fresh, up to date, and appealing. Of course, any radio network has a tremendous appetite for news and information, but RFE faces two unique mechanical difficulties that have forced it to set up a special large and complex department.

The first difficulty concerns language. The reader must remember that RFE is a network of five semiautonomus stations, each operating in a different language. But since no one of these is the "official" language of the network, we must bring in a sixth, English. And even these six do not include the language of the country where the operation is located and which is native to many of the personnel, hence German is added. Finally, because of the importance of events in the Soviet Union and in Yugoslavia much material in the Russian and Serbo-Croatian languages is also necessary. Daily operations involve eight different tongues.

Secondly, there is the matter of the Iron Curtain. This was designed as much to keep people and information in as it was to keep people and information out. If RFE is to succeed in its goal to become a "home service" radio for the captive nations, it must have detailed information about everyday life in these countries.

A large part of the responsibility for collecting and disseminating news and information falls on the Munich operation. In this chapter we shall examine the organization and operation of the News and Information Service, one of the operating divisions of RFE-Munich. This division is made up of four sections: Monitoring, the Field Offices, the Central Newsroom, and Research and Evaluation.

Radio Free Europe
Monitoring

One of the major aims of Radio Free Europe, as we saw in the third chapter, is to break the monopoly on news and information that the Communists try so hard to achieve in the countries they control. But RFE is not physically in a good competitive position. It operates from a foreign land, on only one medium, with only one program schedule to each country. The Soviets have hundreds of newspapers, periodicals, radio stations, and face-to-face agitators with which they hammer home their line day after day. One of the results of this is that in everyday matters related to domestic issues, the Soviets have the news initiative. What they will make news, will be news. The people may listen to the western radio, but as one refugee put it, the "attention cues" for what is perceived, absorbed, and remembered, particularly on domestic issues, is by and large provided by the Communists. Radio Free Europe must take the initiative when it can; where it cannot, it must counterpunch with vigor. But whether leading or countering, it must know what the Communists are saying to their people behind the Iron Curtain and know it quickly so that answers and challenges can be made while the issue is still news.

There is another need for up-to-the-minute news on events behind the Curtain and the Communist reporting of them. We have seen that it is necessary for editors, writers, and researchers to live an imaginary life in their homelands. If the psychological environment of a captive country is to be maintained among the exiles in Munich, they must be confronted with the same blast of propaganda as their countrymen behind the Curtain.

It is the Monitoring Section that supplies RFE with the contents of the home radio transmissions and the wire services of the satellite countries. Monitoring can be looked upon as the "ear" of RFE—a large, sensitive, mechanical ear that picks up the voices from behind the Iron Curtain.

Just outside the little town of Schleissheim, about twenty miles north of Munich, the Monitoring Section has its headquarters, most of its technical equipment, and part of its staff. This is the center of an operation that monitors thirty-five Iron Curtain stations on a regular basis—four to six on a spot basis. A close watch is also kept on Yugoslav broadcasts, both those designed for home consumption and those for export to the satellites, and western stations such as Radio Vatican and the BBC are checked for information that may be of interest to RFE. In addition to aural monitoring, eastern and western press services in Morse, *Hellschreiber*,[1] or teletype are picked up and relayed into the Central Newsroom's teletypes for reproduction and distribution. The aural monitoring averages between 45,000 and 48,000 words daily, the mechanical between 125,000 and 150,000. In the course of a week's time twelve languages will be used.

Because monitoring exists primarily to serve programing, it is broken down into sub-sections that correspond where possible to the programing desks. There are three sub-sections to correspond with the major programing desks—Polish, Czechoslovak, and Hungarian. These are located in the English Garden building in Munich, and the signal is piped in from Schleissheim. This physical arrangement makes possible a very close liaison between the monitors and the program editors, who can keep up with the news, commentary, drama, and music which their audiences are hearing from the Communist radio. Under normal conditions monitors receive the signal on sets equipped with two tape recorders. One can be used for recording a program while the monitor is typing out the contents of the other. Tapes of important events and voices are preserved for possible programing use. If the monitored program is important enough to warrant special attention (for instance, a round-table discussion from Radio Prague dealing with a proposed new currency reform), it can be piped directly into a conference room where editors and writers can hear it, discuss and analyze it, and be prepared to go on the air immediately with their own round table of comments. The Hungarians have worked out a special rotation system of handling important speeches so that programing can have them immediately. One monitor transcribes the first ten or fifteen minutes, rushes it off to the editors and comes back to pick up the fifth ten- or fifteen-minute section. This gives the editors a complete text just half an hour after its completion, and an English translation is available in one hour. Just one hour after a speech ends, the Voice of Free Hungary is ready to go on the air with analysis and comments.

The Rumanian and Bulgarian sub-sections, whose programing desks do not require as much material as the other three, are located at Schleissheim as are the monitors who handle non-target countries. Russian, Albanian, Yugoslav, and East German radio are monitored regularly to keep editors, the Political Adviser's Office, and other interested sections abreast of the up-to-the-minute developments in these countries. The Russian monitoring, for example, gives RFE the daily morning Pravda editorial which sets the political line for the entire satellite press.

In addition to supplying the complete text of monitoring, which goes in the original language to the people interested, editor-translators in Schleissheim and senior monitors, with the assistance of news editors in the English Garden building, select certain items of major importance and translate them into English. These are known as "Monitoring Highlights" and keep Americans both in Munich and New York informed of important events. (A copy is sent by radio teletype to New York every day.) They are also the instrument by which the people on one desk keep themselves informed of developments in other target countries.

Behind RFE's monitoring operation is an engineer and a newsman— an engineer to cope with the many technical problems involved and a newsman to see that the news gets into the hands of the right people, with proper priority given to that which is important. Let us look first at some of the engineering problems involved. Few laymen realize that the cold war is an electronic war of considerable dimensions. The bulk of this story will be told in the next chapter, dealing with how RFE breaks through the jamming and other obstacles designed to keep its programs away from the ears of the intended listeners. Listening in on the Communist domestic radio is an important part of it.

Monitoring is essentially "eavesdropping." We well know that Communist propaganda is specifically tailored for given audiences. The official line is modified in each case for Moscow, Warsaw, or Sophia, and in all these places it differs from what is sent into the West. If the Soviets could, they would certainly halt the Polish home service at the Polish border and limit local stations to the regions they serve. Signal strength is kept at the minimum required to cover the area concerned. The job of the engineer at Schleissheim is to pick up these programs that were never meant for western ears. It involves, for instance, picking up a signal from Radio Sophia at three times the distance it was designed to carry for ordinary reception. In the other major satellites the distances involved are not so great, but in addition to major stations, RFE wants to know what is being discussed on small stations because they are often more frank than large networks and provide a local color not obtainable in another way. Some of these stations have a very low power output and are located hundreds of miles from Schleissheim.

A second obstacle to be overcome is interference—natural and man-made. The radio band in Europe is much more crowded than it is in the United States, and, furthermore, there is no legal limit on station power output. Therefore, not only does the engineer find a number of stations broadcasting on almost the same frequency as the weak signal he is trying to pick up, but there are also powerful stations in the vicinity of Munich that create spurious signals in the sensitive receivers that may show up almost anywhere on the wave band. The Voice of America, for instance, has a million-watt transmitter in the Munich area. (The most powerful radio station in the United States is 50,000 watts.)

In addition to these general problems, each station that the engineer tries to pick up involves a number of special problems. For instance, when trying to pick up Radio Warsaw, he finds that (1) RIAS has a relay station at Hof, almost on a direct line between Schleissheim and Warsaw; (2) the BBC broadcasts to Poland on a frequency very close to that used by Radio Warsaw; (3) a Russian jamming station aimed at blotting out the BBC also booms its signal into Radio Warsaw's frequency and into the ears of RFE's monitors.

This is the situation. And how is it dealt with? Several devices are used to overcome the weak signal. First, extremely sensitive receivers are used—receivers which amplify a signal by as much as a million times and which, incidentally, bear about as much resemblance to a home receiver as the modern automobile does to the horseless carriage. Second, various kinds of special antennas (such as the rhombic and Beveridge) are used which have a gain approximately twenty times greater than that of an ordinary dipole (just a single pole). But these power-boosting devices in themselves create new problems. When one amplifies the desired signal, the interference is also amplified; the sensitive receivers, and some of the power-boosting antennas used, increase the problem of spurious signals.

There are several ways to deal with the problem of interference. A filter can be hooked in between the antenna and the receiver to cut out certain frequencies. If, for instance, the engineer wants to tune in a weak signal on 790 kilocycles which is being blotted out by a powerful station broadcasting on 800 kc., he can by the use of a filter eliminate the 800 kc. signal. A second technique called the "side band selector" is similar in principle to the filter. It is, however, built directly into the receiver. The layman can get a crude idea of how this operates by visualizing the 800 kc. frequency as being made up of three signals occupying the band between 799.5 and 800.5. By use of a side-band selector, the part of the signal in which the disturbance is the greatest can be eliminated. A third device, the loop antenna, can be used on medium and long wave and is useful when interference comes from one specific station. The loop antenna is essentially a ring which will not pick up a station that lies in its own plane. The interfering station can thus be tuned out. And, finally, a small receiving station has been constructed at Moosburg, to the east of Schleissheim, where the interference from transmitters in the Munich area is not so great.

In addition to trying to maximize pickup of all the stations that are of interest to programing, the engineer also tries to achieve maximum flexibility in the use of equipment and in the distribution of the signal. That is, ideally, he would like to be able to hook up any receiver to any antenna and to send the signal from any receiver to any place in Schleissheim or Munich where it is needed. And the ideal has almost been obtained. By use of multicouplers a single antenna can be used to pick up six different signals simultaneously (although this increases the problem of spurious signals). Different receivers can be used with various antennas and the signal sent into any of the various monitoring booths, or if needed, into the conference rooms.[2]

Where the task of the engineer ends, that of the newsman begins. After the signal has been delivered to where it is wanted, the message is transcribed, sometimes translated and edited, and passed on to all concerned. And this must be done quickly, accurately, and the message edited with a judicious eye to what is newsworthy. The story of how this is done has been explained in operational terms above. But part of the story is "unofficial," providing an example of the unofficial aspect of RFE's operation which is so important to its success. The head of monitoring is a former news-agency correspondent. He knows what should be done with the incoming material, but it is physically impossible for him to do all the work. Twelve languages are involved, and monitoring begins at 0400 and continues until 0100 the following morning. The initial task, then, was to train a staff. Part of this involved language training. All monitors, of course, could each handle their own tongue, but translating personnel could always be used, and it was desirable to introduce some flexibility into the staff to cover vacations, illness, and similar contingencies. Thus monitors were encouraged to learn other languages. The most important was English, both for the purpose of intercommunication (although German was used here) and for increasing the size of the translating staff. Many were encouraged to attend classes. And the newsman got into the act himself. He began to hold weekly meetings in his own home to help members of his staff with English. But these weekly meetings were more than social gatherings. Special topics of political importance were taken up. Staff members were occasionally asked to give reports, and these reports were discussed by all. Along with building up language capacity, the newsman was passing on his skills to those who could absorb them—skills that included such intangibles as political sensitivity and awareness—in other words, skills that were essential for a good editor-translator. The result was the development of a more highly skilled, more flexible staff. In this totally unofficial way many of the skills that today carry the monitoring operation were built up.

The RFE Field Offices

If we look at monitoring as the ears of RFE, then it is useful to keep the animal analogy (although changing the phylum) and think of the field offices as large antennae that reach out from the central offices in Munich to almost all parts of Europe. Some are snuggled close to the Iron Curtain—Istanbul, Athens, Vienna, Berlin—and pick up the reverberations of events that are not normally felt in the western world. Others are located in the "international capitals" of Europe—Rome, London, Paris—and are sensitive to events and information, available in these cosmopolitan centers, which may be of particular interest to RFE. But wherever they are located, their function is crucial to operations. Monitoring supplies coverage of the radio in the captive countries with samples from elsewhere. From the Central Newsroom comes the up-to-the-minute news of the world as reported by the major wire services. But this is official news. All that comes directly from Communist sources is designed specifically to serve Communist interests—certainly not those of RFE. And reports that come from accredited correspondents from behind the Curtain are subjected to the heavy hand of Soviet censorship. Although both of these are useful, indeed indispensable, RFE is in need of a source of information on events behind the Curtain that is not directly controlled by the regimes. The field offices provide such a source. They were originally established to supply Munich and New York with reports on happenings behind the Curtain, based on interviews with escapees. Some continue to perform this function, but for others it is but a minor part of their daily routines. They operate almost like a micro-RFE-Munich, collecting news and information, handling some programing, minor public relations, and personnel work.

Because of their varying functions, one might anticipate that there would be some differences in size and organization among the field offices. Each, however, is headed by a correspondent, usually an American. They range in size from the small organization in Istanbul, where there is an interviewer and a typist in addition to the correspondent, to the large offices in Vienna, London, and Athens, where there are nine to twelve full-time employees. In addition to these full-time people, each office uses a number of part-time stringers who are contacted on occasion because they have access to news from behind the Curtain or because they have special language skills for which there is a need. However, there is a strict rule against hiring anybody to go behind the Iron Curtain to get special information for RFE.

The field offices in Istanbul, Athens, Graz, Vienna, Salzburg, Berlin, Munich, and Frankfurt still devote much of their time to the interviewing of escapees. Istanbul is the major source of Bulgarians; in Athens (and its branch office in Salonika), Bulgarians and Rumanians are available, and repatriated Greeks who had been captured and deported during the civil war also provide a valuable source of information. Graz, Salzburg, Vienna, and Munich are congregating points for newly arrived Hungarians and Czechs, and refugee camps located near Salzburg and not far from Munich provide places where refugees are available for longer-term interviewing. Berlin, of course, can be looked upon as sort of a listening post behind the Iron Curtain. In addition to the refugees available there (mostly German), residents of East Berlin are sometimes available as information sources. In the other offices not many refugees are available—an occasional Polish sailor jumps ship in Stockholm, Hamburg, or London, but an office like London gets only about a dozen or so a year for interviewing purposes. This does not mean, however, that these offices are unable to provide information about events behind the Curtain. Their correspondents and interviewers talk to businessmen, athletes, and entertainers who are in the West on official business, and also to westerners who have had occasion to travel in one or more of the captive countries. At times these people know they are talking to RFE reporters; at other times, they do not. Other sources of information in London, Paris, and Rome are the communities of people native to one or more of RFE's target countries. Some of these people have continuing contacts in their homelands, and correspondents tap them for information on events in the satellites.

Another function of the correspondent in a major office like London, Paris, or Berlin is to provide general news coverage of important events. Press-service coverage of these events is not always adequate for RFE's purposes. The press services, by and large, are writing for a western audience, and therefore not only select material which is of particular interest to this audience, but also assume that their readers have a certain fundamental knowledge about the events and situations reported. Many things that would be of considerable interest to a satellite audience may be given only minor consideration, and other events may be presented in a frame of reference which would be meaningless to an eastern European audience. For instance, a House of Commons question period and debate on foreign policy might be reported by Reuters in such a way that news of primary interest to an audience behind the Curtain is given only a kind of parenthetical consideration. An RFE correspondent would cover the same meetings and send stories to the Munich newsroom that are of particular importance to a satellite audience. One of the main functions of the office in Rome is to provide this special kind of coverage on Vatican affairs, which are of interest to the millions of Roman Catholics in the target countries.

Another example would be the reporting of the French general election in January 1956. Western press services wrote their stories for an audience that had a general appreciation of the operation of a parliamentary election and had some personal experiences to which they could relate what they read. But many people in the satellites have had no experience whatsoever with such elections, and therefore the reporting of them must be done within an entirely different frame of reference.

In addition to firsthand coverage of events, the newspapers in the areas are closely watched and stories or editorial comments of interest to RFE are either mailed or phoned into the Central Newsroom. Berlin and Vienna go one step further and send in a daily press roundup.

Some programs are also prepared in a major field office. Both London and Paris have their own small studios. London is particularly important for Polish programing, because of the large Polish community there.

The Central Newsroom

The Central Newsroom can be looked upon as a large switchboard that receives much of the information that comes into RFE and distributes it to the interested persons. Its major function, at least in terms of time priority, is to supply the five programing news desks with material needed for the newscasts. There are twenty-one hourly news deadlines daily, and the editors on duty in the newsroom are responsible for seeing that news is available to fill these holes. An effort is made to expedite the incoming material so that the news chiefs on the desks can develop a "new lead" for each hourly newscast. But the major stories take up only a minor part of the day's time. The teletypes are continually ticking off stories which, however routine, are essential to the continuing newscasts.

Most of the news comes into the newsroom on one of eight teletype machines. Two of these are used to receive the British agency, Reuters, which comes into RFE on a land line from Bonn. Because this is the only English-language land-line service available, it forms a basic part of the news budget. The other western agency to which RFE subscribes is INS.[3] Its reports are sent from New York by radio teletype, picked up at the Schleissheim monitoring station, and relayed into the newsroom by land line. In addition to these services other western news agencies are monitored at Schleissheim and relayed into the newsroom.

But RFE is also interested in news from the East, and thanks to the technical equipment of the monitoring stations the newsroom is supplied with an almost complete coverage of eastern European press agencies. These include TASS (Soviet), Tanjug (Yugoslav), Agerpress (Rumanian), PAP (Polish), CTK (Czechoslovak), MIT (Hungarian), BTA (Bulgarian), ATA (Albanian).

As soon as the material comes into the newsroom it is checked by the editors and sent to the duplicating room, where up to a hundred copies can be made.[4] This is one of the ways in which RFE's newsroom is different from the kind found in an ordinary radio network. In most commercial networks a single copy of each teletype transcript is delivered, in rotation, to those interested in seeing it. But at RFE this material is used not only for programing but also as background for policy formation; accordingly, between fifty and one hundred copies of each item are circulated.

The total amount of news that comes through the newsroom is staggering. It averages 250,000 words a day (550 to 650 pages), seven days a week. The staff that handles this output offers a good example of the multinational character of RFE. In 1956 the news chief, the senior editor, and four editors were all Americans; there were two news assistant-translators (both German) and two news assistants (a Frenchman and a German); a translator (Yugoslav); one secretary (German); two multilingual typists (both German); and seven copy clerks (five German and two Czech).

One should not get the idea that the newsroom is just a passive recipient of the news that comes in its direction. The news chiefs on the desks and some program editors make special requests for information through the newsroom. For instance, the Hungarian sports editor may want special coverage of an international soccer game between Hungary and Belgium being played in Antwerp. The news chief will call Reuters and ask for special reports. Or a political editor may want a particular kind of story on French politics. It is the news chief's task to call the RFE correspondent in Paris and ask him to provide a special story.

The functioning of the newsroom can only be fully appreciated if looked at from the point of view of the news or commentary editors. When an important story breaks, the news editor will first get coverage of it from as many as twelve different press agencies. If the story breaks in Europe and is very important, special reports from RFE's own correspondents will soon be coming in. As soon as the press begins covering and commenting on the event the editors, by looking through the news budgets, may get press reactions ranging geographically from Istanbul to Stockholm and differing in point of view from that expressed by *L'Osservatore Romano* to *L'Unita*. In addition to coverage on current happenings the newsroom tries to provide more general background information and political commentary as it appears in the press throughout the western world.

The Evaluation and Research Section

The other three sections of the News and Information Services are engaged almost exclusively in the process of collecting and distributing raw data. The library unit of the Evaluation and Research Section also collects data by token of the fact that it handles subscriptions to newspapers and periodicals and purchases books. But the major work of this section is devoted to three other tasks: (1) evaluating the accuracy and reliability of incoming reports; (2) storing information; (3) supporting programing with special information and reports.

The Evaluation and Research Section is broken down into two subsections. One (evaluation) is concerned largely with the evaluation and permanent storing of material; the other (reference, research, and library) with the collection and storing of material primarily for the direct support of programing. Evaluation is organized in terms of country desk units while the organization of the reference, research and library unit partially follows country desks but also functions independently of them. The chief of the section is at the same time head of the Evaluation Sub-Section.[5]

The Evaluation Units. We have seen how the field offices prepare and send *reports* into Munich. These reports consist largely of the detailed accounts of interviews, written in the language of the person with whom the correspondent talked. No final attempt is made in the field offices to assess the contents of the report; everything is sent on to Munich exactly as it was heard. But the possibility of error finding its way into a report is great. A refugee who has just risked his life to escape is not the most unbiased commentator on the local scene. His hatred and fear of the regime is likely to be immense. Furthermore, the RFE correspondent interviewing him is in many instances undoubtedly looked upon as an official representative of the nation where the escapee hopes to find political asylum and a new home—a man to be pleased at all costs. This information can serve as the basic stuff of much programing; it may be important for policy decisions; but before it can be of any use whatsoever, its accuracy and reliability must be determined.

Several techniques are used to evaluate the reports. First, the information given in a report is checked against known facts; second, a check is made to see whether or not the source was in a position to know what he reports; a third technique is to check the internal consistency of the report; if the escapee draws his own conclusions from a set of conditions, checking the logic of the conclusions is a fourth manner of evaluating the report; and finally, a kind of intuitive knowledge of the nation from which the reports come is sometimes used.

By far the most important technique of evaluation is to compare the new information with known facts. And the known facts at the disposal of RFE's evaluators are the most complete available in the western world, according to no less an authority on the satellites than Professor Hugh Seton-Watson. Let us take a look, for example, at what the Czech evaluator has available when he begins to evaluate a report. He has two kinds of files, card and subject. The card files contain individual cards on 48,000 people in Czechoslovakia and 26,000 on various concerns such as factories, state farms, mines, and prison camps. If the report being evaluated deals with working conditions in a certain factory, the evaluator will check the information against his cards. Exact location of the plant, products, names of foremen and Stakhanovites, and previous comments on working conditions will be compared with what is said in the report. In the subject files more detailed information is available. For the Czech unit these files contain the reports (called *Items* after they have been evaluated and reproduced) accumulated since 1951, the clippings from twelve daily Czech and Slovak newspapers and numerous periodicals, selections from the daily monitoring reports, and clippings from selected sections of the western press.

When the reports come in they are entered in a ledger and passed to the chief of the Evaluation and Research Section, who runs through them quickly to establish priorities and gives them a preliminary security check. Within half an hour they are on the desks of the evaluators, who check them and provide an English summary of their contents. (Important reports are translated into English by the translation pool.) An evaluation comment is also added in English. Some reports are rejected as untrustworthy; others are held up while queries are sent to the correspondents, asking for further information. The finished product, called an *Item*, is mimeographed and circulated in from 140 to 200 copies.

One further note on organization. Besides the five target-country units there is a non-target desk. This unit collects and files reports and other information on non-target countries. Among the most important are the Soviet Union and East Germany. Because of the shortage of personnel there is no detailed analysis of the material done by this unit, but about 175 reports are processed and published every month.

The Reference, Research, and Library Sub-Section. This sub-section is divided into three operating units: reference, research, and library. The library unit is essentially a small, specialized library containing approximately 24,000 volumes, 15,000 of which are in the languages of the target nations and the rest in western languages. About 4,000 new volumes are received each year. The research unit includes one member from each target desk, who is responsible for keeping his eye on the publications in his country and making recommendations to the chief of the Reference, Research, and Library Sub-Section on what books are of particular interest to RFE. In addition to books, the library handles the subscriptions and distribution of 700 western and 550 satellite periodicals. Every month about 3,000 copies of various publications are routed through the library to the various editors, evaluators, and researchers.[6]

The reference and research units are somewhat amorphous in structure, and their tasks are closely interrelated. The reference unit is responsible for reading, clipping, and filing the satellite and western newspapers, periodicals, and monitoring reports. Fifty dailies alone are read and clipped. But these files are completely separate from those in the evaluation unit. They contain much the same information but it is filed according to a different code, and they exist primarily for use by the program editors and writers. The evaluation files are held inviolate; no material can be taken out of the file room. For the purposes of evaluation they must be complete. But the reference unit's files exist for the editors and writers. If they like, they can borrow material and take it to their offices to work on. The reference files contain information not only on the target countries but also on non-target countries. Elaborate and detailed files are kept, for instance, on the United States and the Soviet Union, which provide the editors with a wealth of information for programs dealing with either of these two countries.

The research units are organized on a target country basis and are physically located with the people from the reference unit who work on the target countries. The primary function of the research units is to provide the program desks with information they request. This involves everything from providing specific facts in response to a phone call (for instance, a request for statistics on oil production in Iran for the past five years) to preparing elaborate target papers. Again there is some variation among the different country units. Three Polish researchers devote their entire time to the preparation of the *Polish Press Digest*. This digest is published five days a week and runs between twenty-five and thirty-five pages an issue. It contains a review of a very large cross-section of the Polish press—metropolitan and provincial, daily, weekly, and monthly. Over forty newspapers and periodicals are regularly covered. The other two Polish researchers supply the editors with answers to their daily questions and work on target papers. Three or four of these are prepared a year to provide the background information necessary. Last year, for instance, four such papers were prepared dealing with the youth problem, the repatriation of Poles from Russia, regime Catholics, and the Polish army. This last report was done by two outside researchers in London, working on contract.

The Hungarian researchers prepare a type of press review called the *Hungarian Daily Survey*, but it differs considerably from the *Polish Press Digest*. It is much shorter, only about ten pages daily, and is particularly concerned with surveying the self-criticism found in the Hungarian press. The reports that the Hungarians put out also differ from those done by the Poles. They are much shorter and are issued three to five times a month. Some are prepared at the suggestion of an editor or the desk chief; others are undertaken on the initiative of the researcher. Typical titles are the "Economic Plan for 1956," the "Hungarian Writers' 'Revolution,'" and "The Standard of Living of a 'Typical' Hungarian Working Family."

The Czech research unit prepares a press review that is shorter than either of the others and serves primarily as a sort of index to the press. It also turns out papers that supply direct support of programing.

In addition to the researchers working on specific countries, there are two "Outside Researchers" that supply information to all desks from the many libraries in the Munich area and in other places in Germany. Another researcher prepares a *Western Magazine Digest* which has a wide circulation in RFE.

The New York Department of Research and Information

The Department of Research and Information in New York provides the information and research support for the New York programing desks. It keeps a close eye on the American press and maintains clipping files of articles that may be of future interest. It also files the vast amount of information that is relayed from the News and Information Services in Munich. From this storehouse of material the department provides script-writers and policy people with newspaper clippings, library reference lists, reports from outside agencies, and original reports, digests, roundups, and summaries written and edited by people in the department.

On the research side, the Research and Information Department has a small Studies Branch, whose purpose is to provide certain depth studies required for specific RFE purposes. For example, RFE is particularly interested in broadcasts that will appeal to the managerial groups in the satellites and possibly exploit their vulnerabilities. The Studies Branch has prepared a series of studies on management and efficiency problems in the target countries which has two purposes: to provide an accurate basis for the planning of a concerted campaign in this field, and to explore the source material and provide an initial store of information that may be of use for actual programs dealing with this problem.

The Studies Branch works closely with the Free Europe Press research people in New York, who maintain running research on conditions in the satellites but are not equipped to undertake long-range research projects for operational purposes like the management study referred to above.

Finally, the Department of Research and Information in New York is equipped to interview travelers and refugees recently arrived from the countries behind the Iron Curtain.

Breaking through the Jammers

Raw materials are gathered, guidances prepared, program schedules developed, programs produced—and there remains the final step of transmitting the spoken word to the target audiences. Radio Free Europe's technical facilities for undertaking this final and all-important task are indeed impressive. At Biblis (in West Germany) there are eight short-wave transmitters—three 50 kw., one 20 kw., and four 10 kw. Just outside Lisbon stands one of the largest transmitter sites in the world—four 100 kw., eight 50 kw., and one 7.5 kw. short-wave transmitters. Near Holzkirchen just fifteen miles from Munich is the 135 kw. medium-wave transmitter, plus six 10 kw. short-wave transmitters.[1] The Biblis site is good for "one-hop" short-wave propagation on the 49, 41, and 31 meter bands while Lisbon is ideal for higher frequencies—25, 19, and 16 meter bands. The medium-wave transmitter is at Holzkirchen (near the Czechoslovak border) because in order to be effective, medium-wave transmitters should be as close to the target as possible.

But with so many of the transmitters many miles from Munich, how does RFE get its programs on the air—particularly news programs which come up every hour? And how are the programs produced in New York fed into the transmitters? In the United States, radio networks are linked by wire. Such facilities are available in Germany, but there are no program lines that run through Spain to Portugal. Nontopical programs are prepared in advance and tapes flown from Munich or New York to the transmitting site. But radio relay is the only answer for news and other topical programs. Programs produced in New York, either in RFE's own studio or in studios leased from WOR, are sent to Munich over the facilities of Press Wireless Service in New York. From Munich programs are sent by land line either to

Biblis or to Holzkirchen, where six short-wave transmitters are used for the Lisbon relay. (Three of these, however, are reversible and can be used to beam programs into the target countries if not needed for relay purposes.) Standards for this kind of broadcasting, of course, are very high. In order to get satisfactory results under all kinds of atmospheric conditions, and in spite of Soviet efforts to jam the relay, the transmitters work in pairs. In other words, the same programs are fed out over two transmitters at the same time. Lisbon can choose the best one for sending on to the target countries.[2] Another device is also used to ensure high-quality reception. A number of frequencies are available for transmission, and if a satisfactory signal is not being picked up on one frequency, changes are requested. As many as 85 to 90 frequency changes may be made each day in order to maintain the high minimum standards.

What happens when a word from a Czechoslovak news items is read into a microphone in a studio at RFE-Munich? When the word enters the microphone it sets up an electronic signal. This little signal runs through cables into the studio control room and from there is fed into the master control room. From the master control room it is routed through lines leased from the German postal authority to Biblis and Holzkirchen. At Biblis it is fed into the transmitters beamed to Czechoslovakia. At Holzkirchen it is fed into three transmitters—the 135 kw. medium wave beamed directly at the Czechoslovak Republic and into two short-wave transmitters for relay to Lisbon. The signal is picked up in Lisbon on the diversity receivers and relayed over VHF circuits via the Lisbon studio and master control room to the transmitting site where it is sent out over the ether to Czechoslovakia. In less than one hundredth of a second after a word in this news item has been uttered in a Munich studio, it can be heard in Czechoslovakia simultaneously on any one of a number of frequencies. In its journeys this electronic signal has encountered hundreds of radio tubes, has traveled many thousands of miles, and has been amplified literally billions of times.

But what about jamming? This is one of the most frequently asked questions about western broadcasts directed behind the Iron Curtain. Is it worth all the time and money and effort to try to talk to the captive peoples if nothing can be heard through the frightful din created by hundreds of jamming stations? In order to answer the question it is necessary to discuss briefly the problem of long-distance radio transmission.

Systematic jamming on a large scale dates from the early days of World War II [3] when it was used by both sides to disrupt military communications and by the axis powers, particularly Germany, to blot out foreign broadcasts aimed at local populations. After the hot war had ceased and the cold war had begun, the Soviet Union engaged in sporadic efforts to jam certain western broadcasts. The effort became deadly serious in 1949. In August of that year Mrs. Anna Kasenkina, a Russian schoolteacher in America, jumped out of a window in the U.S.S.R. consulate in New York. No news of the incident was carried by official agencies behind the Iron Curtain, but the Voice of America broadcast full details. Embassy officials reported that within a few hours the news was being talked about in Moscow. Twenty-four hours later the Russians carried an official version so much at variance with the VOA's story that it "evoked snickers." [4] Walter Bedell Smith (at that time Ambassador to Moscow) feels that it was this incident that "caused the Kremlin to decide to eliminate this source of truthfulness" by engaging in an all-out jamming effort. [5]

In its simplest form jamming consists of setting a noise machine in front of a microphone and broadcasting hoots and howls on the same frequencies as the undesired broadcasts. A slightly different approach is to have the jamming transmitter play loud and boisterous music to drown out the signal. For example, when RFE's Holzkirchen transmitter first went on the air, it was greeted by a jammer in Prague that played loud military music continuously on its frequency. The most refined technique, in the words of an RFE engineer, "is to employ a basic transmitter, tuned to the same channel, modulated by random rumbles, rattles, buzz-saw noises, and high pitched shrieks in a repeating cycle." [6] Another technique is to feed the interference directly into the main power network, creating the effect of a gigantic electric razor being used in every household.

The jamming of short-wave and that of medium-wave transmission present entirely different problems. Medium-wave transmission follows the curvature of the earth. Radio Free Europe's medium-wave transmitter can be looked upon as a large searchlight focused on Czechoslovakia. The special directional antenna has an effect similar to that of a reflector on a searchlight. It takes the waves that would be dissipated on non-target areas and turns them on the Czechoslovak Republic. There are theoretically two ways in which this transmission could be jammed. First, the Communists could build a large, powerful transmitter, at some central point in the Czechoslovak Republic, designed to jam RFE throughout the country. This, however, has several disadvantages from the Communist point of view. Because of the large power output of the Holzkirchen station, the jamming station would require a tremendous power capacity. And even with tremendous power, it would not be effective in all areas. Terrain features between the jammer and the RFE transmitter could create areas that would be "shadowed" from the jamming but able to receive the full power of RFE's signal. And the border areas closer to Holzkirchen than to the central jammer would not be severely affected. The second approach is to build a number of small transmitters concentrated especially in highly populated areas. This is more effective, but it is also more expensive. Ten to twenty 10-kw. transmitters located in Czechoslovakia may be required to mangle RFE's medium-wave service to Prague.[7]

Short-wave jamming is an entirely different problem. Short-wave signals do not follow the curvature of the earth but tend to travel in straight lines. Long-distance transmission is achieved by virtue of the fact that short waves bounce off the Heaviside layer and return to the earth. (The Heaviside layer is created by the ionizing action of the sun's rays on the outer reaches of the atmosphere.) The point at which short waves return to the earth is determined by two factors: (a) the angle of incidence at which they hit the Heaviside layer;[8] (b) the height of the Heaviside layer. The smaller the angle of incidence and the higher the Heaviside layer, the greater will be the distance between the transmitter and the point where the signal returns to the surface of the earth.

There are two ways in which short-wave transmission can be jammed: local jammers and sky-wave jammers. Local jammers are greatly handicapped by the fact that they are effective only within about fifteen miles. But even within this radius they are not efficient because it is the tendency of short waves to go upward; the ground-wave power is weak. Sky-wave jammers are built approximately as far from the target as is the transmitter sending the undesired signal. The object is to bounce the signal off the Heaviside layer and bring it down right on top of the other signal—as in a game of electronic billiards. But a number of problems are involved. The ionosphere (in which the Heaviside layer is located) does not remain at a constant height. It varies at different times of the day and in different seasons of the year. This means that a jammer transmitter located in one area will be effective only when the Heaviside layer is at a given height. In the late afternoon the ionosphere rises and layers compress rapidly. But because the evening comes earlier in the Soviet Union than it does in western Europe, the portion of the Heaviside layer off which the jammer transmitters (located as far east of the target as Lisbon or Biblis are west) must bounce their signals has raised considerably.

Let us look at a practical example of what this means for the Soviet attempts to jam RFE's Lisbon signal to Hungary. Under normal conditions the jammers would have to be at a distance from Hungary equal to that of the Lisbon transmitters—some place in the Ural

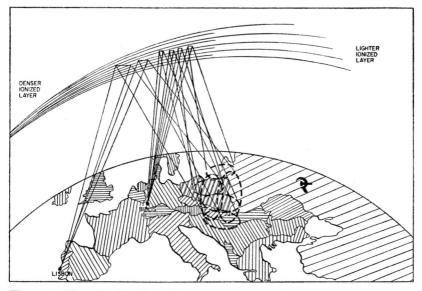

Figure 4. How Radio Free Europe penetrates the target countries. A stylized representation of short-wave broadcasts on two frequencies from Lisbon and four frequencies from Biblis, showing the denser portion of the ionized layer (Heaviside layer) to the west and the lighter portion to the east during the early evening hours. The broken-line circles over the northern target countries roughly approximate RFE's "pattern of bombardment."

117

Mountains. But as the afternoon comes to a close in western Europe the jammer signal may be striking west of Hungary; in the evening hours it may even be reaching listeners in England. If the Soviets wanted to continue to jam the transmission, they would have to bring in another jammer located closer to Hungary.[9] And RFE has another factor working in its favor. In the late afternoon the Heaviside layer (or better, layers) becomes very dense and thus creates an excellent reflecting surface. This is the optimum broadcast time. After several hours of this optimum condition, the layer rapidly becomes more porous. A good portion of a signal pierces it and is dissipated in the stratosphere. But because RFE's transmitters are all to the west of the jammers, it enjoys optimum conditions in this regard after such conditions have diminished for the Communist jamming effort.[10] (See Figure 4.)

The Communists are, of course, engaging in extreme jamming efforts against RFE. Basically, three kinds of jamming transmitters are being used. First, there are the "sky-wave" jammers to blot out short-wave broadcasts. Second, there are the medium-power local jammers (perhaps 5,000 to 10,000 watts) for use against medium wave. (A rough estimate is that there are five or six of these jammers west of Prague to protect that city against RFE's medium-wave transmitter.) Finally, there are a large number of miniature (50–100 watt) local jammers probably installed in the post offices in various communities and effective over a radius of a mile or two.[11]

One theory holds that jammers operate in "wolf packs." Each "pack" has its leader who identifies himself by a Morse signal every minute. Technical monitoring services have identified these repeated Morse signals. The other members of the "pack" follow the leader— they listen for his signal and stay on the same frequency. When the leader changes, all members immediately follow suit. Other theories are current which place the authority and command channel for jammer deployment in a central monitoring unit which communicates with isolated jammers and controls their activity. In any case, the maintenance of its extensive jamming operations must put Communist Europe to a considerable expense.

Radio Free Europe commands several techniques for breaking through the jammers. One is the selection of special wave lengths for optimum propagation at various times of the year. Another involves using transmitters of large power output.[12] A third is to multiply the power of the transmitter by the use of special directional antennas. The Holzkirchen medium-wave transmitter is equipped with an antenna that provides a power gain of six or seven times. Short-wave antennas can be built to multiply effective output directed at the target by twenty times or more. A hundred-thousand-watt transmitter at Lisbon can, in other words, have the effect of a two-million-watt transmitter with a sharp, directive pattern. Another very fruitful technique is to have many such transmitters operating on many frequencies. In order to effectively blot out RFE's short-wave transmitters operating on twenty-one different frequencies on an almost around-the-clock basis, year in and year out, the Soviets would need about twenty times that number of sky-wave jammers plus many local jammers. Even if they forgot about all other western broadcasts, they could not marshal the necessary transmitters to accomplish this task.

It can be seen that, theoretically, the jamming poses difficult problems. Does this mean that RFE gets through to the target audiences? In Berlin, Vienna, Munich, and Istanbul, RFE has technical monitoring facilities that, among other things, monitor RFE's own broadcasts. Data on reception are also punched on IBM cards and monthly averages on reception are worked out. These findings reveal, for example, that during the month of September 1955, the monitor in Berlin reported that a Polish listener could hear RFE on one or more of the eight available frequencies, at a signal strength and with intelligibility of from "good" (the highest) to "fair" (92 per cent of the time). The average for all stations over the few months preceding this period was between 85 and 100 per cent.

The Effectiveness of Radio Free Europe

Few problems faced by Radio Free Europe are more difficult than that of trying to assess the effectiveness of its international propaganda operation. There is no "one-to-one" relationship between communications content and effect. As Davison and George point out:

> The effectiveness of communication in influencing behavior depends in large measure on the *conditions* under which the communications are sent and received. . . . The character imputed by an audience to the communicator—with reference, for example, to his power, prestige, reputation for credibility or sobriety, closeness to the top leadership of his own country, etc.—may affect the listeners' receptivity to what is said. Similarly, acceptance of a particular communication may be enhanced or prejudiced by the character of the medium through which it is conveyed. For example, people may be more critical of what they read in a newspaper than of what they hear over the radio or by word of mouth. The "circumstances" or setting (other *conditions*) of a given communication include such matters as its "timeliness", whether it is forced to compete with rival communications or enjoys a monopoly position, whether events support or contradict the message, whether it comes at a time of great anxiety or discontent in the audience, whether the originator of the communication seems to be winning a war or losing it, etc.[1]

Furthermore, propaganda is not an isolated instrument of waging cold war. Its use is interwoven with the use of diplomatic, economic, and military instruments of statecraft supposedly working for the same or similar ends. To isolate the effect of one from that of another is a task of immeasurable proportions. Nor is RFE the only propaganda agency broadcasting from the West into the satellites. Program content is quite similar. What kind of research technique can one use to determine the effectiveness of just one of these broadcasters?

The obvious point is that actions and opinions are not influenced by single factors. People react attitudinally and behaviorally in terms of a host of stimuli that impinge upon them and in terms of attitudes and behavior patterns which have been accumulated as a result of their past experiences. To determine the effect of a single communications stimulus on one person alone is a task that psychologists have not altogether mastered. To determine the effect of mass communications on a mass audience is a task that psychologists have only in the last decade begun to come to grips with.

One other obvious point should be made. The Iron Curtain stands between RFE and its audience. Therefore, most of the techniques that have been developed to measure the effect of mass communications can not be used.

In this study, if one could use sources outside the organization, it would be most desirable to make an independent investigation of the effectiveness of RFE—desirable, but impossible. Even the government of the United States, when it is interested in assessing the effectiveness of RFE, deems it necessary to turn to RFE's own measurement facilities.[2] This chapter will be based largely on RFE's own "Assessment Memoranda"—it will present a critical report of the sources and content of these memoranda and offer some general conclusions about the effectiveness of RFE. However, the great flood of refugees that left Hungary in November and December of 1956 provided material for independent studies of the impact of western broadcasts to Hungary. The most systematic of these reports will be discussed at the end of the chapter.

One further point of introduction should be made. At the time of this writing it appears as if the success of the Polish "national" Communists and the bloody suppression of the Hungarian uprising in the fall of 1956 form a kind of watershed in the recent history of the satellites. These events created some fundamental changes in the relations of the satellites with both the East and the West. It is still too early to assess the role of western radio in this new situation. Except for a few paragraphs at the end, this chapter will deal with the impact of RFE in the captive countries before the momentous events of October and November, 1956. In later chapters the changed position of RFE will be discussed.

Let us look briefly at RFE's assessment machinery and how the problem of measuring "impact" or "effectiveness" is tackled. The raw material that is used for assessing effectiveness is by and large collected through the facilities of the News and Information Services described in Chapter 6 above. Each day material flows from this branch into the Audience Analysis Section. By and large it is material collected for the purposes of programing, but all field interviewers are provided with an elaborate "Audience Analysis Interview Schedule" which they use as a guide in their refugee interviews. Therefore, a certain amount of information is prepared specifically to meet the needs of the Audience Analysis Section.

The Audience Analysis Section produces two kinds of reports for general distribution throughout RFE: (a) a monthly report which, as the name indicates, reviews the audience and regime responses[3] to RFE's activities in all target countries at monthly intervals; (b) Audience Analysis Assessment Memoranda. The latter can be divided into three different types. First, there is the analysis of the audience response in a given country over a period of from four to six months. A second kind of memoranda deals with the regime response in a given target country over a four-month period. Finally, there are special reports which deal with subjects such as trends in radio registration and the development of attitudes in the target countries.[4]

Before getting into the content of these reports, it would be wise to review RFE's approach to the problem of measuring effectiveness. The Audience Analysis Section, created in 1954, is one of the newest departments in RFE's vast organization. Its approach has been highly empirical, involving the analysis, organization, and final presentation of its raw data with a minimal amount of interpretation.

The problems facing the section are immense. The magnitude of the methodological problem was hinted at in the opening paragraphs of this chapter. But before the section chief could even begin to come to grips with these, he was faced with the task of recruiting a staff. Where is one going to find people with a background that will enable them to cope with the methodological problems involved, who must at the same time be fluent in the use of the language of one of the target countries? The answer is, they simply are not to be found, and in the initial stages methodological skill was occasionally sacrificed to gain language competence. This is one of the factors explaining the development of a highly empirical approach.

The section chief began to plot a new course in 1956. He began orienting his study of effectiveness around the search for techniques that would enable him to answer a number of pertinent questions concerning audience and regime response. In regard to audience response, the following questions are emphasized:

1. What role does radio (including regime radio) play in the lives of the target audiences?

2. What do the target audiences get from western radio?

3. In what manner is the behavior and attitude of the target audiences affected by western broadcasts?

4. What would be the effect if RFE stopped broadcasting? [5]

In regard to regime response:

1. What actions and attitudes of the peoples does the regime attribute to western broadcasting and particularly to RFE?

2. To what degree does the regime feel that RFE contributes to the maintenance of an attitudinal *status quo* among the target peoples?

3. What is the meaning of regime attacks in terms of the "effectiveness" of RFE?

4. Are some aspects of RFE's activities more disturbing than others? [6]

Although one may argue whether these are the most pertinent questions or whether this is the most promising approach to the measurement of effectiveness, such speculation is beyond the scope of this chapter. They are included merely to give the reader an idea of the direction the work of the Audience Analysis Section is likely to take in the future. Our principal concern here is to review the evidence that RFE has already collected and analyzed in order to measure its effectiveness.

Audience Response to Radio Free Europe

This section on audience response is taken from three of the Audience Analysis Assessment Memoranda dealing with audience response in Czechoslovakia, Hungary, and Poland.[7] Before going into the contents of these reports, however, it is necessary to review briefly the sources from which the information was drawn. The Polish report (No. 25) is based on 127 interviews and 107 letters received by the Voice of Free Poland.[8] The social and ethnic composition of the interviewees is something less than representative of RFE's listening audience in Poland. Seventy-three of the interview sources were Polish citizens—refugees, emigrants, or legal travelers in the West. Forty-one of these were members of the intelligentsia, including (a) regime delegates traveling officially in the West ("always far from representing the regime point of view"); (b) private individuals traveling in the West; (c) a number of Jews who were allowed by the regime to emigrate to Israel; (d) refugees. Other members of the middle classes (tradesmen, merchants, etc.) made up another large segment—thirteen of the total number. There were fourteen representatives of the working-class elements in Poland including five sailors. No peasants were represented in the sample. The socioeconomic background of five individuals was undetermined.

In addition to the Polish citizens there were fifty-four foreigners interviewed. The majority of these (thirty-eight) were German, most of whom spoke Polish. The rest represented various European nationalities.

All of the seventeen Polish *voivodships* except Bialystok, Lublin, and Kielce in the east and Zielona Gora in the west were represented. There was one source from Soviet-annexed eastern Poland and one from a labor camp in the Soviet Union (Vorkuta).[9] The absence of reports from the eastern areas is easily explained by the facts that (a) it is difficult to escape from these areas; (b) no German repatriates come from there; (c) there are few official travelers in the West from these *voivodships*. The *voivodships* of Warszawa and Wroclaw were the most heavily represented.[10]

It is far more difficult to identify the social origin of letter writers than it is of interviewees. The former very rarely explicitly identify themselves in these (or any) terms. However, on the basis of careful analysis of handwriting and use of language, in addition to comments made in the letter about occupation and living conditions, it is possible to arrive at some rough estimation of the socioeconomic status and usually possible to determine the sex of the writer.

Of the 107 letters received during the period under consideration, only 39 of them had any relationship to RFE's programs. The others were descriptions of living conditions and expressions of political opinions, without any reference to RFE, or were requests for help—medical advice or help in tracing relatives in the West. In the following breakdown into sex and socioeconomic status only the former 39 are considered.[11]

Sex		Socioeconomic Status	
Men	14	Workers	3
Women	13	Peasants	4
Undetermined	4	Unidentifiable working class	6
Group letters	8	Middle class	8
	—	Intelligentsia	5
	39	Undetermined	2
			—
			39

Letters were received from all parts of Poland (every *voivodship* was represented), with the largest concentration from Warszawa and Wroclaw.

The Czechoslovak study was based on 190 interviews and 93 letters. The interviewees can be broken down into five nationality groups: Czechs, Slovaks, Germans, Greeks, and other foreign nationals. The Czechs and Slovaks were either refugees or legal travelers. The Germans were mostly people who had been imprisoned in 1945 and were at this time returning legally to Germany. The Greeks, numbering twenty in all, were also largely repatriates—people who had been captured during the Greek civil war. Most of them were under twenty-one years of age, and since they could not speak Czech or Slovak, they were not very useful sources. The other nationals, of whom there were only fifteen, were either travelers from the West or people from one of the other satellites who spent some time in Czechoslovakia before escaping to the West.[12] These five groups of interviewees included 151 men and 39 women. All but two of the nineteen provinces in Czechoslovakia were represented.[13] The tabulations below give the socioeconomic composition and age distribution of the interviewees.[14]

Very few of the letters received by the Voice of Free Czechoslovakia

Nationality and Socioeconomic Status *

	CZECHS	SLOVAKS	GERMANS
White-collar workers	43	4	7
Workers	30	9	14
Farmers	10	..	3
Undetermined	17	4	14
	—	—	—
	100	17	38

* Omitting the afore-mentioned 20 Greeks and 15 other nationals among the 190 interviewees.

Age

Under 21	28
21–65	112
Over 65	5
Undetermined	45
	——
	190

during this period were of substantive interest for audience analysis purposes.[15]

The Hungarian study was based on 238 interviews and 203 letters. In addition to Hungarian nationals the group of interviewees included a number of Germans and some Jewish emigrants to Israel. In the breakdown of sources national origin was not considered. Socioeconomic status, age, sex, and geographic location of sources are indicated below.[16]

Socioeconomic Status		*Geographic Location of Source*	
White-collar workers	65	Western Hungary	67
Workers	85	Middle Hungary	79
Peasants	39	Northwestern Hungary ..	15
Undetermined *	49	Southeastern Hungary ...	0
	——	Undetermined	77
	238		——
			238

Age		*Sex*	
Under 21	62	Males	208
21–65	114	Females	30
Over 65	5		——
Undetermined	57		238
	——		
	238		

As was the case above, very few of the letters were of substantive interest in the study. Most of them made some kind of specific request, carried greetings to RFE or to specific editors, or commented on the general situation in Hungary.[17]

These are the sources from which audience assessment memos on audience response are built. One could hardly be called a skeptic for lifting an eyebrow and questioning both the reliability and validity of any conclusions that might be drawn from this kind of sample. But

* Includes border guards, soldiers, housewives, unidentified confidential sources, etc.

this is what RFE has to work with, and so let us look at it critically
and estimate sources of error and the general usefulness of the material.

Concerning the interviews, the most damaging criticism possible
would maintain that the very fact of the interviewees' presence in the
West must be "opinion linked" in highly significant ways.[18] The group
is self-selected, and it could be argued that their leaving the homelands
differentiates these refugees, as a subject for audience research, from
the people that remained behind. In other words, could these refugee
groups provide truly representative samples of the audience behind
the Iron Curtain? Specifically, it could be claimed that the refugees
would have an extreme anti-Communist bias while official travelers
would be at the opposite end of the continuum; the vast majority of
people who are usually found someplace between these two extremes
are entirely unrepresented. Sheldon and Dutkowski have indicated,
however, that certain kinds of refugee interviews are projectable.[19]
They conclude that in cases where flight is not primarily politically
or ideologically motivated, refugees *at the time of escape* express opinions that do not differ significantly from those held by the people in
their social class that remained at home.[20] A vast majority of RFE's
refugee interviewees would fit into this category. They flee because the
material conditions of life are so bad—they do not earn enough to
live on, food is scarce, working conditions bad, working hours long.
These pressures are at work on a large majority of people in the satellites. Escape is related to factors that make escape possible: (a) access
to the border area (residence there or reasons for legitimate travel in
the area); (b) absence of family and property obligations; (c) age. In
these cases Sheldon and Dutkowski conclude "that individuals . . .
reveal a considerable similarity to what appears to be a plausible char-
acterization of the satellite populations themselves. . . . This is especially true of the disillusioned workers, peasants, and artisans in the
sample who seem to be much the same as the disgruntled working
masses at home whom the Communist system has failed to attract, or
whom it did attract in the early period but later lost . . ."[21] Of course,
the opinions of refugees should not be considered as representative of
the members of their class who are Communist or pro-Communist,
which is in any case a small proportion of the population.

But even if the refugee has opinions similar to those held by people remaining in the homeland at the time he leaves, there is no sure indication that his own outlook will not change between the time he crosses the border and is finally interviewed by an RFE representative. Sometimes as much as several months may be involved—months that may be quite traumatic. There is the usually harrowing experience of crossing the border, the utter strangeness of the new world, the despair and frustration that are likely to result from even a few weeks in a refugee camp. Any one of these could result in significant changes in attitude over a few months' period. Furthermore, the RFE interviewer is usually looked upon as a man to be pleased—a man who can perhaps help the refugee find a new home in the West. The refugee may think it to his advantage to express opinions that are likely to be popular with the interviewer. A skilled depth interviewer could perhaps overcome these sources of bias, but RFE's representatives in its field offices are, by and large, journalists—skilled in interviewing for items of broadcast interest, but understandably not qualified (and perhaps not interested) in probing for basic attitude complexes that were prominent before the man escaped.

However, this is not a significant source of bias as far as some of the more simple questions go. For example, "Did you listen to RFE?" and similar questions can be followed up by a discussion of wave lengths and radio personalities in which the degree to which a person listened becomes rather obvious.[22]

There is still a third source of bias—the purely statistical bias. Radio Free Europe's sample by no means represents the universe of RFE's listeners. Certain groups are over-represented; other groups are hardly included in the sample. Thus very wisely RFE does not project its findings directly from its sample, but uses the representatives from each socioeconomic or national group to draw conclusions about audience response from that particular group. If, for instance, all twenty-five workers in a sample of Czechs and Slovaks comment on the popularity of a given program, this is taken as evidence that that particular program has some popularity among workers in Czechoslovakia. Although these twenty-five workers may make up 90 per cent of a given sample, their response is not taken to indicate that the program in question is popular among 90 per cent of the population in Poland.

The question of reliability and validity of the interviews is even more serious among the non-native sources. What can a former German prisoner of war say about Czech attitudes toward RFE after spending ten years in a prison camp in Czechoslovakia? Obviously not very much, but if he knows about RFE and perhaps can even comment on some of its radio personalities, it is very good evidence that RFE's news, information, and reputation are spread by word of mouth among nonlisteners. If it penetrates a prison camp, it is reasonable to assume that it is disseminated rather widely throughout the country.

Travelers from the West who go behind the Iron Curtain provide a rich source of information—rich, but difficult to evaluate. They are usually questioned about the conditions of life as they have seen them, about the attitudes and opinions of the people they came into contact with, etc. In other words, they are looked upon as "unconscious observers" who did not know they would be interviewed on their return at the time they entered one of the captive countries. The problems involved in the use of this kind of evidence are obvious. But the intimate contacts achieved by some of the travelers from neutral countries (particularly Sweden and Switzerland) make them an invaluable source of information. When travel first became freer in the satellites, these sources were useful largely as they corroborated or refuted information from other sources. But as travel in the satellites becomes more common, these sources will tend to provide a more and more valuable base from which independent conclusions can be drawn.

Letters are not considered by RFE to provide reliable data for listener research. Studies undertaken among audiences in the United States have demonstrated their shortcomings for this purpose. Apart from the factors that operate in the United States to make letters unreliable for this kind of research, RFE feels that conditions behind the Iron Curtain make correspondence from the satellites even less useful for its purposes:

(a) The habit of letter writing for discussion purposes has never been as widespread in Poland as it is in the Anglo-Saxon countries. The serious press—similar in this to the French or Swiss press—never carried anything similar to the letters to the *New York Times* or the *London Times*. Instead, letters to the editor were found in specialized women's papers, bearing on particularly feminine subjects, and generally in the lighter type of press. Generally speaking, letters to press and radio were never the generally accepted media of public expression under normal conditions. It is hardly to be expected that it should develop under abnormal conditions and in an atmosphere of danger. (b)The risk of letter writing must not be underestimated. A relationship of this sort between a Polish citizen and RFE, if discovered, could have serious consequences for the writer. [In most cases letters to a foreign address must be taken and handed in unsealed at the post office.] Of the interviewees, very few had written letters to RFE. No intellectuals interviewed had ever written to RFE. One of them answered curtly, "I am not crazy." [23]

This combination of lack of tradition and the danger involved causes RFE to view its letter writers as particularly naïve or unusually reckless, and motivated by an intense desire to write. "The least frequent type of person among RFE correspondents is the predominantly well-balanced person, in full possession of his self-control, soberly appreciating the risks and profits—if any—of letter writing and having a reasoned and critical attitude to problems." [24] As was mentioned above, letters are valued mostly because they indicate the distribution of RFE's listeners and contain specific factual comments about conditions of life (prices, incomes, etc.).

What can one learn about the impact of RFE from this sample? The first question to be asked—and happily the most easy to answer— is, "Is RFE listened to by the people behind the Iron Curtain?" The answer is as close to an unqualified "yes" as it is possible to give on the basis of the sample available. Every source interviewed during the periods on which the various reports are based had heard of the existence of western broadcasts—even the Greek prisoners in Czechoslovakia who could not understand the local tongue. A large majority of the sample had listened themselves to broadcasts from western stations. This was evidenced not only by their affirmative statements to that effect, but by their ability to discuss wave-length information, radio personalities, and program content. [25]

These reports indicate that RFE is the most popular of the western stations. It received twice as many "votes" as its nearest rival, both in terms of the personal preference expressed by the interview source and in terms of what he felt to be generally the most popular of the western broadcasters in his country. The BBC and VOA were about tied for second and third place. [26]

The popularity of RFE seems to be based primarily on two factors. First, in contrast to any other western station, it is on the air all day long. The listener may tune in at his convenience and has a variety of programs at his disposal.[27] The second factor is the native character of the station. The BBC, VOA, and all the others (except perhaps Madrid's Polish service) are considered to be merely the foreign-language service of a western broadcasting company. (However, in the case of VOA, especially in Hungary, this seems to be an advantage. Its popularity is largely based on the fact that it speaks officially for the United States government.) The evidence indicates that RFE has succeeded in supplying a "home service." Czechs, Slovaks, Poles, and Hungarians regard it as "their" station. As a Hungarian lawyer put it, "RFE is like a secret broadcasting station operating in Hungary, while VOA and BBC represent the official broadcasts of the American and British Governments respectively."[28] A Czech comments, "RFE takes the place of a home broadcasting station; it is situated in the West because it cannot exist at home."[29] However, a readily available "home service" is not *ipso facto* popular. Witness the regime radios. To be popular a radio must fulfill the listening needs of its audience. The major need is for an objective, reliable news and information source. Radio Free Europe apparently fulfills this need.[30]

However, RFE's top popularity position is not maintained among every element of the satellite audiences. The evidence shows that the BBC outranks RFE in prestige and popularity among the better educated elements of the population in Czechoslovakia, Hungary, and Poland. Its virtues are its objectivity, reliability, and high intellectual level; its popularity dates from the dark days of World War II.[31]

Criticism of RFE (and other western stations) is not lacking. Particularly, those who favor the BBC complain that RFE lacks objectivity and speaks in an exaggerated and immoderate tone.[32] Some accuse RFE of raising "false hopes"; others, of reporting inaccurately on internal affairs.[33] It should be pointed out, however, that RFE has set a far more difficult task for itself than has either the BBC or VOA. The latter two restrict their comments and news largely to events in the West or local happenings that are well documented. Radio Free Europe tries to carry a full line of news and local commentary. This is apparently appreciated by people who have almost no way of hearing about events in other parts of their own country if the official Communist organs decide not to cover them. It is understandable that it would be least appreciated by members of the intelligentsia who might

131

have good "grapevine" sources for this kind of information.[34] This is also the group that is the most critical about any inaccuracies in RFE's reporting of internal events.

If RFE is widely listened to, what results does it have? This is a far more difficult thing to determine than the mere fact of listenership, but RFE's findings on the question will be reported. The most direct result of RFE's (and other western) broadcasts is that of keeping the local populations informed about international and foreign events.[35] The desire for such information is apparently one of the main reasons for listening. Radio Free Europe is frequently singled out by refugees for particular notice. Its hourly newscasts and up-to-the-minute reporting are appreciated. Several sources have mentioned particular news items that they were aware of only because they were carried by RFE; others comment favorably because news of specific important events was carried first by RFE.[36]

The second most frequently commented-upon function of RFE's broadcasts is that of providing a much-needed *moral support* for the captive peoples. This is not a complimentary term dreamed up by some young RFE researcher; it is a term used by the interviewees themselves and repeated in many letters. "You alone keep up our morale," "We call RFE simply 'Radio Hope'" are typical comments.[37] What is meant by this is well expressed by a Polish refugee:

In the present situation of the Polish community [pre-1956], it is most important to keep up independent thought and the morale of the population, to give it encouragement by means of opposing Communist propaganda. This is an absolutely necessary task which must be performed by somebody. In a situation where an organized, regular underground movement could be catastrophic in Poland, the Western radio has taken over this role, thus "deputizing"—so to say—for an underground movement which otherwise would be necessary. It is the best solution, since the Western radio performs this function from abroad, in all security, with the necessary means at its disposal. It thus relieves the national from the necessity of performing this task himself under highly difficult circumstances and with no adequate means.[38]

Three factors seem to be directly related to this function of providing moral support. The first is that merely by being on the air, western stations indicate that the West has not lost interest in the fate of the captive peoples. As long as this interest is maintained, there is hope for the future.[39] A second factor is that western stations provide an answer to the powerful regime propaganda that the ordinary man cannot. This apparently is most important among the less sophisticated elements of the population who cannot supply intellectually or emotionally satisfying answers themselves. Polemical and satirical programs are highly appreciated by this group. The final factor, and one that applies almost exclusively to RFE, is that western radio provides a source of entertainment. This factor is apparently becoming less important as the quality of regime radio improves, but undoubtedly it still retains some significance.

Aside from these two functions, which are fairly well documented, it is difficult to say anything about the impact of RFE on the basis of interviews with listeners and observers. A reasonable question to ask is, "Does RFE have any impact on listener attitudes and opinions?" The best way to provide an answer would be to conduct some kind of "before and after" study, but this, of course, is out of the question. And even if it could be done (for instance, on the basis of refugees escaping from satellite countries at different periods), there would still be the problem of determining whether or not any changes came about because of RFE's broadcasts or for other reasons. In the absence of this kind of study RFE asks its interview sources if they or any of their friends were influenced in thought or attitude by RFE broadcasts. This rather flimsy evidence suggests that western broadcasts may play a role in shaping certain attitudes about the international situation, particularly about events and happenings not reported in the Communist press or reported in a blatantly obvious, propagandistic manner. In the main, however, the role of RFE (and other western stations) seems to be that of supporting and reinforcing certain existing attitudes and beliefs, contributing, one might say, to the maintenance of an attitudinal *status quo*. Comments like "RFE is the most effective encouragement for resistance to Communism" or "RFE influences persons who are potential opponents of the regime" suggest that RFE does play this kind of supporting role.[40]

The acid test of any propaganda operation is whether or not it can influence or precipitate action. There is clear evidence that RFE can precipitate some action—perhaps inconsequential in western eyes but politically significant in a police state. The letters that RFE receives are representations of acts, and it is apparent that the hundreds of letters received every year are only a fraction of those actually sent. Some correspondents write, for example, that this is their third or fourth letter although it is the first actually received.

The most convincing cases of RFE influencing action consist of relatively frequent reports that Communist officials and agents mend their ways after having been denounced by RFE. (Each of RFE's voices broadcasts a kind of "black book" program on which, on the basis of very carefully screened evidence, it denounces particularly unscrupulous local Communist officials and regime supporters.) There are more than a dozen individual reports of zealous Communists losing their enthusiasm after being mentioned by RFE.

Thus, a source who generally affirms that naming of regime spies and agents makes a great impression on them, tells the story of a cadre leader in one of the Warsaw institutions who changed his behavior completely after having been named by RFE in 1953. There is another story of a UB [secret police] agent whom people started avoiding after RFE had named him and who consequently grew "much calmer and quieter." A person, suspected of spying in a village, inquired ironically of the village inhabitants whether anything had been said about him from abroad. Similarly, a UB chief in a small town tried to find out from his chauffeur whether RFE had said anything about the bad treatment of prisoners in that town. A communist manager of a factory is said to have completely changed his attitude to the workers after having bought a radio set on which he listened to RFE even while being driven in his car.[41]

These reports are not interpreted to indicate any genuine "conversion" or change of heart. They do indicate, however, a certain amount of insecurity on the part of the "middle bureaucracy" of the Communist party, and that RFE has discovered a way to work on these feelings to produce minor changes in behavior.

Aside from these isolated cases, there is little evidence that RFE affects the behavior of its broad mass of listeners. The exception may have occurred during the Hungarian uprising in 1956. This incident will be discussed below.

Regime Response to the Activities of Radio Free Europe

The response of the regimes to RFE's broadcasting may also be used as an indicator of effectiveness. Three kinds of behavior may be examined in this regard: (a) regime attacks on RFE; (b) comments on RFE that reflect its impact on a target country, found in the self-criticism columns of the local press; and (c) direct action precipitated by RFE (or action the regimes take in attempting to offset or neutralize what they feel to be the effect of RFE).

Regime Attacks. Shortly after RFE first went on the air, it was greeted by a rising crescendo of invective from the regime press and radio. Here are a few typical lines from Radio Prague:

The United States, the arch-villain behind a vast conspiracy against peace and socialism, has brought havoc to innocent Koreans, Indochinese and countless colonial people who desire liberty. The traitors of Radio Free Europe, steeped in this mud, serve that part of America where criminals and gangsters are protected so much that nothing happens to them even when they kill another person. What a difference when you listen to Radio Moscow's broadcasts to Czechoslovakia! From Moscow we hear about the Soviet People's work, leisure and education. From Radio Free Europe we just hear the rattle of arms.[42]

The object and number of regime press and radio attacks emanating from the Czechoslovak Republic, Hungary, and Poland, covering a period of almost two years, are shown in Table 4.

The three countries have always differed respecting the kind and frequency of attacks. As indicated in Table 4 the Czechoslovaks have been the most vociferous; they have also been the most bitter and blatant. Czechoslovak attacks have been characterized by the vio-

Table 4. Regime Press and Radio Attacks on Western Broadcasters from
April 1954 through February 1956

Object of Attacks*	CSR	Hung.	Pol.	Total
RFE-FEP operations	1319	153†	680	2152
VOA	131	22	325	478
BBC	26	2	139	167
Other specific western broadcasts	52	...	52	104
Unspecified western broadcasts	226	46	147	419
Total	1754	223	1343	3320

Source: RFE, *Audience Analysis Monthly Report,* Vol. II, No. 2 (February 1956), p. 1.

* An attack is a single press or radio item. One attack sometimes has more than one western station as a target. Figures do not include repeats of radio press reviews.

† Fifty-eight of these attacks occurred during the month of February 1956, and were generally part of the Soviet-Satellite large-scale propaganda attack against balloon operations.

lence with which they denounce the exiles (traitors, Nazis, rebuilders of the *Wehrmacht*, etc.) and by a general tendency to attempt to discredit RFE rather than to deal specifically with the arguments it advances. The Polish regime in the beginning responded in a similar manner, but in early 1955 a change became apparent. Following a spate of self-criticism that occurred in the press,[43] the propaganda organs of the regime began to come to grips more specifically with the content of RFE broadcasts. Programs were answered by name and articles would appear in the regime press, attacking the "enemy's" line a few days after an RFE broadcast on the same subject.

A comparatively insignificant number of attacks have come out of Budapest. The Hungarian regime seems less concerned than the others with western broadcasts,[44] apparently preferring to ignore them rather than attack.

When analyzing data on impact gathered from interview sources, one is always concerned with the question, "How reliable are they?" When concerned with regime attacks, however, one asks, "What do they mean?" or "Why does the regime attack?" Persons arguing on the assumption that it is a cardinal rule of every propagandist not to advertise or dignify the enemy's propaganda by attacking it unless it is absolutely necessary, maintain that every attack is a cry of pain and that frequency of attacks is therefore an excellent index of effectiveness. At best, this is an unsophisticated view not held by anyone in RFE, although there has been little systematic analysis to determine precisely what the regime attacks mean as reactions. However, this author feels there are four major reasons why the regimes attack RFE.

1. Regimes attack when they feel that RFE is particularly vulnerable. There are a number of examples of attacks apparently based on this kind of appraisal. For instance, on December 30, 1954, one of RFE's labor programs broadcast the following statement: "It is unfortunately true that our country would breathe more freely today if instead of the scoundrel sitting there today a man of, let us say, Adenauer's qualities were sitting at the Prague castle." Time and time again, during the following month, regime press and radio echoed this sentence, presenting it to the Czechs and Slovaks as "evidence" that RFE was dominated by Germans and that the exiles were merely the "heirs of Hitler." [45]

2. Attacks may be only an incidental part of a general propaganda campaign. The large number of attacks that originate in Prague during the anniversaries of the February *coup* and the German occupation of Czechoslovakia in 1939 seem to have little relationship to anything except generally increased propaganda activity at these times.

3. Radio Free Europe could be attacked as a "scapegoat" in an attempt to absolve somebody, or some unit of the party, of responsibility for a failure. At the end of 1953 the Prime Minister and the First Secretary of the Communist party in Hungary blamed RFE for the fact that almost 50 per cent of the peasants in agricultural collectives had abandoned them during the previous six months' period and returned to individual farming. Although RFE was carrying on an "anticollective" campaign at the time, it is hardly likely that it was largely responsible for the exodus, but it provided a handy "scapegoat" for Nagy's young "new course" government.[46]

4. Attacks may actually indicate that the regime feels that it is being hurt by RFE's activities or that these activities hold a potential danger. The Czech regime has good reason to fear the power of exiles, in view of the twentieth-century history of Czechoslovakia, and attempts to discredit RFE because it feels endangered by such a weapon in exile hands.* When the regimes come to grips directly with the substantive content of programs in a defensive rather than an offensive way, it is an indication that broadcasts are causing concern. But to accept this as evidence of RFE's influence among the people is to assume that the regimes are making an accurate assessment of the role of RFE. With the usual Communist tendency to exaggerate the influence of propaganda—both their own and the opponents'—this assumption is open to question.

The Role of RFE as Revealed in Self-Criticism. Self-criticism theoretically has always been a part of the Communist system. However, at certain times it is tolerated much more than is usual. It is this one part of the press that western experts keep their eyes fixed upon because of what it teaches them about the major problems being encountered by the regimes. In Poland during the cultural "thaw," self-criticism appeared in unprecedented proportions. Some of this un-

* See note 44 to this chapter.

doubtedly represented merely the attempt of writers to participate in the current "fad." But one gets the impression that much of it was sincere and that the Communists were going through a period of genuine soul-searching in regard to some of their important tactical and strategical assumptions. Two articles that appeared at this time will be reviewed in some detail because of the interesting picture they present of the way some Communists look at RFE.

Kronika carried an article entitled "About Propaganda." Part of it read as follows:

The name of defamer can well be given to anyone who might say that our propaganda has specialized in providing false information. This was never the case. It is true, however, that it has always reduced all information to the bare minimum, making sure that the reader or listener should not have too much to cope with. Such a formulation of course requires some qualifications. We have always been informed with the utmost detail about, say the progress of the livestock purchasing campaign in the Lowicz district or about the progress of the hunting season in the Ussuri province in Russia. But here an additional condition is introduced. We usually learned about livestock purchasing when the plan was exceeded or about the hunting season when it was successful. Information, on the other hand, about events which are generally regarded as important has usually been rare, especially where events unpleasant for our point of view have been concerned. Our propaganda kept mum when a fire broke out in a mine or when hooliganism became a universal calamity. It said nothing about the fact that we are building very few houses and that there are workers in Poland who live in extremely difficult conditions. It has remained silent about very many things. It has ignored the existence of counterpropaganda.

There can be no question in the twentieth century of a no man's land. Such ground is immediately taken over by the enemy. In the twentieth century the radio is an article of everyday use for many people. In the twentieth century balloons may be sent with propaganda leaflets or booklets to countries which are 100 or even 200 kilometers distant. . . . Facts which were true but unfavorable to us and which were ignored by our propaganda, have been seized upon by the enemy. And the enemy propagated them immediately for all to see and hear. Such information had great propaganda value. It was true. It was not afraid of censorship. Only after interpretation did it become false. RFE broadcasts all day long. Apart from RFE there are also VOA, London, Paris, Madrid. They are listened to not only by foreign agents sent to Poland. And I fear that when one hears true information—especially when one can easily verify it—information which has been passed over in silence by our propaganda, at best he loses confidence in the latter. At worst, he believes the other side's interpretation; he listens to the enemy. It seems to me that the very fact that important matters have been ignored can give rise to little confidence among people who have had the chance to see the facts with their own eyes.[47]

The second article is called "An Answer to an Old Friend."[48] The writer was reflecting on a talk he had had with an old friend. His friend was of middle-class origin and had not fared too well in prewar Poland. He had survived the war without excessive hardships and was now working in an office contributing to the building of a "new" Poland. Fundamental issues concerning Communist Poland were raised in their conversation. His friend was critical, although not without recognizing that there had been some improvements. He praised some of the developments in new Poland but complained of the lack of freedom, of social evils such as low standards of living, labor exploitation, and abuses by security authorities. However, his greatest concern was that he lived in a world completely incomprehensible to him.

Reflecting on his friend's views, the writer remarked that similar attitudes prevailed among the intelligentsia and also among workers. They were hostile to the Communist system and their hostility sprang from the feeling of being lost in a new world that was unintelligible to them. The writer went on to say that these people, and there were plenty of them, were justly described as constituting an "internal emigration." Both the real emigrees in the West and internal emigrees in Poland had sealed themselves off. The key notion with which they armed themselves in this isolation was that everything written officially or semiofficially in Poland was mere propaganda.

In this way many people have ceased to believe *a priori* in the veracity of any public statements. Some have ceased altogether to read the press and listen to the home radio. Their outlook on Poland's internal affairs was being shaped by the programs of the *Voice of Free Poland* that were always at hand.[49]

These two statements (and there are others, although admittedly not as striking) suggest that the regime attributes to RFE a role in the discrediting of its propaganda and in the maintenance of an attitudinal *status quo* among the people. They thus support the conclusions in this regard that were drawn from the refugee interviews.

Direct Regime Response to RFE's Activities. The third kind of regime response that it is important to assess is the direct action taken to counteract the effects of western broadcasting. The establishment of an elaborate system of jammers * is the most clear-cut example. And powerful evidence it is that the regimes fear at least the potential if not the immediate impact of foreign radio. However, this is an atypical example. It is rare indeed for the actions of any government to be determined by a specific event or series of events, particularly by the activities of a foreign radio station. The difficulties in measuring effectiveness mentioned in the introduction to this chapter manifest themselves with particular force when attempts to measure the direct regime response are undertaken. However, there is some evidence to indicate that RFE was at least partially—perhaps largely—responsible for a major turnover in the Polish Ministry of State Security. The details of the case are worth presenting.

In December 1953, Josef Swiatlo, head of Department Ten (Security of the Party) of the Polish Ministry of Public Security, escaped to the West. Agreeing to appear on RFE in an especially prepared series of interviews, Swiatlo personally described the organization and operation of the state security apparatus. But he went further than this. He revealed unsavory details in the private lives of the top leaders in the party. Facts concerning the luxury in which they lived, evidence to prove their subservience to Moscow, tales of intrigues and jealousies, incompetence and cruelty, were laid before the Polish people. For the first time the public received an authoritative picture of their leaders, stripped of the glamour and patriotism with which they had been portrayed for almost ten years. It is also likely that many party and regime officials, some of them in relatively high positions, heard facts about the life of the party and its leaders which were hitherto unknown to them.

Between September 28 and December 31, 1954, the *Voice of Free Poland* featured Swiatlo on 101 broadcasts and mentioned him in 146 separate news items (not counting repeats).

On October 25 the regime, which previously had been relatively quiet on the matter of Swiatlo's defection, accused him of being an "American agent and provocateur" who was responsible for the arrest, on unfounded charges, of Herman Field [50] and a number of Polish Communists. Field was immediately released from prison. The fol-

* See Chapter 7.

lowing day the official organ of the Communist party in Poland, *Trybuna Ludu*, carried an editorial restating the charge that Swiatlo was an American agent and accusing him of spreading "idiotic and vile lies [and] false information." The article went on to say: "If the matter concerned merely vile calumnies which are being spread by American yapping stations, it could be contemptuously ignored. However, the case of *agent-provocateur* Swiatlo deserves attention for different reasons."[51] Among these "different reasons" was the embarrassment to the state at having blindly suffered the presence of an "American *agent provocateur*" in the Ministry of State Security. The editorial lamented the "lack of vigilance in certain branches of our Party and State apparatus, and in particular, in the security apparatus." There had been a "criminal lack of control"—the guilty will be severely punished.[52]

On December 23, the regime announced that General Radkiewicz had been removed as Minister of Public Security (a post he had held for ten years) and shifted to a relatively minor position. In January the head of the Security Ministry's Investigation Department, Rozanski, was arrested, and Fejgin and Momkowski, Swiatlo's immediate superiors, were expelled from the party. All four of these men had been heavily compromised by the Swiatlo broadcasts. These personnel changes were part of a general reorganization of the state security apparatus.

The question is "To what degree were these changes precipitated by RFE's broadcasts?" A definitive answer is impossible; all we can do is speculate on possible relationships. On the one hand, the very fact that a man in Swiatlo's position and with his knowledge escaped would be grounds for some changes. Furthermore, the security systems in all the satellites underwent considerable reorganization following the fall of Beria. One could argue that changes were due in Poland regardless of Swiatlo's broadcasts. But on the other hand, it was over a year after Swiatlo left the country that the first change was undertaken. The regime had barely mentioned the case before the RFE broadcasts began. The reorganization of the security apparatus also followed by almost eighteen months the fall of Beria. By December 1954, it had already survived the roughest storms of the post-Beria period.

Radio Free Europe stated its conclusions about the impact of the

Swiatlo broadcasts in a number of tentative hypotheses, four of which are worth repeating in full.

1. These broadcasts disseminated the Swiatlo interview so widely throughout Poland that the regime felt compelled to produce an "explanation" to the Polish people, i.e., that Swiatlo was an American agent.

2. Under these circumstances the regime deemed it useful to use Swiatlo as the *bête noire* in releasing Herman Field and other political prisoners. It seems unlikely that political decisions of such importance were either directly precipitated or caused by the Swiatlo broadcasts, but his statements may well have been a factor in reaching these decisions and timing their execution. A note from the United States Government demanding the release of Herman Field was based on Swiatlo data, but sent before he began his series of broadcasts.

3. The *Trybuna Ludu* editorial cited above seems to clearly establish a direct causal link between Swiatlo, his broadcasts, and the subsequent re-organization of the security service, including the removal of Radkiewicz and the disgrace of three other officials. Again it appears unlikely that Swiatlo's broadcasts "forced" the regime to carry out a re-organization which in any case followed a pattern set by the USSR. However, it seems reasonable to conclude that the Swiatlo broadcasts were an important factor both in the timing of these actions and in the selection and punishment of scapegoats.

4. Regime response to these broadcasts provides strong evidence both of the regime's extreme sensitivity to material directed against the party apparatus and of the regime's conviction that these broadcasts reached and influenced a large audience in Poland, including pro- and anti-regime elements. The regime's denunciation of Swiatlo and subsequent "corrective measures" indicate that the regime was anxious to provide the public with an official explanation for his revelations and convince party members that those responsible would be punished. These actions are explicable only on the assumption that a large part of the Polish people were aware of the Swiatlo broadcasts.[53]

The Effectiveness of RFE as Revealed by Hungarian Refugees in 1956

One of the great exoduses of history occurred in the final months of 1956. When Soviet troops, tanks and artillery poured into Hungary to quell the revolution, tens of thousands of Hungarians escaped into Austria. By early February 1957, 170,000 had sought refuge in the West. This figure represents almost 2 per cent of the total population of Hungary. This group of refugees provided an excellent opportunity to apply systematic public-opinion polling techniques to the study of attitudes and opinion in a captive country. International Research Associates, Inc., conducted such a study.[54] The sample consisted of 1,007 refugees personally interviewed between December 6 and 14, 1956, in twenty refugee camps in and around Vienna. This study can be assumed to be the most reliable of the various refugee studies that have been done, because the sample was drawn from a group representing a larger proportion of the total population and was tailored to *"include the proportions of selected sub-segments of the parent population as exist in fact in the parent population."* [55]

This study supports the view that foreign radio is an important source of news in the satellites. Eighty-six per cent of the respondents listed foreign radio as a source of news in Hungary before the uprising; 21 per cent listed balloon leaflets.[56] When asked which source of news was most relied upon for information on events that were taking place inside Hungary before the uprising, 80 per cent mentioned foreign radio (10 per cent, balloon leaflets) while only 8 per cent listed regime press and radio. For news on foreign events, the percentage figures were even more striking: 84 per cent relied most on foreign radio (8 per cent, balloon leaflets) while only 5 per cent relied most heavily on regime sources.[57]

Radio Free Europe, the Voice of America and the British Broadcasting Corporation were the "big three" among the foreign stations. In the year preceding their escape, 96 per cent of the respondents said they had listened to RFE, while the figures for VOA and BBC were 82 per cent and 67 per cent respectively. More significantly, when the listeners to foreign radio were asked, "How often did you hear the foreign radio stations?" 81 per cent of RFE's listeners responded "frequently" (the choice being "frequently," "occasionally," "rarely"), while 67 per cent made a similar response for both VOA and the BBC.[58] These figures are particularly interesting when interpreted in the light of two other pieces of information. It is considerably more difficult to receive RFE than it is the BBC and somewhat more difficult than receiving VOA,[59] presumably because of jamming. Furthermore, the listening audience is more critical of RFE than of the other two stations. Seven out of ten feel that RFE is reliable, whereas the figures are 85 per cent and 90 per cent for VOA and BBC respectively on this issue.[60]

It should also be pointed out that the three western stations most widely listened to appeal to different types of audiences. While RFE's listening audience was distributed fairly well among all the sub-groups of the sample, the VOA appealed more to the professionals and less to the very young, the least educated, to unskilled workers, and to housewives. The BBC was listened to principally by the best educated, the very young, and the high income groups.[61]

This study by a skilled, independent research organization indicates the crucial role that western radio plays in the lives of some of the captive peoples, and demonstrates the dominant position that RFE holds among the "big three" western broadcasters. Finally, where the findings are comparable, it corroborates the studies that RFE makes of itself and therefore adds some validity to its reports.

9

Operations from the Berlin to the Poznan Riots

In the previous chapters we have described the organization of RFE and how this organization functions to produce policy and propaganda. In this and the following chapter attention will be focused on the development of a propaganda campaign.

Radio Free Europe began its operations with an optimistic assumption of success based on the biblical authority that "the truth shall make them free." "But it's a tough fight," remarked Jan Masaryk, and it was not long before the full import of this twentieth-century comment on sacred teaching became obvious. One gets the impression that, by the beginning of 1953, RFE was beset by a certain amount of frustration. It had forged a mighty technical weapon with which it could pierce the Iron Curtain and bring its message to the captive peoples. Its goal of liberation had the official support of the new administration in Washington. But how could it use its instrument to achieve its goal? It could not build up the hope that western armies would soon come smashing through eastern Europe. Not only was this contrary to American policy, but in the age of thermonuclear weapons, war meant total destruction. No promise of liberation could be appealing if it followed in the wake of atomic annihilation. Nor could RFE incite violence or call for mass uprisings and revolution. Even if the listeners would respond, RFE felt itself in no position to call for action that would lead to a blood bath. Radio Free Europe seemed fated merely to support the morale of the captive peoples and to harass the regimes in its daily polemic broadcasts. What was needed was an action program. But an action program has two prerequisites. Propaganda is no "ultimate weapon." It is effective only when it is part of a general strategy which plans for the integrated use of all instruments of statecraft to reach a given goal. Until the outlines of some general strategy of liberation were devised, no action program for RFE could be developed. This was the first prerequisite. The second was a thorough analysis of the target countries to determine what kind of action was feasible in the situation as it existed. This kind of analysis was begun following the Czech and East German riots of June 1953.

The Significance of Events in June 1953

In Czechoslovakia, the youngest of the People's Democracies, 1952 ended on a note of terror. Slansky, Clementis, and several other Communists were tried on a number of charges ranging from ideological deviation to sabotaging the economic plan. They were, of course, found guilty. The major offenders were executed, and the whole affair was used as a pretext for introducing new and harsher economic policies. In the spring the repressive measures were intensified by Zapotocky (who took over the reins of government when Gottwald died shortly after returning from Stalin's funeral). The most drastic step was taken on May 30, when rationing was abolished and a currency reform instituted. This action swept away savings, depressed the already low standards of living, and forced workers to increase production by keeping them on the job longer.

But at this point something happened that the police state fears, but rarely has to deal with. On June 1, large-scale riots broke out at the famous Skoda works in Pilsen and rapidly spread to a number of other cities. The workers were protesting the new reform. The demonstrations were violent but short-lived; on June 15 the regime was able to sponsor a large workers' rally in Bratislava which passed off without incident. The stringent economic course was (for the time being) maintained. But something had happened that neither the regime nor the people could forget, although its full import was not evident until some time later.

While the Communist oppression was being increased in Czechoslovakia, the old policies were suddenly reversed in East Germany. The collectivization drive was curtailed, workers' norms were lowered, the investment rate in heavy industry reduced, and an "agreement" was signed with the Evangelical Church. However, the people were not in a grateful mood. They had caught the glimpse of a better life and rose in what was almost a rebellion to force the regime into even greater concessions. On June 17 the uprising started in Berlin and rapidly spread to many other places in the East Zone. The people were brought under control only when the Red Army, in full battle array, took charge. Stones would not stop tanks, and rioters were subdued.

The Czech and the German demonstrations developed out of entirely different situations. The Czech workers rioted when they felt themselves being pushed deeper into the trough of misery; the Germans interpreted the granting of concessions as signs of weakness, and they rose to push their advantage. But there was one all-important similarity. In neither case were the demonstrators put down with the ruthless brutality that RFE had expected would follow acts of overt opposition. Tanks moved into Berlin streets, but, by and large, their guns remained silent. Arrests were surprisingly few; mass executions unknown.

From these events RFE drew three important conclusions: First and most important, there existed behind the Iron Curtain a large opposition. It was unorganized; it was inarticulate.. But in Czechoslovakia (where our interest is focused for the moment) it included large sections of the working class and of the youth who in 1948 supplied the mass support for the Communist party. It even included members of the Communist party. Some shop stewards at Pilsen threw in their lot with their fellow workers. Second, the rulers were disorganized and uncertain of themselves. Their leader of thirty years was dead. They were not sure of the new policy of the Kremlin; they did not know what course the power struggle might take. They hesitated to move vigorously against the rioters not because they had renounced brutality, but because they had lost confidence—not because they were more merciful, but because they needed the workers in order to meet the production demands made by the Kremlin. The third point follows from the first two. The workers, if they stood firm, could make demands on the regime that the regime would have to honor. These three assumptions arising out of an analysis of the June demonstrations underlie the VETO and FOCUS operations that were started the following year.

New Themes Developed after the June Riots

After a few days of initial confusion RFE developed a new propaganda line for its broadcasts to Czechoslovakia. Its purpose was to convince the people—most of all the industrial workers—to use their own strength and ingenuity to begin hacking away at the Iron Curtain from the inside.[1] Radio Free Europe's policy guidance for workers programs called for scripts that would make the workers aware of the significance of the events in Pilsen and Berlin. It was crucial to convince the industrial workers that their strength was increasing while the rulers were confused and disorganized.[2]

In speaking to the police and to the army RFE tried to undermine any loyalty that they might have to the regime—to make them unreliable instruments of control, particularly in times of crisis. Broadcasts to the police were to follow the line suggested by this paragraph:

It is true under a true people's regime or under a reactionary regime that the police fire upon the oppressed and striking workers? What is the mark of a Fascist? Is it not that he takes sadistic pleasure from shooting and beating the workers in his own country? Must a man be hated by his neighbors simply because he wears the uniform of a policeman? [3]

To the army the questions were similar. Radio Free Europe wanted to remind the officers that they owed allegiance not to the Communist leaders but to their country and to their people. The rank and file were told that they might some day be asked to shoot at their brothers in the streets of their own cities. Radio Free Europe had reported that when the German *Volkspolizei* were called into the street to suppress rioters, they were something more than embarrassed. They held their fire because they could not shoot down their brothers. Some even put their guns into the hands of the workers. And the Czech and Slovak soldier was asked, "If that day should come for you . . . would you do less than the East German *Vopos* did?" [4]

Next to the workers, officials in the party and in the regime were the most important targets in RFE's revised campaign. Officials were reminded that chances of their living to a ripe old age were not great. Most servants of the Kremlin, great or small, live to be disgraced, purged, imprisoned, perhaps shot. The risks were even greater during the period of uncertainty when they did not know what turn the power struggle in the Kremlin might take. In a situation like this, party loyalty means nothing and personal loyalty is dangerous because one never knows when the object of that loyalty in the Kremlin may fall. And all the time the officials are known by the people to be agents of a foreign power. When the people are free, the officials may expect to be torn to pieces as was the case with the collaborators with the Nazis in France in 1945.[5]

The appeal to the officials was concentrated on giving them two action alternatives. Either they could cross the "golden bridge" of forgiveness by the people and use their positions to sabotage the Muscovites and protect the people in that part of the nation under their charge, or they could defect to the West.[6]

And finally there were the youth groups. For three years RFE had been addressing the students and telling them not to manifest their resentment against the regime—not to show their disbelief at the preposterous Communist teachings—not to cry out that a "poem written by an illiterate sycophant to celebrate the manufacture of a tractor is not literature." Rather the student was told to be quiet and learn what he could from his parents. He was told to learn a profession, to learn about firearms and how to handle a platoon of soldiers, because someday his country might need his skills. Following the June riots, the students were told in addition:

Be suspicious. Do not be taken in by strangers who talk about resistance. Be not tempted by the promise of adventure, of secret meetings. Do not look for leaders. But at the same time, think about what you can do, what part will be yours when the time comes. And when you think, remember how great will be the reward—to be a free man rebuilding a free country in a free, fraternal United Europe; to have a *Koruno* that will actually buy something—an English motor-bike, a French literary review, a novel by Hemingway, a honeymoon on the Italian lakes, all in a world without police. It is you who will rebuild our society according to your ideas, not a foreigner's ideas, of what the life of our country should be.[7]

These themes suggested action but they did not yet constitute an *action program* because they were not related to any obtainable goal. The *action program* in Czechoslovakia (Operation VETO) did not start until the following year. In order to understand how it was developed, it is necessary to review events behind the Iron Curtain in the summer and fall of 1953 and RFE's response to them.

The "New Course"

In the first days of July 1953, Nagy replaced Rakosi as head of the Hungarian government. Four days later he repudiated some of the stringent policies of the old regime, and launched Hungary on the "New Course." In August it became evident that the "investment in moderation" was spreading to Czechoslovakia, when President Zapotocky criticized the policy of rapid, forced collectivization and announced that peasants would be free to leave the collectives. Although the "New Course" went further in Hungary than in the other satellites, we will trace its development in Czechoslovakia because of the close relationship between the unfolding of events there and the development of Operation VETO.

The "New Course" really got under way in Czechoslovakia in the middle of September when the regime announced a new economic program which included the following points: (a) curtailment of the investment rate in heavy industry; (b) greater investment in all sectors of agriculture and higher prices allowed peasants for grain; (c) relaxing of the pressures that had been exerted against the independent (noncollectivized) peasant; (d) increase in quality and quantity of consumer goods; (e) augmentation of the housing program; (f) broadening of the raw material base specifically in order to increase production of thermal and electric power.

And there was soon some evidence that the program was not merely an empty propaganda gesture. By the end of September prices were reduced on 23,000 consumer items. In November new assistance programs for both the collective and independent peasant were announced. In December food prices were cut, income taxes favorably revised, buying restrictions on some consumer items reduced, and delivery quotas on many agricultural products lowered.

The "New Course" involved not only economic measures; speeches made in December by Viliam Siroky and Antonin Novotny made it clear that it also contained important political and ideological elements. The following schedule of political events was announced to take place in the late winter and early spring: (a) elections to party committees of lower rank in February; (b) elections to shop committees in late February or early March; (c) elections to local, district, city and regional National Committees* probably in May; (d) parlia-

---

* These committees came spontaneously into existence during the liberation of Czechoslovakia in 1945. They were given legal standing and wide powers as organs of local government in the draft constitutions of 1946 and were placed under the Ministry of Interior. Siroky declared in December 1953 that jurisdiction over them had been transferred to the cabinet.

mentary elections (required by the constitution); (e) Tenth Congress of the Czechoslovak Communist party, June 11–13.

At the same time this political program was announced, the ideological line was laid down. Siroky and Novotny, in their December speeches, made it clear that the new policy represented no retreat from basic Marxist principles. In fact, the success of the "New Course" was predicated on the reaffirmation of these principles. It represented the tactical changes of the party to meet a new situation. The Communists made it clear that it was not a compromise with bourgeois nationalism, social democracy, or "Masarykism," which were singled out for specific criticism—the first because it would open the old sores of Czech-Slovak dissension; the second because it would introduce anti-Marxist concepts of "equalitarianism"; the last because it was merely the old bourgeois capitalism masked behind a fraudulent humanitarianism.

The whole party apparatus would also have to be revitalized. A new spirit of militancy would be needed to uproot functionaries who were living in isolation from the masses and merely repeating the old slogans. All the instruments of propaganda and agitation would be used to instill a new enthusiasm among party members and, through them, among the masses.

This was the situation in January 1954. The policy advisers at RFE felt there were two main aspects of the "New Course." The first was purely economic. The Communist world was beginning to realize that if it were to achieve its goal of catching up economically with the West, it would have to increase productivity (output per man hour) as well as production. This could not be done without eliminating the grosser errors and inefficiencies in the whole planning structure. But more important, in the last analysis it meant gaining the cooperation of the workers. Terrorism could enforce high norms and reduce absenteeism, and thus increase production; but it could not raise productivity. This could only be done by granting concessions including more consumer goods. It was hoped that the resultant increased productivity by more satisfied workers would result in the production of both more guns and more butter.[8]

But the concessions could not be granted unless they were strictly controlled. The Communists were determined not to let concessions in Czechoslovakia have the result that they had had in Germany the previous June. And so the second part of the "New Course" involved a strengthening of the party apparatus to actually increase the degree to which the masses in their new economic freedom were controlled by the regime. New elections were being held in shop committees because during the June riots the old committeemen had either thrown their lot in with the workers—and therefore could not be trusted by the regime—or they had so earned the contempt of the workers that they no longer had any influence over them. New, local party chairmen and secretaries were needed because the old ones were either living in isolation from the masses or had grown so fond of their friends and neighbors that they were protecting them from the decrees of the regime rather than enforcing them. New National Committees were needed because the regime needed a fresh, enthusiastic, and trustworthy instrument with which it could enforce its will throughout the countryside.[9]

At the end of January 1954, RFE developed a plan to deal with this new situation.[10] It had three phases. The first was to run during the pre-election period or until about the twentieth of February. During this phase RFE would explain to the people of Czechoslovakia the real meaning of the "New Course"—how the age-old combination of the carrot and the stick was being used to accelerate the process of sovietization. The reasons for the economic concessions and the new elections, and the relationship between the two, would be broadcast across the countryside.

The second phase would run from mid-February until mid-May. During this period RFE would actively engage in the campaigns for election of new shop committees and new National Committees as the "Voice of the Opposition." It could not, of course, support candidates of the opposition, but it would present the demands of the people and let the candidates know what course of action the workers expected them to pursue.

The third phase would correspond to the period of the campaign for elections to the parliament. Although RFE felt that the shop committees and National Committees could be used by the people for their ends, the parliament could only be a rubber stamp for the regime. Thus, during the third phase its efforts would be devoted to discrediting the parliament and discounting the elections as a shameless travesty of democracy.

Operation VETO
All the basic tactical elements of the first phase of the VETO operation were contained in this January Plan. Operation VETO, which began in late April, represents a refinement of these elements and a general intensification of activities in an integrated, long-range *action program*. The January Plan laid out a tactical maneuver designed to frustrate the regime's intentions of using the round of elections to revitalize and consolidate the state and party machinery. Operation VETO was a long-term campaign aimed at achieving eventual liberation. The election fight would merely be the first step in a long-range program to return political initiative to the people. The development of VETO rested on a number of assumptions that had been debated in RFE since the death of Stalin and the beginning of the "New Course." The debates concerned the meaning of events that were taking place in the Soviet orbit. Some people argued that the post-Stalin reforms were superficial, insignificant, and likely to be revoked. They could draw on a great deal of historical evidence to support this view. Others felt, however, that powerful forces present in the Soviet Union even before the death of Stalin were behind the reforms and that once reforms were begun, reversals in policy could only be temporary. Operation VETO (and later Operation FOCUS) was based on the assumption that RFE (and its sister organization, the Free Europe Press) should encourage the captive peoples to work for specific, short-range reforms, and that success in this policy would lead to the gradual erosion of Communist authority. The people in RFE who objected to this interpretation resisted its adoption for some time. They felt that it was not right to give the listening audiences hope that their condition could be improved without the complete destruction of the Communist dictatorship. They believed that it was dangerous to concentrate popular hopes upon a continuation of the post-Stalin reforms. The more the captive peoples thought about specific grievances and their possible alleviation, the less they would think about the over-all question of abolishing Communism altogether. But by the spring of 1954 this position was held by only a small group in RFE.

Behind the change from the tactical maneuver of the January Plan to the long-term campaign that was Operation VETO, lay the development of the concept of liberation as the result of a confluence of forces in operation within and outside the satellites. The outside force is the strength of the free world; the inside, the strength of the people's opposition. Radio Free Europe saw its long-range task under Operation VETO as building up the strength and action potential of the internal force until the day should come when a favorable relationship between the internal and external components finally coincided with an international situation in which the Soviet Union would find it more painful to intervene than not to intervene. This was considered to be a realistic view of events that would lead to liberation.

We stated above that in its first phases VETO represented a refinement of the tactical elements involved in the January Plan and a general intensification of activities. The important refinement was in the concept of the "People's Opposition"; the intensification consisted of the combining and integrating of the radio with the balloon-leaflet campaign.

The realization that there was a large, unorganized opposition in Czechoslovakia that was capable of engaging in politically significant action came out of the June riots. The January Plan spoke of RFE as the "Voice of the Opposition." The idea was extended to its logical conclusion in Operation VETO. In broadcasts to the people of Czechoslovakia, RFE emphasized the existence of a "People's Opposition." It was a movement without formal organization, without a headquarters, without material means, but to which every Czech and Slovak belonged if he was opposed to the process of sovietization that was taking place in his country. It was neither a conspiracy nor an underground. Essentially, it was a spiritual union of all patriotic Czechs and Slovaks. In VETO, RFE spoke as the "Voice of the People's Opposition." The people themselves had to be careful even about what they said in private. No internal voice of the opposition would have the means or the opportunity of commanding a mass audience. Radio Free Europe tried to fill this gap. It could speak clearly, forcefully, and, it hoped, authoritatively.[11]

An effective opposition must have a platform, however, and RFE articulated and disseminated the Ten Demands of the People's Opposition as its platform, expressed briefly in the following terms:

1. Trade Unions for Trade Unionists
2. Better Pay—Less Talk
3. Workers must not be Chained
4. No Meddling with Workers' Free Time

5. No More Farmers' Bondage
6. Smaller Quotas—Larger Crops
7. Local Autonomy instead of Bureaucracy
8. Goods for the People, not for the Soviets
9. Back to Serving the Customer
10. Housing for Families, not for the State

Radio Free Europe developed these demands from an analysis of numerous information items and a careful coverage of the regime press and radio. They were not the dream of some American sitting in a comfortable chair in Munich, reflecting on the situation in Czechoslovakia.

Operation VETO marked a refinement in the concept of the "Voice of the Opposition"; it involved an intensification due to the integrated use of radio and balloon-leaflets. The relative advantages of the spoken and written word have long been recognized by propagandists. The tactical flexibility of radio, its all-pervasive nature, and its ability to capitalize on the emotional power of the human voice are all limited by the transitory nature of any given program and the problem of dealing both adequately and briefly with complex and difficult thoughts. But its weaknesses may be compensated by the strengths of the written word. The VETO plan was devised to take advantage of the complementary nature of radio and leaflets. Basic messages were carried in by balloons launched by the Free Europe Press. They were then commented on and interpreted in the light of day-to-day events on various programs on the Voice of Free Czechoslovakia.

In discussing the development of VETO it is useful to look at a number of phases identified by certain specific objectives and themes. Phase one was short and introductory. It was designed to capture the interest and stir up the curiosity of the Czechoslovak public, and to plant the idea of the Ten Demands as the platform of the "People's Opposition." It began late in April 1954, with the dropping of a sticker containing only the number "10" and with a campaign of radio spot announcements designed to stimulate interest in the number "10." Starting just after the first of May 1954, (scheduled beginning on May 1 was postponed because of unfavorable winds) the small newssheet *Svobodna Europa* (Free Europe) was carried into Czechoslovakia by balloons, listing the Ten Demands and commenting on them. This publication was dropped over the country until shortly after the middle of May. In the meantime four other leaflets were dropped with the aim of popularizing the Ten Demands and making special appeals to specific groups (farmers, workers, party functionaries, etc.). These leaflets were in the form of stickers and gave the people the means of participating in the electoral campaign by pasting them up in public places. The themes developed in leaflets were also carried in radio programs.[12] On May 1, some of the May Day programs dealt with the Ten Demands and their meaning. On the next day (a Sunday), the radio audience was informed about the publications that were being flown into Czechoslovakia and a special VETO song was introduced. On May 3, five programs dealt specifically with VETO, three of them directed at special groups—farmers, civil servants, workers—spelling out what the Ten Demands meant to them. This level of activity was continued throughout the week.

The second phase got underway in the latter part of May. It had two important objectives. The first was to explain exactly what the Ten Demands really meant to individuals; the second and more important task was to try to get the people to understand why the opposition campaign was based on specific and attainable demands (i.e., why an *action program*). The first involved relating the demands to the specific needs of individuals in Czechoslovakia and penetrating so deeply that it would be impossible for them to hear or see the number "10" without political connotations coming to mind. The balloon-leaflet implementation of this was accomplished by two leaflets. The first was the "Ballot of the People's Opposition," issued in 20 million copies. It carried a statement and exposition of the Ten Demands. (The releasing of this leaflet marked the transition between phase one and phase two.) The second was an eight-page picture edition of *Svobodna Europa*, "designed to translate the Ten Demands into human and individual terms by photographs and text written in more readable, informal language." [13]

The second and far more delicate mission of phase two was to explain the shift to an *action program* based on the Ten Demands. Why, instead of sustaining the assumption that liberation would come, albeit eventually, from the free world, did RFE begin to speak to the people of Czechoslovakia as essential partners in the struggle? Why, instead of polemics and exhortatory slogans, did RFE now talk about the "People's Opposition" and its ten specific demands? The answer to these questions involved an exposition of the thinking that lay behind the whole VETO operation. In brief, the reasoning was presented to the Czechs and Slovaks as follows: Liberation as the consequence of an aggressive war waged by the West was unrealistic. Liberation as the result of a reformed Kremlin voluntarily withdrawing from the satellites, or liberation as the result of successful Titoism, was a fantasy. Viewed seriously,

. . . liberation of the Soviet satellites is likely to occur only as the result of a *favorable confluence of events within and outside* of the country. Inside this means that *coordinated mass opposition* must evolve and gather strength during the pre-liberation period. Outside the country it means that the "People's Opposition Center in the Free World" must provide initiative, tangible symbols and (in part) the ideological basis for sustained resistance. Without external support the People's Opposition would wither in isolation. Without internal receptivity the efforts of the free world would indeed become pointless and unnecessary attempts at "interference."

Given, however, a favorable relationship of internal and external components, and given the right moment when in the course of international events the Soviet Union finds it less painful not to intervene than to intervene, *then* coordinated mass opposition becomes coordinated mass action actively supported by the "Opposition Center" outside.

This "favorable confluence of events" lies in the future—quite possibly in the distant future. Neither the internal nor the external components are yet prepared to take advantage of any unlikely turn of events which might make non-intervention a realistic possibility. But it is clear that every day that passes without some form of increment in the strength of the internal opposition is a day which must be counted in favor of a *Pax Sovietica* in Eastern Europe. That is why the first steps must be taken now to assist the people to act in unison, why an action program, with limited but realistic goals, must be introduced and firmly planted in the minds of those who form our audiences, and on whom we rely and who rely on us.[14]

Getting this kind of a message across is a difficult propaganda task. It involves subtle and sophisticated reasoning. Subtlety and sophistication are not the strong points of any propaganda. But more than that was involved. The answer to the question "Why an *action program?*" is based on a specific interpretation of world events following the death of Stalin. The acceptance of RFE's answer was predicated on an acceptance of RFE's view of the world. In short, the fundamental task of VETO was to get the Czechs and Slovaks to accept a certain *Weltanschauung.* Creating a picture of the world of the future and an appreciation of the forces at work to build that world was one of VETO's tasks.

It was during this second phase that the full power of radio was brought to bear. In addition to carrying the substance of the VETO message, the radio suggested things that could be done to make the "People's Opposition" a living reality. Broadcasts informed the Czechs and Slovaks, for instance, that one of the leaflets—the "Ballot of the People's Opposition"—was not to be used in the official election. Instead it could be affixed to walls and bulletin boards, mailed to party members and candidates for election, slipped under thresholds. In short, its ballot box was all of Czechoslovakia.

Programs also reminded the people (and the electoral commissions) of all their legal rights in the elections. The regime had promised that the voting would be free and secret. Election results were to be announced as soon as known, and in all cases where candidates did not receive a majority of the votes, new elections were to be held. (It is obvious that RFE did not expect the law to be enforced in all cases. It was making a propaganda demand within the framework of the regime's own legalistic election guarantees, designed to make the regime pay dearly in terms of loss of prestige for everything it gained by tampering with the electoral process.)

Although the elections did not give the people a choice among a number of candidates, they had the legal right of crossing out the names of candidates they objected to. Thus, RFE advised the voters to examine carefully the lists of candidates. Any candidate who could be of direct or indirect use to the cause of the "People's Opposition" should be supported. The hard Communist or crude opportunist should be struck from the list. People should go to the polls with a pencil, prepared to exercise their rights if the opportunity presented itself.

Care was taken to answer the possible response of the defeatist, i.e., that the regime would announce the results of the elections according to its own needs, and that any manifestation of opposition would be purely futile. This may well be the case, as RFE admitted, but even if the regime refused to acknowledge the strength of the opposition it would nonetheless know that it existed and how strong it was. Individual candidates would be made aware that they had incurred the quiet wrath of the people, and all this would contribute to the wavering and hesitancy the regime had shown since the death of Stalin.

The emphasis on elections built up to a crescendo on May 15, the day before the National Committee elections. Original plans called for another peak in early June, just before the parliamentary election, but this was cancelled when the regime announced that the elections would be postponed until fall.

It should be pointed out that the regime responded to VETO with vigorous counterpropaganda. The first reaction was diversionary—it did not deal with the substance of VETO, but attacked the exiles in RFE who "strive to sell the independence of Czechoslovakia to the American imperialists" and "to seek a liberation of Czechoslovakia with the aid of SS-men," and force it to join a "German dominated European Federation." But soon the regime began to deal directly with VETO. It argued with VETO's proposals and even adopted its terminology in speaking about "the ten demands of the so-called peoples' opposition." [15]

The first two phases of VETO were laid out before the operation got under way. It is only proper to speak of phases after that in terms of RFE shifting its emphasis and modifying its tactics to fit the changing conditions and situations in Czechoslovakia in 1954. In July through September, for instance, Operation VETO was tied in with the "Harvest of Self-Defense" campaign that RFE waged during the harvest season. The "Harvest of Self-Defense" dealt with the peasants' struggle against the requisitioning process. The project was carried out within the context of the Ten Demands, with particular emphasis on the fifth and sixth demands which concerned agricultural policy and the eighth demand which asked for more goods (foodstuffs) for the people.[16] When heavy rains and floods inflicted severe damage in July, RFE reminded its listeners of the way natural catastrophes had been handled by democratic Czechoslovak governments in the past and described how western governments were dealing with similar situations. It demanded that the regime make compensation for individual losses and reduce the delivery quotas after an honest and just appraisal of the storm and flood damage.[17]

What might be called phase four of VETO was in reality a repetition of the tactics that had been planned and only partially used in the spring because of the postponement of the elections. The election campaign in the fall gave RFE a chance to draw on the experience gained in the application of VETO concepts in the spring and to refine techniques and adapt new ones. The policy posture toward the Czechoslovak National Assembly was essentially the same as that developed in the spring; namely, that the parliament is merely a rubber stamp and since the people have no means of influencing the elections or the candidates, it would not be advisable to try to develop an action campaign. The campaign was used as a hook on which to hang programs designed to further discredit the parliament. Scripts were written, for instance, describing the operations of democratic parliaments (Britain, the United States, Sweden), how they functioned as a bulwark against the assumption of dictatorial powers by any one group, and how they arrived at social and political programs as the result of free debate and study.

The Slovak National Council was treated in a different manner. Without any references to Czech-Slovak antagonisms the Council was attacked as merely the agency which legitimated decisions made in Prague; in other words, it was merely an instrument of "Communist centralism" that frustrated rather than fulfilled Slovak demands for self-government within a federated Czechoslovak Republic.

But it was in regard to the shop committee elections that the *action program* of VETO was truly implemented in the fall of 1954. A number of speeches given in July by Joseph Tesla, chairman of the URO (Revolutionary Trade Union Movement), indicated that perhaps the appeals of RFE to the workers were worrying Communist officials. On July 2, 1954, Tesla gave a speech in which he said:

All cases of 'social democratism' in Union activity lead to protection of unjustified low norms, to various theories of egalitarianism, to the misuse of bonuses . . . A trade Union organization yielding to such opinions will yield to the pressure for wage increases not based on higher productivity. . . . The danger of 'social democratism' is always evident where Union officials . . . succumb to the elementary pressure of employees. . . .[18]

Other newspaper stories indicated a similar concern. For example, "In the Metz works in Stepanov and the ZPS works in Lisen, Union officers directly opposed the norm setters in order to protect low norms and unjustified high earnings."[19]

Such official comments reassured the policy advisers at RFE that they were on the right path. They felt that although it was true of Czechoslovakia (as of other countries behind the Iron Curtain) that the peasants were the most dogged opponents of the regime, the allegiance of the industrial worker was nevertheless more important to the regime than subduing the peasants. It was this prize that was being contested in the shop committee elections.

During the pre-election phases (i.e., before the regime announced a definite date for the elections) RFE, in the name of the "People's Opposition," demanded that the promise made in the spring to hold fall elections be fulfilled. The time had come to begin the return to industrial democracy. Nobody had to teach the prewar Czechoslovak worker anything about democratic trade unionism, but for the benefit of the younger men, RFE broadcast a "course" in trade unionism based on Czechoslovak and western experience. The scripts were calm in tone; expository and not polemical.[20]

After the elections were announced, the "Workers' Opposition" based its approach on three basic points: (a) that no good can come of the elections if the ROH (Trade Union Federation) puts up candidates known to be its stooges; workers must have freedom to examine the list of candidates in advance, in each mine and factory, and to discuss the list at a plant meeting; (b) that the Shop Council's powers and functions shall be printed and distributed to all workers and that workers shall be free to assemble with candidates and examine them on their knowledge of the powers and functions and their interpretation thereof; (c) that elections shall be truly democratic; candidates to be drawn from among workers in the mine or factory; secret ballot; election by simple majority; mine or factory's own workers as tellers of the vote.[21]

These three points were conceived as part of the basic doctrine that the function of shop councils is to represent and protect the interests of the workers.

During the whole campaign two basic cautions were observed. No instructions were given on the selection of candidates or how to vote. There was no talk of "infiltrating" or "capturing" the councils. It was felt that apart from the fact that it might put individual citizens in jeopardy of being charged with "acting in obedience to instructions from the western radio," such comment was not necessary. People in the factories knew much more about the specific situation than did RFE and were aware of the kind of action that could be undertaken. RFE looked at its task as perceiving "what the people themselves are doing, [making] the value and meaning of their own acts clear to them by looking farther ahead than they are looking and [formulating] their demands [not RFE's] in a concise, easily remembered language which will persuade them that we are truly their brothers because we say exactly what is in their hearts." [22]

The second caution observed was that violent language and strong attack was reserved for those people whom the workers genuinely disliked—the higher functionaries of the ROH who were almost never in the factories. Local functionaries sometimes have the sympathy and support of the workers because of the peculiar pressures that the regime can exert upon them or because they have already crossed the "golden bridge" by seeking to promote the workers' interests. [23]

Operation FOCUS

The Hungarian Operation FOCUS was the second large-scale radio balloon-leaflet campaign. Its basic elements were identical to those of VETO. It tried to build up the idea of an internal resistance movement (called the National Opposition Movement). Twelve demands of the opposition were propagated, and the campaign was launched during an electoral period. However, there were three important differences between the Hungarian and Czechoslovak situations which led to differences in implementation. First, the "New Course" had gone further in Hungary than it had in Czechoslovakia. More concessions were actually granted and a program of administrative and economic decentralization had begun. Second, the opposition in Hungary was more diffuse and was more significant in the countryside than it was in the industrial and urban centers. Finally, RFE felt that the Hungarian party apparatus showed signs of greater internal strain than did the Czechoslovakian. [24]

By and large, however, VETO and FOCUS are so similar that it is not necessary here to discuss the detailed implementation of the latter.

The Evolution of the Propaganda Concepts of VETO and FOCUS

Operations VETO and FOCUS were developed as *action programs* to frustrate the political aims of the "New Course" while encouraging the listeners to apply what pressure they could to force the regimes into granting more and more economic concessions. The action emphasis was terminated following the reversal of the "New Course" in early 1955 (symbolized by the overthrow of the Nagy regime in Hungary). In a period of "crackdown" RFE felt it would be futile to encourage people to work for concessions. But the other aspect of VETO and FOCUS—the attempt to get the listening audiences to accept a view of the world which included the prospects of liberation—was continued.

Bulganin's and Khrushchev's visit to Yugoslavia in May and June of 1955 provided material which caused RFE to refine its concept of liberation through the operation of a "confluence of forces." This visit was undertaken to heal the breach that had developed in 1948. The price the Russians had to pay was one paragraph in the Belgrade Declaration of June 2, 1955, signed by Tito and Bulganin, which read:

Compliance with the principle of mutual respect for, and non-interference in, internal affairs, for whatever reason, whether of an economic, political or ideological nature, because of questions of internal organization or differences in social system, and of different forms of socialist development, are solely the concerns of the individual countries.[25]

Two months later Tito indicated in no uncertain terms that he interpreted this paragraph to apply not only to Yugoslavia but also to other Communist states in eastern and central Europe. On July 27 he unleashed a biting attack against the Hungarian regime. The essence of his charge was that there were still "Stalinists" in Budapest. "They are still putting people in prison . . . who express opinions freely and approve the statements of Khrushchev and other Soviet leaders" (i.e., the statements made at Belgrade). Similar charges were later directed at Prague and Bucharest.[26]

Radio Free Europe felt that the Belgrade Declaration and Tito's application of its principle to all the captive countries could be a tremendous centrifugal force in the satellite system. Its vast information-gathering agency had provided evidence to show that a number of high Communists in the captive countries would like to have more freedom from Moscow. This conclusion was reinforced by RFE's correspondent at the second Geneva conference in the fall of 1955, who got the impression that non-Russian Communists were "disgruntled and disillusioned" by the intransigence of the Soviet delegation. They had expected, he wrote, that the Russians "were going to let loose of them a bit and let them manage their own affairs a little more." Molotov, he added, "must have shocked many of those people badly."

Radio Free Europe further reasoned that the Belgrade principle might conceivably influence the relationships between the party leaders and the rest of the populace. Prior to the summer of 1955 every satellite regime was partially protected from local demands (both from within and outside the party) by the general knowledge that the "Kremlin would not allow it." But if Moscow says that it respects the principle of "non-interference in internal affairs" and recognizes "different forms of socialist development," then the regimes stood in a different position both in relation to Moscow and to their own people.

While the Belgrade Declaration provided a foundation on which RFE could carry the propaganda wars to the enemy following the official abandonment of the "New Course," other events in 1955 forced RFE to assume a somewhat defensive position. The Summit Conference in Geneva in the summer of 1955 was hailed in some parts of the world as signaling the end of the cold war. This interpretation supported the Soviet position in the captive nations because it meant that the western powers had agreed to a permanent Soviet hegemony in eastern Europe. The photograph of the beaming, genial Eisenhower shaking hands with the respectable, goateed Bulganin could be interpreted by the peoples in the satellite countries as a symbol of an agreement that would seal their fate for generations. And the UN membership "package deal" at about the same time, which gave the puppet governments of the satellites a legitimate place in the UN, could be used as further evidence to support the thesis that the captive peoples were a pawn sacrificed to perpetuate the *status quo*. Fortunately for RFE, President Eisenhower said on August 24, 1955:

Eagerness to avoid war—if we think no deeper than this single desire —can produce outright or implicit agreement that the injustices and wrongs of the present shall be perpetuated in the future. Thereby we would outrage our own conscience. In the eyes of those who suffer injustice we would become partners with their oppressors. In the judgment of history we would have sold out the freedom of men for a pottage of a false peace. . . . The domination of captive countries cannot longer be justified by a claim that this is needed for purposes of security.[27]

RFE used this statement to support its claims that the United States government would agree to no Soviet peace terms that involved an acceptance of the *status quo* in central and eastern Europe.[28]

While the Geneva conferences and the Belgrade Declaration were providing themes for all RFE stations in 1955, a situation known as the "thaw" was developing in Poland that furnished important programing material for the Voice of Free Poland. The debates on culture during this period will be reviewed here briefly because they offered a convenient opening for fresh attacks and because they demonstrate the difficulties encountered by a totalitarian regime as it tries to control every aspect of human existence. A failure in one area sometimes exposes weaknesses throughout the entire structure.

The debates on culture were touched off by a relatively insignificant event in 1953—the publication by the Institute for Literary Research (IBL) of a work entitled *Literary Periodicals in the Kingdom of Poland in the Years 1832–48*. In a review of this esoteric work in an equally esoteric journal, an author and critic, Chalasinski, questioned one of the fundamental tenets of Marxist-Leninist theory. He questioned the existence of two distinct currents in every national culture. The review did not go unchallenged, and soon Chalasinski found himself accused of liberalism, of attempting to revise "sacred" teaching, and of an eclecticism inspired by bourgeois ideology.

In February 1955, the Department of Social Sciences of the Polish Academy of Science organized a conference in Zakopane, attended by notable academic and literary personalities. By this time Chalasinski's position was based on three major points, summed up by an RFE researcher as follows:

(1) A disciple of historical materialism is not in duty bound to accept every thesis propounded by the so-called classical marxist thinkers but, basing himself on the theories formulated by Marx, he can develop a notion of the "Existence which determines consciousness" which will answer the requirements of those aspects of cultural life in the examination of which he is engaged. *The validity of supplementary hypotheses is decided on by facts and not by the agreement with this or that statement made by one of the classical marxist thinkers.*

(2) Historical materialism must be supplemented if it is to supply the base for a full and complete theory of culture which will provide a comprehensive explanation of man's activities and of the products of those activities. Historical materialism must also be supplemented if it is to become an adequate "weltanschauung" explaining to the individual the meaning and purpose of life. Such a "weltanschauung"

must also deal with values which cannot be derived from the teachings of marxism-leninism. Values are drawn from historical experience and from the cultural achievements of mankind from which marxism-leninism has cut itself off and to which *a return must be made if marxism-leninism is to become a comprehensive theory dealing with all the aspects of human thought and action.*

(3) Marxist humanism is in decline. It is characterised by: "Scholarly incompetence, a lack of understanding of relevant issues, or the downright falsification of the true picture of bourgeois learning." [29]

Until June 1955, the debates on culture were restricted to a very small group of intellectuals. In that month, however, Zolkiewski published an article in *Nowe Drogi* attacking the literary revisionists and pointing out that their "rightest warpings" called not only for a revised basis for artistic and scientific formulations, but in the last analysis, they amounted to a political attack that struck at the very foundations of the people's democracy and of the dictatorship of the proletariat. This article and others following in *Przeglad Kulturalny* reopened the debate with Chalasinski and his followers, but this time the audience was much larger. And in this debate before a larger audience the defenders of orthodoxy were on the defensive. One of the defenders closed his article with these words: "I regret if I have been unable to convince you. I recognize that I am sometimes short of arguments. This does not mean, however, that I intend to give way." [30]

The Polish desk followed these debates very closely and reported to the Polish people the truly momentous issues that were raised by a critical review of an obscure work on literature. It pointed out to intellectuals the debilitating consequences of a state-controlled culture and indicated how the unanswerable arguments of the intellectual dissidents undermined the rational foundations of the entire Communist society.[31]

If a number of events in 1955 caused RFE to assume a somewhat defensive posture, the Twentieth Congress of the Communist Party of the Soviet Union in February 1956—and the de-Stalinization campaign—enabled RFE to seize the initiative. Never in its history had RFE been presented with an issue that was so favorable for engaging the enemy on his own ground, for searching out "his vulnerable places, and [striking] them at the foundation of his being." So many themes and variations were used during the ensuing months that it is impossible to repeat them all here. However, they seem to fit into three interrelated general categories: (1) Adding fuel to the fire—that is, applying the logic of de-Stalinization in areas where the Communist leaders had never intended them to apply; (2) indicating that the monstrous Stalin was in fact a product of the Soviet system and that the only method of ensuring that another Stalin will not come to power is to change that system; (3) pointing out that the West was not being deceived by the de-Stalinization program and that it recognized that the basic aims of Soviet imperialism have not indeed been fundamentally altered.

Literally dozens of themes fit into the first category. Radio Free Europe reminded its listeners that editorials and speeches really did not go very far in repudiating Stalin. His face still spoiled hundreds of public places, buildings, and books. Everything from mountain peaks to factories had been named after him. To make the record straight all these should be removed and books rewritten. But more important, how about the "little Stalins" who still rule in the satellites? Should not their faces—and with their faces, their influence—be removed from the places of power? Indeed, since Stalin touched every aspect of human existence, should not every aspect of human existence feel the effects of de-Stalinization? A major policy guidance stated the problem this way:

To stimulate a greater variety and intensity of legitimate and realistic demands, we should ask what stalinism means, what it is that has now been denounced, rejected, and the removal of which our peoples have now been promised. In each country, our peoples have the right to look at what is most abusive and ask, "Is this not stalinism? If yes, when is it to be abolished?" When are we to have opposition parties? A free press? Free elections? Dissolution of collective farms? Free trade unions? More and better consumer goods? Freedom of travel? Freedom of communications with the free world—Western radio, journals of news, opinion, learning, science? Open trade with the West? Is it now to be denounced? . . . Teheran, Yalta, Potsdam: Were they Stalin's personal work? Was the brutal denial of free elections, as demanded by the Potsdam arrangement, Stalin's work? When the United Nations condemned certain "Satellite" regimes for maintaining armies in excess of treaty rights, and for disregard of treaty clauses on human rights, was it condemning stalinism? Will the forces now be decreased and the human rights now be respected by the new anti-stalinists? What is there in the mode of governing our people, the mode of exploiting farmers and workers, the mode of poisoning their children's minds, the mode of preventing them from learning what is going on in the free world and even in the communist world—what is there in all this that is not stalinist? Tell us, the people, and let us judge for ourselves.[32]

The themes which hammered home the point that since Stalin was no more and no less than a product of the Soviet system, the logic of de-Stalinization demands revising the system in order to make it impossible for any new Stalin to arise, were not mentioned explicitly in the New York Guidances but were developed at Munich. The propaganda point to be made is obvious. If Stalin was the monster Khrushchev makes him out to be (and Khrushchev should know), then Krushchev and all other Communists are obligated to alter the system that created the monster.

Finally, RFE felt that it was important to let the captive peoples know that the West was not being taken in by the apparent changes in the Soviet Union. Diplomatically, this meant that it would not grant concessions to the "new" Soviet Union which would enable the Communists to tighten their strangle-hold on the satellites. Domestically, it meant that socialist parties throughout the world would not yield to Communist demands for "popular front" governments; that the decanonization of Stalin was a Trojan horse which created confusion among the Communists but was met with skepticism by the socialist parties.[33]

Guidances during this period pointed out explicitly that all scripts should be written in the light of RFE's basic policy, which held that (1) "there is no likelihood of military action by the West to liberate [the satellites]"; (2) "The two Geneva conferences made it clear that there is no present likelihood that any degree of liberation, beyond some slight lifting of the Iron Curtain, can be achieved by diplomatic negotiation." Listening audiences were then reminded that liberation could be achieved only by the operation of a confluence of forces. A small booklet dropped on Czechoslovakia in the spring of 1956 spelled out explicitly RFE's policy posture at that time. (See appendix for translation.) This booklet, entitled *Kdy to Skonci?* (How Long Will This Go On?), begins with a frank answer to its basic question—nobody knows how long the occupation of the satellites can last, but nobody believes that it can endure forever. The booklet then discusses developments in the international situation. The growth of western strength, the change in Soviet tactics, the unlikelihood of a general war, the "cold peace," the "Belgrade Principle," are all commented upon. Next, the importance of internal passive resistance and what it can hope to accomplish is considered. The last section of the booklet discusses the "confluence of forces" and RFE's vision of a world in which liberation will be a possibility. The tone is not in the least polemic. It reads almost like a lesson in contemporary history—a lesson from which a vision of the future can be gained. It is not a call for specific action; it is rather an attempt to instill in the minds of the Czech and Slovak people a certain view of the world—a view that includes the possibility of liberation.

Events in the spring and summer of 1956 were rapidly leading to a climax. That climax and RFE's reaction to it is the subject of the next chapter.

The Uprisings in Poland and Hungary

N_{IKITA} Khrushchev included in his now-famous speech on the "cult of the individual" a warning to the Communist faithful: "We should in all seriousness consider the question of the cult of the individual. We cannot let this matter get out of the Party, especially not to the press. . . . We should know the limits . . ."

In the Soviet Union, Krushchev was able to keep the campaign to eradicate the "cult of the individual" fairly well within the intended limits. The debate could not be restricted to party circles; it could not be kept out of the press. But there is little evidence to indicate that it trespassed the limits set by the solemn *Pravda* editorial of March 20, 1956.[1] Nobody extended the attack to include those aspects of Stalinism that were perpetuated in the interests of the dead dictator's successors in the Kremlin. Indeed, if it served its interests, the "collective leadership" could out-Stalin Stalin, as the agricultural decrees of March 1956 indicated. But in the satellites the de-Stalinization campaign went far beyond what Krushchev could have intended.

The first spectacular results of the campaign in the satellites were the revisions of the "show trials" of the 1949–53 period. The lead for revising famous trials involving crimes against the state was taken by Moscow when the name of Antonov-Ovseyenko was restored to a place of honor. He was shortly followed by a number of old Bolsheviks who had been executed in the great purge of the thirties. In the Soviet Union only corpses were rehabilitated, and their ghosts could find nobody of importance to haunt. But the situation in the satellites was different. The show trials that were revised had originated as part of Stalin's attack on Yugoslavia and his efforts to see that "national Communism" did not spread. If the repudiation of that attack was to have any meaning, its victims would have to be cleared. But this was a far more serious matter than clearing the names of a number of old Bolsheviks. Some of the victims were still alive and some of the men who were most responsible for the trials were still in positions of power. The most embarrassing situation was in Hungary; the most serious in Poland.

In Budapest, in September 1949, Laszlo Rajk was tried for high treason. He confessed his guilt on all counts and said, ". . . it is undoubtedly true that to a certain extent I became an instrument of Tito, or rather of Tito's policy—of the same Tito who followed in Hitler's wake and followed Hitler's policy in the Balkans and in eastern Europe and who was backed by the American imperialists, his ruling masters." First Party Secretary Matyas Rakosi took credit for exposing the plot against the state. On March 29, 1956, the same Matyas Rakosi announced over Radio Budapest that the Rajk trial had been based on provocation. An attempt was made to transfer the blame for the trial to Gabor Peter, a secret police chief who had met his fate in another trial in 1954. But that Rakosi's prestige had suffered a blow was obvious to all.

The reassessment of Titoist crimes in Poland was not as embarrassing as it was in Hungary. Poland was unique among the satellites in that it had produced no great "show trial." Victims of the Titoist purge had been merely spirited away. There were fewer official statements that now had to be retracted. Furthermore, the "little Stalin" most responsible for the purge, Boleslaw Bierut, had conveniently died in Moscow in March 1956. But the most significant contrast with the Hungarian situation was that the chief victim, Wladyslaw Gomulka, was still alive. The Poles soon found out that rehabilitating a man with blood still running through his veins is a more serious matter than eulogizing a corpse.[2]

In Czechoslovakia a different course was pursued. As in Poland, the man most responsible for destroying the Titoists (Slansky, Clementis, and their followers) was not on the scene in the spring of 1956. Gottwald had died in Moscow while attending Stalin's funeral. As in Hungary, the victims had been executed. Although it would seem to have been easier for the Czechs than for either the Poles or Hungarians to rehabilitate the accused Titoists, they in fact did not. They continued to maintain that Slansky and Clementis were imperialist agents, but withdrew the Titoist charges. In a manner of speaking, Slansky and

171

Clementis, who were tried and executed in 1953 as imperialist agents *a la* Tito, in 1956 were condemned to continue their term in the Communist Hades as imperialist agents *a la* Beria.

The compromise that marked the Czechoslovak revision of its Titoist *cause célèbre* was typical of the temperate course the anti-Stalin campaign took in that satellite state. Comments by the leadership and by the official press were careful to recognize Stalin's accomplishments at the same time the "cult of the individual" was being weeded out. One important figure, Alexej Ceprika, First Deputy Premier and Defense Minister, was dismissed from his official posts and expelled from the party for "fostering the cult of the individual," but most of the blame for past mistakes was heaped on the heads of those already safely dead—Slansky, Stalin, and Beria. The only relatively serious post-Congress unrest in the spring of 1956 came from student groups. In April a series of student meetings were called, presumably for the purpose of propagating the post-Congress line. But throughout the country the students seized upon these meetings and used them as a platform from which to present their demands to the Communist leaders. These demands were far-reaching; they called for a freer press, the abolishment of jamming, a greater role for the national assembly, and a revision of judicial procedure. The students also raised some questions concerning the ownership of uranium resources in Czechoslovakia and the special privileges that Soviet citizens had in their country. But after a few embarrassing weeks, the regime restored the range of public discussion to its "proper" limits.

In Hungary the reaction was more significant. By the middle of May the regime had taken steps to raise living standards by raising the basic wage minimums of most industrial workers. Concessive decrees were also issued, aimed at trimming the size of the bureaucracy and at decentralizing the administration. Moves were made in the direction of reducing the use of terror as an instrument of social control by such devices as a recommendation that certain minor offences "hithertofore treated as crimes should be classified in the future as regular offenses punishable by monetary fines." [3] In this same vein an editorial in *Szabad Nep*, party organ in Budapest, called for a continuation of the " 'class struggle' within the framework of the 'rule of law.' " Intellectuals also were permitted to make demands for such things as greater cultural contact with the West and with Yugoslavia.

Perhaps the most important single piece of evidence that the "thaw" was coming to Hungary was the dismissal of Rakosi as First Secretary on July 18.

But by the spring and summer of 1956 the de-Stalinization campaign had a greater impact and went farther in Poland than in any of the satellites. In the last chapter we pointed out that the cultural "thaw" had reached sizable proportions in Poland even before the Twentieth Congress. A criticism aimed originally at the debilitating effect of party domination in the arts had expanded into a questioning of some of the fundamentals of Marxism-Leninism. After the Congress, in attacks on the "cult of the individual," Polish writers lashed out at the entire Zhdanov-Stalinist line on art—something they had done only by implication the previous year.[4] In April 1956, writers even went so far as to question certain aspects of the relationship between Poland and the Soviet Union.[5]

Intellectuals were not the only vocal critics in Poland in the spring of 1956. No less a figure than Premier Cyrankiewicz got into the act. In addressing the opening of the eighth session of the Seym (parliament) on April 23, he called for greater "democratization." He admitted that the past sessions of the Seym had been too short and the debates too infrequent; he complained that its activities consisted merely of formalizing action already taken by various ministers. And in the session that followed more deputies participated in debate and five deputies even voted against an abortion law, thus destroying the Seym's previous record of unanimous votes on all bills.

The government also took action that was in keeping with the spirit of the "thaw." On May 6 the Polish press announced the "resignation" of Jakub Berman from his position as Deputy Premier and as a member of the Politburo. Berman was one of the leading "Stalinists" in the party. Steps were also taken to raise the standard of living, to reduce the size of the administrative bureaucracy, and to reduce the powers of the secret police.

The Poznan Riots

There is evidence to indicate that the discussion in the press and the remarks of party leaders hinting that the lot of the people might be improved had a large audience—an audience impatiently waiting for action. Referring to the causes of the French Revolution, Alexis de Tocqueville wrote: "The evils which are endured with patience

173

so long as they are inevitable seem intolerable as soon as a hope can be entertained of escaping from them." The same line could be written about Poland in June 1956. Reports from throughout the country indicated a state of unrest. The city of Poznan seemed to be the center of particularly strong discontent. Throughout April and May the local newspaper, *Gazeta Poznanska*, had been crying out against the shortage of consumer goods, low wages, and a miserable housing situation.

The largest industrial establishment in Poznan is the Stalin locomotive works, known by the abbreviated name ZISPO. The workers in the ZISPO plant were not happy with the management. The intellectual climate of the "thaw" allowed them to protest, but their protests, according to the *Gazeta Poznanska*, went unheeded. The complaints of the workers did not only involve general grumbling. They concerned specifics—misapplication of wage regulations, excessive payroll deductions, and misallocation of raw materials that left piece-rate workers idle, with no chance to earn even while on the job. When the workers received no satisfaction locally, they sent a delegation to Warsaw where they presented their case to the Ministry of Machine Industry. What happened from this point on is difficult to reconstruct. Some reports said that the demands had been met, but obviously the workers were not entirely satisfied with the response to their delegation. Then, on June 27, a mass meeting was held at the ZISPO plant and an increase in work norms was announced. The next morning, at seven o'clock, the workers gathered at the factory and began to march toward the center of the city.

As the workers moved along the streets they were joined by other citizens. And what started as a simple demand for fair treatment in the factory became a general demonstration against the regime. Improvised placards appeared bearing such slogans as "Freedom and Bread," "Out with the Russians," "Down with Phony Communism." As the demonstrators came down Stalingradska Street toward Wolnosc Square they numbered nearly 30,000 strong. Barricades were hastily thrown up while troops armed with automatic weapons and tanks massed on the edge of the city. Before noon all main traffic arteries were closed, the barrels of antiaircraft guns were lowered for horizontal fire, and the first T34 tanks began moving into the city. The crowd began chanting "Bread, Bread, Bread." Forbidden patriotic songs were sung.

The Uprisings in Poland and Hungary

By 11:30 A.M. a full scale skirmish had begun. There are conflicting reports on just how it got started. Some reports say a police official fired into the crowd. The regime maintains that small-arms fire from the crowd was directed at the headquarters of the secret police.

For hours after that, the mob raged out of control. Rioters destroyed a jamming station, smashed into the prison, released the inmates, destroyed its records and set it on fire, and captured the Communist party headquarters. But by Friday evening the regime was back in control.

The first news of the demonstrations caused great concern in Radio Free Europe. Its policy advisers did not believe that uprisings and revolutions would drive the Russians out of the satellites. At the best they would lead to useless bloodshed; at the worst, to severe reprisals. One of the first guidances issued at Munich, after news of the events was studied, contained this warning to all writers:

We understand and appreciate the motivations which have driven the workers of Poznan to desperate measures. However, riots and revolts are not likely to improve matters in Poland, for the police may be given an opportunity for reprisals which only make things worse. No government which bases itself exclusively upon the tanks and bayonets of armed forces, will endure. But the Polish people must husband their strength and hold on for the time of freedom.

This theme was contained in the first special program on the situation in Poznan, broadcast to Poland on June 29. The writer of this program maintained that the major question to ask in regard to Poznan was: "Will the Poznan holocaust bring an improvement to the people's situation?" A part of the answer went as follows:

Let us have no illusions. Incidents like that play into the hands of Ochab and his Stalinist clique, who want the return of terror and oppression. The struggle for freedom must end in victory, for no regime based on repression can last. But in that struggle prudence is necessary. And therefore in the name of the ardent desire, common to us all, Poland's freedom, we must call on the people to preserve calm and refrain from acts of despair.

But while RFE felt obligated to speak words of caution and calm at the very time that a part of its audience was venting its spleen on a ten-year oppressor, it also assumed as part of its function the task of assuring the Poles that their struggle was being observed with sympathy in the West. Radio Free Europe argued that if the workers of

Poznan felt completely abandoned by the West, they would become docile tools in the hands of the Communists after the riots had been put down. This problem was dealt with by reporting in detail newspaper comment in the West. As soon as word of the rebellion was received, the field correspondents were notified to send into Munich excerpts of the sympathetic press in England, France, Italy, Austria, and Sweden. Radio Free Europe also generated much of its own ammunition by soliciting comments from well-known Americans, particularly labor leaders. Among those who responded were George Meany, AFL-CIO President, Governor Averill Harriman of New York, David J. MacDonald, President, United Steel Workers, and Jacob Potofsky, President of the Amalgamated Clothing Workers.

A second major function of RFE was to report accurately to both Poland and the other satellites on the events in Poznan. In periods of crisis the captive peoples apparently trust their own news agencies even less than in normal times and thus become more dependent on news from the West. It was fortunate that the Poznan riots broke out while the Poznan International Trade Fair was in session and that in 1956, for the first time since the war, western businessmen attended in large numbers. These westerners returning from Poznan, plus a number of refugees, provided RFE with a good source of eyewitness reports of the events which were used in programs. For instance, the second special program broadcast on June 29 was an account of the riots based on eyewitness accounts. Similar reports were broadcast to the other satellites.

While the Voice of Free Poland was still primarily concerned with warning the rioters and reporting on the events of Poznan, the other stations were already using the riots as a point of departure from which to attack the Communist rule. The International Commentary broadcast to Czechoslovakia on June 29 was devoted entirely to Poznan. Part of it went as follows:

It has been said that there has been relaxation inside the Communist countries and in Poland in particular. Is this really so? How benevolent is a regime which uses troops and guns and tanks against workers? The Communists have attacked Stalin's brutality and spoken of the restoration of socialist legality. Where is that legality in Poznan? Khrushchev has announced an era of reconciliation in which the first care will be for the workers. What kind of care is this that the world has seen at Poznan?

The Uprisings in Poland and Hungary

A Hungarian Special Midnight Commentary on June 29 warned the Hungarian workers to remain "patient and disciplined," in the following words, "The system of oppression is increasingly unstable everywhere, with the people's battle for freedom gaining hope. Success, however, depends upon unity, patience and discipline."

On the day after an uneasy peace had been restored, the Voice of Free Poland was directing its attention somewhat away from the immediate event and looking toward the future. It was concerned specifically with the fate of the people who would be arrested as instigators. Cyrankiewicz announced over Radio Warsaw shortly after the demonstration broke out that "Everyone who raises his hand against the people may be sure it will be hacked off in the interest of the working class . . ." The "Reflector" on June 30 was the first of a number of programs that addressed itself precisely to this problem. It asked the Communist authorities, "Will the defendants be tried publicly by an independent court? Will they be able to call witnesses for their defense? Will they be able to name the true culprits who drove them to misery and despair? Will they be defended by genuine advocates?" A special program on the same day quoted from a Polish edition of Lenin's works a passage in which Lenin recognized the right of workers to strike in a Communist-ruled country. The program said that in the 1920s strikes took place in Soviet Russia and Lenin considered them admissible and justified as a protest against bureaucratic distortions. It then remarked, "Stalin's infamous dictatorship banned strikes, but the Communists speak now of the return to Leninist norms. But between the return to Leninist norms and the suppression of the Poznan strike, there is an obvious contradiction."

On July 2 RFE recognized its major task for the immediate future to be that of protecting the workers of Poznan from brutal retaliation. The daily guidance of July 3 stated the problem this way:

As we pointed out yesterday, it is now RFE's first and foremost task to make the maximum contribution towards saving the surviving victims of Stalinist brutality. Not only do we owe that much to the heroes of Poznan, but we can—by pressing our demands that trials be held in public, that the names of the arrested be published immediately, and that no one who might be condemned be sent to Russia—put the Communists into a dilemma that should greatly advance their present predicament. The fight for justice for the victims of communist brutality in Poznan should spotlight the fact that the

177

Communist regime repressed a strike, a workers' movement, as no "capitalist" nation would have dreamt of doing. It should spotlight the fact that the workers of Poznan demonstrated for legitimate demands—demands recognized as legitimate by the Communists themselves. It should spotlight the fact that the Polish people are at the mercy of Soviet colonialism which exploits the country (and which sends 8,000 lbs. of rice to Pakistan at precisely the time that Poles are short of food . . .).

The taking on of such a task was predicated on the assumption that RFE could affect the actions of the Communist officials in Poland. This assumption in turn was based on an analysis of the situation, which led RFE to believe that the investment in liberalization and de-Stalinization in the entire Soviet bloc was so great that even an event such as the Poznan riots could not reverse it. Radio Free Europe could thus keep the treatment of the Poznan rioters before the people as a test case of the sincerity of the de-Stalinization campaign. It could point out that summary executions, "show trials," and severe prison terms were the worst manifestations of Stalinism and therefore it was the duty of the regime not to use these techniques in Poznan.

Events of the next few weeks indicated that the RFE analysis was correct. Perhaps the most perceptive western correspondent in Poland is M. Philippe Ben, who writes for *Le Monde* (Paris). His dispatches from July 11 to July 18 describe and analyze the struggle between the "tough" and the "liberal" wing of the party. On July 18 he indicated that there was evidence that the "liberals" were becoming dominant. He reported that it was already certain the upcoming meeting of the Central Committee would approve of a Five Year Plan that would provide for an increase in living standards by 30 per cent. Furthermore, a "New Economic Policy" would be introduced, providing for some private enterprise and considerable concessions to the peasants. On August 3 he commented from Warsaw:

One can carefully prepare for this trip—read for weeks Polish newspapers which arrive abroad, try to enter the mystery of "democratization", interrogate the now numerous people returning from that country. Once arrived there, one quickly understands that he knew few things. One had heard about the freedom of speech, but could one imagine that high government functionaries, important journalists, engineers, would phone your hotel, would openly discuss their problems and their difficulties? There are even passers-by, people one meets in a restaurant or in the streetcar . . . This liberty of expression, resembling a current of fresh air, strikes the newcomer.

On August 7 he continued:

The most bitter enemies of the Polish regime have repeatedly told us that for about a year they have had no fear of nighttime visits from the secret police or arbitrary arrests, made after denunciations or anonymous letters, nor do they fear questioning in jails without a warrant—a traditional technique of dictatorships.

The words and actions of the top Communist officials also indicated a continuation of the "thaw." The original official explanation of the riots, i.e., that they were precipitated by *agents provocateurs* was abandoned, and Warsaw (but not Moscow) admitted that the economic plight of the workers was to blame. The *New York Times* quoted *Trybuna Ludu* as accusing the "heartless bureaucracy" of party and trade unions of having "lost every contact with the workers . . ." [6] The investigation revealed facts, *Trybuna Ludu* continued, that "show that the basis for the bloody riots was the dissatisfaction of the workers. They had sufficient cause to be embittered but the form of protest employed by them was incorrect."

The results of the Poznan riots were similar to those of the other riots in the Soviet bloc since 1953. Berlin, Vorkuta, Pilsen—all had led to new or continued liberalization. Radio Free Europe did not conclude from this observation that more riots were in order—indeed, we have seen how its first commentary on Poznan called for caution and moderation—but it did indicate that the "people's opposition" was gaining strength and that the Communists respected this strength by making concessions. In other words, by the end of July 1956, RFE had evidence to indicate that its concept of the confluence of forces was a realistic one.

The Victory of Gomulka

The eyes of Soviet experts were focused on Poland in the late summer of 1956. The treatment of Gomulka and the fate of those arrested after the riots seemed to be key indices in evaluating the direction events would take in the satellites. As early as July 11, M. Ben reported in *Le Monde* that many members of the Central Committee wanted Gomulka back in a position of power. But Gomulka had set

179

a high price—the dismissal of a number of high-ranking Communists including Hilary Minc, Deputy Premier and for years the Polish economic czar. It was Gomulka's criticism of his policy that helped lead to his imprisonment in 1948. In August Gomulka was readmitted to the party. In September the first sentences for Poznan rioters were announced. They were exceedingly light. Two weeks later Minc resigned his official position in the government.

As the time approached for the first meeting of the Central Committee since Poznan, western correspondents reported a wave of excitement sweeping through the Polish capital. Newspapers carried the headlines "No Bread without Freedom, No Freedom without Bread." Rumors of "peaceful revolution" were heard. On Friday, October 19, the Central Committee met. The first order of business was the re-election of Gomulka and three of his closest advisers to full membership in the Central Committee. These four men were elected, and in quick succession all the members of the Politburo submitted their resignations. A Gomulka supporter then rose to move that Gomulka be elected First Secretary of the party, replacing Ochab, and that a new Politburo be formed excluding all Stalinists. Then the Stalinists played their trump. They announced to a stunned audience that Comrades Khrushchev, Molotov, Kaganovich, and Mikoyan had landed in Warsaw and were at that very moment being driven to Belvedere Palace. A few minutes later the top-ranking Polish Communists, including both Gomulka and Ochab, left to meet the Russians.

The reports of what happened at that tense meeting are in remarkable agreement. The Russians apparently were adamant in their demand that the Stalinists be kept in control of the party. The moderates and the Gomulka supporters responded with their firmest no. But the Russians had not put their puppets in key positions in Poland for nothing. They reported that Marshal Rokossovsky was moving Polish troops toward Warsaw and, more important, that a Soviet division in southwestern Poland was moving in full battle gear. At that point Ochab firmly set the conditions for further negotiation: He warned Khrushchev, "If you do not stop them immediately we will walk out of here and break off all contact." That would mean war. Ochab recognized this and added, "The party and our workers have been warned and they are ready."

Krushchev for a moment seized the mantle of Stalin. He shouted in reply, "I will show you what the way to Socialism looks like. If you don't obey we will crush you. We are going to use force to kill all sorts of risings in this country. Russian soldiers were slain [liberating Poland]. We will never permit this country to be sold to the American imperialists."

But apparently, then, both sides retreated slightly.

Radio Free Europe's reaction to these events was immediate; its analysis of the happenings in Poland and the mood of the Polish people proved to be very accurate. On Saturday (the day after the arrival of the Soviet delegation in Warsaw), RFE-New York sent an urgent message to Munich spelling out the policy lines. Two major points were made. The first was a warning not to broadcast programs that might incite mass, violent action. The second was to try to focus the wrath of the Polish people on the Soviets by, for instance, intensive comment on the Soviet visit as unwanted and illegal interference. Three other points were made: (a) sympathy should be expressed for the Polish people and they should be made aware of the fact that RFE understood the very difficult situation they were in; (b) the emphasis should be placed on straight, factual reporting; (c) RFE should seek no credit for creating or helping to create the present situation. Any progress made toward greater democratization and independence is to the credit of the Polish people alone.

By the time this message had gone out from New York, Munich had been dealing with these events for almost twelve hours. The assumptions made in Munich about the situation in Poland, and the propaganda lines developed, were congruous with those being developed in New York. The Munich analysis of October 20 contained the following points:

1. The Nationalist-Liberal group led by Gomulka, supported by Cyrankiewicz and Ochab, is in control of the party apparatus and receiving vast popular support throughout the countryside.

2. The new leaders do not desire any complete break with Moscow for two main reasons: (a) The USSR is the only guarantor of Poland's western boundaries; (b) they realize that any efforts for a complete break might provoke the Russians into armed intervention which they otherwise would not undertake.

3. The reports of western correspondents and the violent tone of a

Pravda editorial on Poland indicate it is likely that there are still grave differences between the Russian leaders and the new Polish Politburo. The danger of Soviet armed intervention is great.

4. Although Gomulka and his followers are convinced Communists, the success of their program is the only chance Poland has in the immediate future to obtain a measure of independence from Moscow.

5. Although the Polish people overwhelmingly support Gomulka, there is a great and ever present possibility that the intensity of their plight and their hate for the Russians will push the new leadership into a position which will leave the Russians with no alternative but intervention. There is even some evidence that the Russians wanted to see violence and demonstrations in order to have an excuse to intervene.

From this analysis came the policy line and the numerous programs broadcast by the Voice of Free Poland. On Saturday, October 20, the Voice of Free Poland abandoned its normal schedule and began to broadcast special newscasts and commentaries to keep its listeners in touch with developments in Warsaw. During the following week as many as ten special programs were broadcast in one day.

Two of the special programs broadcast the first day (October 20) indicate very well the manner in which RFE was implementing its propaganda line. The first of these programs, "Unwanted Visitors," began by referring to the catastrophic economic and social conditions in Poland that created the mood of the people and their demands that something be done. It went on to point out the fact that the man who was leading the Soviet delegation was Nikita Khrushchev, who not many months before had attacked Stalin and the methods he used. But now, this same Nikita Khrushchev was taking action that belied his own words. He came to Poland to try to prevent the process of de-Stalinization; he was an advocate of the idea that the principle of separate roads to socialism must stop before it reaches Poland. The script then contains a crucial paragraph in which the Polish people were advised, in an oblique and subtle manner, not to push their demands or their leaders too far.

The Politburo delegation, having landed in Warsaw and taken up its quarters at the Belvedere in order to open its talks with the Politburo of the PZPR, knew very well that no one either in that Politburo nor in the party rank and file, nor even among the people, i.e., among the vast majority of Poles, can envisage for a moment a break with that political make-up in which our country found itself against its will and in which it must continue against its will until objective conditions favouring a radical change are established. The attitude of the people within the last twelve years has shown that it is a nation full of political wisdom, a nation which can subordinate its feelings to the existing situation without losing, at the same time, its ideological objectives from sight. Poles know very well that Soviet Russia has at its disposal both military and economic means which would enable it to interfere in Poland.

The second script, "What is the Issue of the Conflict?"—written by the chief of the Polish desk—closed by dealing with the question, "Who will emerge victorious?" In answering the question, the script pointed out that the Soviets could crush the new Polish leadership with overwhelming brute force if they deemed it necessary. But such action would be costly. It would demonstrate to the whole world a return to Stalinism, a revival of methods that had been severely condemned by the Soviets themselves. It would produce ramifications of doubt and criticism in the colonial areas of the world where the Communists' propaganda is now so appealing.

But there is another factor which may affect the Soviet decision to intervene or not to intervene: the behavior of the Polish people. Violent action would probably precipitate a violent response. The script ends with this warning:

We have information that a group of Stalinists headed by Konstanty Rokossovski and Zenon Novak, is consciously making towards anarchy and chaos, trying on purpose to increase the boiling atmosphere, in order to justify the necessity of Soviet intervention from the outside. In this connection there arises the most important question, Will the community let itself be provoked or will it keep the necessary calm? The development in the next few days will depend first and foremost on whether the new administration convoked by the VIII Plenum will be able to get the situation in hand, calm the atmosphere, and find some immediate means to heal the economy. The group of Stalinists will doubtlessly do all in its power to make this task more difficult and to deepen the existing confusion. If they succeed, then there is no doubt that any excuse will be used to put Soviet tanks into action.

Although this type of commentary was an important part of RFE's programing during those crucial days, even more important were the straight, factual news reports on events taking place in Warsaw and the world's reaction to them. Some of the western newspapermen in Warsaw apparently had very close contacts with important figures in the new Polish leadership. During the first few days the Polish press was somewhat limited in what it could print, but RFE kept up a steady stream of broadcasts reporting in amazing detail and accuracy what was going on in Poland. Western press comment and statements by important western statesmen and politicians such as Eisenhower, Dulles, and Stevenson were also poured into Poland.

By October 22, RFE was basing its policy on the following estimate of the situation:

1. Gomulka had won the first round; Soviet armed intervention, at least in the immediate future, was unlikely.

2. Gomulka did not intend a complete break with the USSR if only because he was still a convinced Communist and more important, because the Soviet Union was the only guarantor of the Polish western boundary.

3. Poland was tremendously important to the Soviet Union for strategic reasons and thus the Russians would not permit Gomulka to go so far as to seriously threaten this security position.

4. For the moment Gomulka had widespread support, but the maintenance of this support was dependent on meeting the pressing needs of the people.

In short, RFE felt that it was operating in an entirely new situation. It was broadcasting to a country in which the Communist party had achieved substantial independence from Moscow and in which the Communist government was no longer looked upon by the people as a tool of foreign domination. Throughout the next few weeks commentaries were designed to (1) keep the Polish people (particularly extremist elements) from taking any action which might lead to Soviet military intervention; (2) keep the Polish people informed of events in their own country and of western reaction to them.

While this approach meant that RFE was supporting Gomulka, one should not assume that its idea of an ideal future Poland would be congruent with Gomulka's; rather, at that particular time, the interests of RFE and those of Gomulka were similar. Guidances and scripts of this period read as if they were partially based on a "two stage" theory of liberation.[7] Gomulka was the instrument of the first stage. But even in this period RFE tried to draw a sharp line between support for the nationalist leadership in its attempt to gain independence from Moscow and support of the Communist party. A dialogue on the "Other Side of the Coin" program for October 25, 1956, went as follows:

Voice I: . . . If I say that I would be out there listening to Gomulka, if I were in Warsaw, it is because he represents our only chance for winning a little freedom without provoking a national tragedy. I am prepared to swear that nine out of ten in the crowd which cheered Gomulka were just as much Communist as I am.

Voice II: Would you really applaud Gomulka's speech?

Voice I: I certainly would, but not Gomulka! I would cheer like mad at every sign that the iron vise which grips Poland is loosening if only an inch, that we have more right to our own lives than we had a week before, that the deadlock has finally and happily been broken. And I don't need to be in Warsaw to feel that way about it!

While this point of view was advanced in many scripts, the Voice of Free Poland did not lose its vision of a Poland in which the people themselves could choose without coercion or violence among alternative solutions to their economic, social, and political problems.

Of course the present improvement in the political and economic situation does not even in part satisfy the demands of the people. The people do not want to be ruled by an insignificant minority. They reject dictatorship under any form. They demand full freedom of thought and speech . . . They yearn for peace and security. The present reforms will certainly not satisfy all those longings . . . In our present situation, no prospects for a better future can either be underestimated or overlooked. This does not mean, however, that the people of Poland must reconcile themselves once and for all to the present state of affairs . . . The success of the struggle [for the full implementation of their aspirations] will depend upon our ability to perceive the difference and limits separating what constitutes our long-term aim and what lends itself to achievement at the given moment.[8]

The independence of the States is a victory achieved through the struggle of the entire nation, with its own forces, without any help from outside.[9]

The Tragedy in Hungary

Heated to the incendiary point by the same pressures, one people may quickly catch the flame once it has been ignited by another. Earlier in this chapter we referred to the rehabilitation of Rajk and

185

the dismissal of Rakosi. In early October, Rajk's remains were disinterred and he was given a state funeral with honors. While 200,000 Hungarians marched past Rajk's coffin, Imre Nagy kissed his widow and thus identified himself with the executed Titoist. On October 13 Nagy was reinstated in the party, which had expelled him just ten months before as a "Titoist."

One week later the Communist party organ, *Szabad Nep*, called for a "Hungarian Road to Socialism" while Radio Budapest "welcomed" the readmission of Gomulka to a position of power in Poland and complimented the Polish Communists who were not afraid of the implications of their march forward. These statements from official organs apparently were taken as clues by student and worker groups in the country. On October 21 students of the Universities of Szeged, Pecs, and the Technology University in Budapest were calling for more freedom both for individuals and for the country. The next day their demands were circulated among the population. In Gyor the popular demands and demonstrations called, significantly, for the withdrawal of all Soviet troops from Hungary. At about the same time in Budapest crowds gathered, calling for the return to power of Imre Nagy and for the withdrawal of Russian troops.

The demonstrations had a strong pro-Polish flavor. The statue of General Bem, a Polish officer who fought in the Kossuth army of 1849 against the Russians, was decorated and the crowd carried banners reading "Long Live the Polish Youth." The demonstrators also demanded the withdrawal of Soviet troops and the re-instatement of Nagy as premier. On October 23, crowds gathered in Parliament Square and other places in Budapest and the demands were reiterated. They were fired upon by units of the AVH (secret police) and the demonstrations turned into a revolution.

On the evening of October 23 the Central Committee of the Communist party convened for what developed into an all-night session. As close as it is possible to reconstruct, the Committee made a decision to ask for Soviet help in quelling the disturbances. First Secretary Gero called Moscow and apparently described a situation so serious the Soviet leaders ordered their units in Hungary to take steps to restore order. On the morning of October 24 Russian and Hungarian troop units moved into Budapest. At about the same time Nagy was made premier, but his program fell far short of that demanded by his supporters in the streets. He appealed to the insurgents to lay down their arms, promising amnesty for those who did—destruction for those who refused. He said further that his program including plans for greater democratization and liberalization would be announced shortly.[10]

As these events were just beginning (on October 22), a wave of optimism had swept through RFE. The Poles appeared to have won a tremendous victory, and if the Soviets were unwilling to intervene in Poland where their security and economic interests were greater than in the other satellites, it was reasonable—one might say necessary—to assume that similar successes could be achieved in other countries. Radio Free Europe felt that its role in this regard was to broadcast to all its target countries factual reports on the developments in Poland. From this information its listeners could decide on proper action on the basis of their own estimate of the situation. The daily guidance on October 22 advised:

Detailed cross reporting of the Polish story—consequences of which cannot yet be foreseen—will be our task for today and for some time to come. Today's commentaries should, of course, also include the demands of Hungarian students.

And the next day:

. . . the developing Hungarian situation seems to be offering continuing opportunities to draw parallels with Poland, implying potential for similar developments throughout the orbit.

Within hours of the time this message went out on the air to Munich, the Hungarian demonstrators were fired upon and the revolution had begun. And within twenty-four hours it was not the parallels but the dissimilarities between events in Poland and in Hungary that were RFE's major concern. It is true that both situations had developed out of similar conditions and pressures. But here the parallel ceases. In Poland Gomulka was in full control almost from the beginning and was widely supported by the party. Even Ochab, whom nobody had looked upon as a great nationalist, stood firm with the new leader and was willing to fight the Soviets, if necessary. And the Poles, thanks to the installation of General Komar as head of the security forces several weeks before, had a strong and centrally controlled force it could use if necessary. Most important, the demands made by the Poles were issued by the leadership.

But in Hungary there was no Gomulka; there was not even an Ochab. Gero, who was in a position similar to that of Ochab, did not defy the Soviets but asked for their armed intervention. Nagy, whom many Hungarians thought might play Gomulka's role at this crucial stage, made no demands on the Russians. Indeed, there was evidence to indicate that he had been in on the decision to call in the Russian tanks. The demands of the Hungarian revolution were not voiced by a national Communist leader with strong support from all segments of society; they were articulated by the insurgents with no central leadership.

This put RFE in an extremely difficult position. After the Soviet intervention the main demand of the insurgents was the withdrawal of all Soviet troops from Hungarian soil, but RFE in New York could only see this being accomplished by a resolute stand of Hungarian leaders actually in office. Nagy was the only hope, but would the insurgents follow a Nagy with no program, a Nagy who was in office when the Russians moved in? And did not Nagy deserve severe criticism for his behavior on October 23 and 24? The policy decision in New York was to broadcast extensive factual accounts of the momentous events in Hungary and not to discuss personalities. The daily guidance of October 24 contained this paragraph:

Heavy and detailed coverage of the Hungarian and Polish stories is our obvious job for today. The total participation in the Hungarian events, paralleling that in Poznan, shows the irresistible desire of the captive peoples for real freedom and for a decent way of life. Nagy and Gomulka will have to move very far to satisfy that desire . . . Actions of the new Communist leaders in Budapest and Warsaw are better not prejudged at this time. That Nagy called upon foreign troops to restore "order" is a fact he will have to live down. He can live it down only by keeping his promises and helping to establish the climate for freedom and material satisfaction for which the people yearn and which they will achieve with or without the cooperation of present Communist leaders.

And the next day:

To repeat: The guilt for the shedding of Hungarian blood lies with the Kremlin and with the Hungarian and other Satellite leaders who helped strengthen and perpetuate the Soviet Empire . . . Who called out the Soviet troops is less important to the ends we seek than the question of whether Nagy can and will fulfill his promise to try to have all Soviet troops withdrawn for good. It was for this purpose, and the restoration of sovereignty to Hungary and its fellow captive countries, that Hungarians have died.

It is at this point that the policy autonomy of Munich, which, as we have seen, is absolutely essential in maintaining an effective tactical operation, shows its corresponding weakness. Munich was much closer to the blood being shed in Budapest. The frenzied excitement of the situation was more commanding there. The policy advisers apparently did not deem it so urgent to spare a man who called in Soviet troops. And for the exiles it was next to impossible to maintain a neutral attitude toward the man who was responsible, it appeared, for the blood of their brothers that was flowing in the streets. In a number of scripts from October 25 until November 1, Nagy and other figures in the new government were bitterly attacked.

On October 25 a Special Commentary (No. IX) was broadcast, denouncing Nagy's actions:

The regime maintains artificial dimness around the events of Oct. 24 and 25, and for this reason it is impossible in these hours to get a clear answer to the question of responsibility. In these moments I. Nagy can still claim that it was not he but the government of his insignificant predecessor, Hegedus, who asked for the intervention of the Soviet troops. But this is no extenuating circumstance because the question arises—why did I. Nagy accept this legacy? Why did he have to accept the Premiership in the shadow of Soviet bayonets, of Russian fusilades and tanks? By accepting the Premiership why did he have to express solidarity with the shameful treachery of Muscovite leadership? We well know that in those fateful hours the situation in Hungary was completely unbalanced; the leaders of the nation and the Party lost their heads and trembled for their own skins. Everyone knew that at this stage of confusion and chaos the key to the situation was in the hands of I. Nagy; his cornered comrades would have paid any price for him to get them out of their tight spot. Why did not I. Nagy accept the Premiership on condition that the Government and Party immediately put an end to Soviet intervention? Why did he not bind his help and cooperation to the demand that the Government and Party, executing the demands of the masses, should find an honest solution to the disturbances?

And on the next day:

Imre Nagy, Janos Kadar and his companions among the leaders of the Party could have overthrown Gero and his Stalinist clique in good time thereby avoiding bloodshed and the outbreak of the revolution. Instead they not only betrayed the nation but also the majority of

Party members who expected them to bring about the slogans of democratization.[11]

To be sure, one or two scripts asked that judgment on Nagy be withheld, but it was not until November 2 that the New York line was implemented in Munich. When Nagy made a speech calling for the unified support of the nation, RFE commented:

Under such circumstances, the first question is this—what moral and political right does the present Prime Minister have to request the nation's unity and trust? Only a few days ago, we called attention on our radio to the stunning reason represented by a call for help to Soviet troops at the moment when the fight for freedom broke out. We raised the question of the serious responsibility for this action which went to the present Prime Minister. Ever since, Prime Minister Imre Nagy has made incessant attempts to clear himself of the accusation, and to shove all responsibility for this desperate act of treason upon his two predecessors, Erno Gero and Andras Hegedus. We here, at a distance of several hundred kilometers and under today's tragic circumstances, are not in a position to decide this debate. The sentence in this trial will be determined under more peaceful conditions, by the nation, possibly only by history. Nor can we concern ourselves unduly with this debate in these so tremendously grave hours. There has never been as much need for national unity, as requested by the Prime Minister, as today.[12]

On the major policy matter during this period, however, Munich and New York were in full agreement. Radio Free Europe had always operated on the assumption that it could not lead the captive peoples to freedom; it could only assist them in the struggle they might initiate with policies they had devised. From the first day of the demonstrations the insurgents had a program. Their demands were clearly articulated. In just a few days most of western Hungary was under nationalist control, and a number of "Freedom Stations" began broadcasting the programs developed in local areas. Radio Free Europe carefully monitored these broadcasts and rebroadcast common points from the lists of demands local areas were developing. In this way it hoped to help unify the freedom movement on the basis of a common program. On October 28 Munich cabled New York, "We are utilizing from these broadcasts [monitored from the insurgent radios] those parts [mainly withdrawal of Soviet troops and the disbanding of the AVH] which are in accord in our opinion with the genuine demands of the insurgents but not repeating the rest." The same day New

York cabled back to Munich what it felt to be the minimum conditions acceptable to the freedom fighters:

1. Immediate and total withdrawal of all Soviet troops from Hungarian soil.

2. Total dissolution of the AVH immediately, and placement of the direction of any new police or security forces and the army in the hands of a minister not associated with any previous cabinet or Central Communist body.

3. Full amnesty to all freedom fighters who participated in the uprisings.

4. Exclusion from the new temporary governments of all persons associated in any way with the regime government or top party command since Imre Nagy's previous premiership.

5. The majority of the cabinet of the new temporary government to be drawn from the various patriot groups on a representative basis.

6. Immediate calling of a Constituent Assembly, selected by free secret popular vote, to frame a new charter of government and action program—this charter and program to be submitted to the people for free, secret voting on acceptance or rejection within a stated period, such as six months.

7. Withdrawal from the Warsaw Pact of Hungary.

8. Continuation of local workers' and other councils and patriot committees which have been formed during the crisis and continuous communication between them, until all the above conditions have been achieved.

A special commentary from Munich on October 29 carried these demands in full.[13]

Throughout the entire Hungarian revolt things were moving so rapidly that it was difficult for RFE to keep up with them. On October 25, Mikoyan and Suslov flew to Budapest and forced Gero to resign his position as party boss.[14] On October 26, Nagy made a speech in which he recognized the legitimacy of some of the patriots' demands. He blamed the riots on the "mistakes and crimes" of the past ten years, and promised to negotiate for eventual Russian withdrawal. On the next day a new government was announced which included the non-Communists Zolta Tildy and Bela Kovacs. Finally, on October 28, Radio Budapest announced to the rebels, "You have won." The army and the police were reorganized, patriotic Hungarian symbols were to replace Communist emblems on flags and uniforms. The next day saw the abolishment of the AVH, and the government requested Soviet withdrawal—but this was based on the condition that the rebels stop fighting. On Tuesday, October 30, Nagy told the triumphant nation that free elections would be held, with all the parties participating in the 1945 elections to be given a place on the ballot. Victory seemed to be in the grasp of the rebels. On October 31 Munich teletyped New York that it appeared possible "that multi-party democracy may be restored to Hungary and that Hungary may be able to assume a position of freedom and neutrality on the Austrian pattern."

This optimistic assessment of the situation proved to be false.[15] The "victory" of the freedom fighters lasted only four days, but these four days indicated clearly the path a free Hungary would take. On November 1 Nagy formally announced to the Soviet ambassador that Hungary would withdraw immediately from the Warsaw Pact, would declare a neutral position in the cold war and seek guarantees of its neutrality from the Big Four. Two days later Nagy told the people that negotiations for withdrawal of Soviet troops had gotten off to an "encouraging start," but Tildy indicated in a press conference, broadcast over Radio Budapest the same day, that "the Soviet reply given so far was not satisfactory." [16]

But during this short period of "glory" Soviet troops were being redeployed in Hungary. At dawn on the morning of Sunday, November 4, they came smashing into Budapest.

Radio Free Europe's New York daily guidances during the period from October 31 to November 4 continued on the same course they had taken previously. Continued admonitions were made to avoid any discussion of personalities in the temporary government set up on October 27. "It will be for Hungarians in the country to decide whether any individual should stay or go," read a part of the daily guidance on November 2. "RFE's place is to help them implement their desires and plans by publicizing and reiterating them."

Radio Free Europe also felt that one of its responsibilities, during those crucial days when the Nagy government was making more and more demands and new Soviet troops were digging in around Budapest, was to inform its listeners about the American position. The daily guidance on November 1 suggested that two passages from Eisenhower's speech to the nation on the previous evening be quoted:

The United States has made clear its readiness to assist economically the new and independent governments of these countries . . . We have also publicly declared that we do not demand of these governments their adoption of any particular form of society as a condition upon economic assistance. Our one concern is that they be free . . .

We have also, with respect to the Soviet Union, sought clearly to remove any false fears that we would look upon new governments in these Eastern European countries as potential military allies.

This speech, of course, was carefully reported in news broadcasts, and on November 3 a special commentary from Munich clearly outlined the American position.[17]

As dawn broke over Budapest on the morning of Sunday, November 4, Soviet troops supported by armor, artillery, and aircraft smashed into Budapest. At 5:00 A.M. Imre Nagy announced: "Early this morning Soviet troops attacked Budapest. . . . Hungarian troops are in combat and the Hungarian Government at its post. This I announce to the people and to the world."

It was his last public statement. The Russians immediately set up a new government under Janos Kadar, which, although it paid lip-service to the goal of Hungarian freedom, supported the Soviet use of armed might to suppress the rebellion. The Hungarians fought with small arms and bottles filled with gasoline until they were physically subdued. By the end of the week Budapest was a quiet, smoking city of horror—a tragic testimony to the fact that the age of the barricade revolution had passed with the coming of the machine gun.

Even before the second Soviet armed intervention, the United Nations had taken up the Hungarian question. On November 3 a special session of the Security Council was called by the United States, Great Britain, and France. A United States resolution called for the United Nations to "affirm the right of the Hungarian people to a Government responsible to its national aspirations and dedicated to its independence and well-being." With action in the Security Council blocked by the Soviet veto, the matter was turned over to the General Assembly, which met in a special session on Sunday afternoon. When this body assembled, news of the brutal Soviet intervention was known throughout the world. The Assembly passed a resolution introduced by Ambassador Lodge, calling for a United Nations investigation.

Radio Free Europe covered the UN story on November 3. Commentaries before the Security Council meeting explained to the Hungarian people the significance of the meeting and the procedures that would be followed. Directly after the meeting RFE was on the air with a detailed report on what had taken place. On Sunday UN news was continued, including a verbatim report of the General Assembly's resolution and commentaries on the UN action and the difficulties involved in sending a delegation to Hungary. But the Russian intervention caused a change in RFE's programs. On November 5 the daily guidance read in part: "There can be no question but that none of our audiences will be too receptive to strong propaganda words and strident voices while the victims of Soviet imperialism lie unburied. . . . If ever there was a time to broadcast humbly, this is it."

On November 4 Munich concentrated on straight news broadcasts. What commentaries were sent out over the air covered the Soviet intervention and attacked the Kadar regime. No commentary position was taken on the desirability or possibility of resistance by the Hungarian revolutionaries. News held the spotlight for the next few days. On November 6 RFE began to report on the intense world reaction to the events in Hungary and on the wave of anti-Soviet feeling that was spreading around the world. Comments and declarations by statesmen expressing sympathy with the Hungarians were also broadcast. On November 7 the news of Eisenhower's re-election was broadcast and commented upon, and there was coverage of the situation in the Middle East. But throughout the week news and western press reviews took up a large part of total broadcast time.

The Role of RFE in the Polish and Hungarian Uprisings

Just five days after the Soviets launched their final attack on Budapest, *Freies Wort*, the official organ of the Free Democratic Party (FDP) in West Germany, carried a blistering editorial attacking RFE. It read in part:

We are convinced that . . . RFE's aggressive propaganda is responsible to a large extent for the blood-bath that has occurred in Hungary during the last two weeks.

A propaganda whose opportunistic agitation has to be paid for finally with the blood of people who have been led astray, is a crime against humanity, no matter from whom it may come or to whom it may be addressed. This holds true just as much for the strategists of the cold war in the so-called "Fighting Group against Inhumanity" in Berlin as for Radio Free Europe in Munich; since the bloody suppression of the national revolution in Hungary, this station bears its name with even less justification than before.[18]

This editorial marked a turning point in both European and American press reaction to RFE during the Polish and Hungarian crises. Comment until this time was largely favorable, but the argument advanced by *Freies Wort* was picked up in Germany and the United States and reverberated through the press for almost three months. The comment on RFE ranged all the way from accusations that it had almost single-handedly triggered the Hungarian revolution to the observation that it was at worst an innocent commentator on tragic events. In the last two months of 1956 the attacks far outnumbered the defenses. It is interesting, however, that only RFE's programs to Hungary were considered. Journalistic accounts fail to assess or even to consider the role that RFE played during Gomulka's *coup d'état*. But it seems obvious that a fair and balanced evaluation of RFE's role during the crises-ladened months of October and November, 1956, can only be achieved by considering its role in both Hungary and Poland.

THE ROLE OF RFE IN GOMULKA'S VICTORY

Unfortunately there is little material available from which one can assess the role of RFE during the crucial events in Poland in late October. However, the brief evidence available suggests that it was not insignificant. We pointed out earlier in this chapter that the Voice of Free Poland had two purposes. The first and most important was to carry strictly factual accounts of what was going on in Poland; the second, to appeal to the people to remain calm and not give the Russians any excuse for armed intervention. There is evidence from both Polish and neutral sources that RFE was an important source of information during this crucial period. When the official press could not carry certain kinds of information, it was spread among the people by RFE. At times RFE bulletins were even pinned up on university bulletin boards. On November 25 a Polish newspaper, *Zycie Literackie*, carried a complaint: "I have recently been hearing more and more of the propaganda activities carried on by the revolutionary committees. . . . Is it a reason for boasting that the bulletin boards of a university were enriched by a display of Free Europe communiques?" On December 2, the same paper carried an answer: "Comrade Machejek is asking if one can boast that the bulletin boards at a university were enriched by a display of RFE communiques? . . . These bulletins were published at a time when our own press, for obvious reasons, could not broadcast many facts such as, for instance, events in Hungary." Apparently, at least among some people, RFE performed a useful function in disseminating information during this period.

There are also some data on the effectiveness and usefulness of RFE's appeals for calm and discipline. On December 20, 1956, M. Ben, writing in *Le Monde*, commented directly on this matter: "In a conversation with us one of the most representative regime journalists praised the broadcasts of Radio Free Europe which appealed to Poles to preserve discipline and calm and recommended that the Poles avoid manifestations and public disorders."

Zycie Literackie of November 11 also complimented RFE (and the BBC) for recognizing that prudence and calm were fundamental prerequisites for the gaining of any kind of escape from Soviet domination. And finally, one of RFE's own evaluation interviews with a "neutral" (meaning either Swiss or Swedish), who was in Poland in October, supports the same conclusion. He quoted a party member and Gomulka supporter, with whom he talked, to this effect: "Had RFE not told our people to be calm, I am not sure whether we alone would have managed to cope with the situation."

This is scanty evidence from which to draw any conclusions, but it does indicate, at a minimum, that RFE policy was acutely attuned to the needs of the Polish "revolutionists" during this period and, at a maximum, that it was of importance in preventing the Polish situation from degenerating into what developed in Hungary.

RADIO FREE EUROPE'S ROLE AND RESPONSIBILITY DURING
THE TRAGEDY IN HUNGARY

The problem of evaluating RFE's role, complicated in regard to Poland by the lack of pertinent data, is equally complex in regard to Hungary for the opposite reason. Hundreds of contradictory articles appeared in the American and European press in November and December 1956. Few made the sources of their information explicit; many of those that did were based on interviews with one or two Hungarian refugees. In analyzing these articles it is possible to divide them into three groups, (a) those that accuse RFE of inciting the

Hungarians to revolution; (b) those that claim that although the scripts do not appear to the American reader to be inciting, the effect on the Hungarian audience in a charged situation was in fact inciting; (c) those that argue that no matter what RFE actually said, the very fact that it had been on the air for six years (along with VOA) could be legitimately taken by the Hungarians as prima-facie evidence that the Americans would come to the aid of any armed attempt to drive the Soviets out of Hungary.

The most serious indictment, namely, that RFE incited the revolution and, when it had burst into flame, added oil to the fire by promising western armed intervention, is simply not supported by a study of RFE's scripts.[19] One can argue that some of RFE's broadcasts to Hungary were innocuous and others contradictory. For instance, on October 25 a special broadcast referred to Nagy as a traitor while Special Commentary No. iv on the same day ended with a statement that the Nagy government still may prove itself. On October 28 the writer of International Commentary C-524 argued that the UN had both the right and the duty to intervene in Hungary, while following broadcasts clearly pointed out difficulties that made intervention next to impossible. However, only one broadcast came close to suggesting that the Americans would intervene, and that was the result of clumsiness rather than intent. In a review of the western press, broadcast on November 4, the comment of a responsible British publication was quoted as follows:

This morning the British *Observer* published a report of its Washington correspondent. This situation report was written before the Soviet attack early this morning. In spite of this the *Observer* correspondent writes that the Russians have probably decided to beat down the Hungarian revolution with arms. The article goes on: "If the Soviet troops really attack Hungary, if this our apprehension should become true and the Hungarians will hold out for three or four days, then the pressure upon the government of the United States to send military help to the freedom fighters will become irresistible." This is what the *Observer* writes in today's number. The paper observes that the American Congress cannot vote for war as long as the presidential elections have not been held. The article continues: "If the Hungarians continue to fight until Wednesday, we shall be closer to a world war than at any time since 1939." [20]

This one press review is hardly grounds for the claim that RFE promised the freedom fighters that Americans would come to their aid. The portion relevant to American intervention is clearly attributed to a British source. However, there were some broadcasts from the West that could have been confused with RFE, and these freely indicated that western help was in the offing. A small transmitter located just outside Frankfurt, used by the NTS (a Russian emigree organization known as the "Solidarists"), was turned over to a Hungarian veterans' group in Germany. Some of the broadcasts from this station were irresponsible—indicating that the West was coming to the aid of the Hungarians. Apparently, some of these broadcasts were confused with RFE's.

The furor that was created by RFE in the German press caused the German government to conduct a formal investigation of RFE's broadcasts during the Hungarian uprising. In a press conference on January 25, Chancellor Adenauer said the investigation had shown that RFE did not incite the revolt with promises of western aid.

The second charge, that RFE's scripts, although appearing innocent enough to the dispassionate American reader after the event, were, in effect, incitements to action to the Hungarian insurgents fighting for their independence is difficult to prove or disprove. It was widely circulated in Europe and America, particularly after an interview by Anna Kethly, exiled president of the Hungarian Social Democratic Party, in Brussels on November 29. She told the press that RFE had "gravely sinned," albeit unintentionally, and implied that it was partially responsible for the tragic course of the Hungarian revolution.[21] Walter Ridder stated this argument most clearly when he said, ". . . the important propaganda fact is not what people hear, but what they think they hear. To a certain extent, the Hungarians believed they had heard what they wanted to hear. From the phrasing of RFE scripts the gap between the actual promises and implied promises is easy to bridge for a people under the maximum of mental stress."[22] Benzedrine, harmless enough when taken by a normal person, might be exceedingly dangerous if fed to a patient already dangerously overexcited. But the effect of radio broadcasts is not as well known as that of benzedrine, and the condition of a patient hundreds of miles away cannot be accurately determined.

It is obvious that for some of RFE's listeners in Hungary, the most innocent broadcast had the effect of benzedrine being fed to an overexcited person. One refugee in this country reported to the author that he was hiding in a basement in Budapest after the second Russian intervention. When he heard over RFE a broadcast of the United Nations' decision to send a delegation to Hungary, he thought immediately of the American participation in Korea, picked up his rifle and went back on the streets to fight. It was not that anybody had promised armed intervention. It was simply (and tragically) that "sending a delegation to Hungary" meant something entirely different to a Hungarian freedom fighter from what it meant to a UN delegate. The question is, however, how many Hungarians reacted this way to RFE's broadcasts which were not in themselves inflammatory? It is difficult to answer. But evidence points to that fact that western radio was not an important factor in precipitating the revolution by direct provocation. The International Research Associates study cited in Chapter 8 provides convincing evidence for this statement. No refugee interviewed listed RFE or western radio in general as a cause of the revolution. Even when sources were asked the reasons why they felt the uprising came at the particular moment it did, western radio was an insignificant response.[23] There are no questions in this study which get at the problem of whether or not the Hungarians felt that RFE's broadcasts contributed to the continuation of resistance after it was hopeless to continue.

With the unrefined data on hand it is impossible to separate the charge that specific broadcasts of RFE during the uprising were interpreted by the listeners as indicating that the West would come to their aid, from the more general charge that the very fact that the West was broadcasting to the captive peoples would be interpreted to mean military support when a revolution broke out. But there is no doubt that the very existence of the American stations gave many Hungarians the impression that the United States would be willing to fight to save Hungary. One half of the International Research Associates sample had this impression whereas only 38 per cent received a contrary impression from the broadcasts.

If the very fact of broadcasting, no matter what the nature of the content may be, has this effect, we are confronted with a grave question of responsibility—not primarily the responsibility of RFE, but the responsibility of the United States government. This question will be opened for discussion in the next chapter.

A Nonofficial Instrument of American Foreign Policy

BOTH at home and abroad Radio Free Europe is generally looked upon as an American institution. The Crusade for Freedom's advertising campaigns to solicit funds to support the activities of the Free Europe Committee tell the American people that RFE is their station. The western European press refers to RFE as the "private American propaganda network." Even significant parts of the audiences in the captive countries are aware of the American sponsorship, and although they appreciate the native character of the programing, the fact of American sponsorship actually seems to lend prestige to the activities of the exiles. However private the organization may be, it must, therefore, be assessed as an instrument of American foreign policy.[1]

Any analysis of RFE as an instrument of American foreign policy must first come to grips with the advantages and disadvantages arising from its private nature. Edward L. Bernays, who perhaps has had as long an association with American foreign propaganda operations as any man in the country, both as participant and observer, feels that there are three obvious advantages of a private agency:

First, it is undoubtedly true that a private agency in foreign countries does not suffer from its being stamped as a governmental propaganda agency. In that way it may possibly develop greater credibility for what it disseminates.

Second, a private agency has somewhat more flexibility in discussing affairs because it is not bound by whatever limitation any government is bound to have as to what it can and cannot say.

Third, it is not subject to possible political pressures of one sort or another that are bound to encumber any organization that is dependent upon yearly appropriations made by the national legislature.[2]

A Nonofficial Instrument of Foreign Policy

People who have experience in an official governmental propaganda operation generally tend to emphasize the importance of the quickness and flexibility that a private agency has because it does not have to clear its propaganda response to events through a large government bureaucracy. It has greater latitude in what can be said, how it is said, and in the techniques that may be used to carry the messages than does a government agency that has the obligations of diplomatic recognition of the target countries to observe.[3] The latter point was particularly emphasized by Lloyd Free, former head of the U.S. information program in Italy, who thought that the fact that the United States government could officially disavow RFE was one of its unique advantages.[4]

These operational advantages are obvious; we do not have to belabor them here. However, the last point raised by Mr. Bernays opens a much larger field for discussion and one that Edward W. Barrett and Lloyd Free, both of whom have had extensive experience in postwar governmental propaganda operations, have dwelt on at length. Both men feel that perhaps the most significant advantage of RFE is its "freedom from Congress." In addition to the general and well-documented criticism that Congress has hampered the operations of the Voice of America by its inconsistency in allocating funds for its operation, the degree to which Congress, congressional committees, and individual congressmen interfered in the daily operations of the "Voice" is bitterly resented.[5] Lloyd Free agrees with Barrett's published views on the role of Congress in the conduct of an American overseas information program.[6]

Barrett is particularly concerned with the damaging effect of congressional investigations. He concludes a vivid account of the effect of the "Voice of McCarthy" on the Voice of America with a comment that by its very nature an agency of international propaganda will be "easy prey for headline-hunting inquisitors" and that "America can never conduct an effective operation in international persuasion if the whole plant is to be pulled up by the roots and publicly dissected every few months by men who have not conscientiously studied the intricacies of the work."[7]

Barrett feels that although the very nature of congressional-administrative relations affects all operations of government, "they hamper the operations of international persuasion with particular severity." He offers four basic reasons:

First, because of the sensitive and subtle nature of an international information and propaganda program, it suffers when it is dissected in the halls of Congress while TASS correspondents and others take careful notes. It is hardly wise to warn a totalitarian power of the next propaganda move by debating it in Congress, and it may be embarrassing at the least to publicly reveal the plans that have been worked out for conducting an information program in a friendly country.

Second, an international information and propaganda program requires a tremendous amount of study and special training before its intricacies can be comprehended. Few congressmen have such skill and training, and therefore congressional debate on the subject is usually uninformed and often dangerous.

Third, international propaganda is a subtle business. Its effectiveness sometimes may not be known for years if, indeed, it is ever fully known. Therefore, the need for mantaining a propaganda program is extremely hard to justify before the hard-headed, practical men who tend to find their way into the appropriations committees.

Finally, an international propaganda operation will always be "controversial" because of the difficulty of measuring with accuracy its results. Since its results can never be proved, any campaign strategy will be subject to attacks. This tends to encourage open debate, but debate which cannot really settle anything.[8]

But there are also disadvantages that may result from a private organization being so actively engaged in international relations. All writers on propaganda as an instrument of foreign policy agree that one of the prerequisites of a successful operation is that it be integrated with basic foreign policy. Barrett makes this point with particular emphasis:

By its very nature, international persuasion is *inter*-dependent with the other foreign programs and policies of the government. If it should ever become truly "independent", it will become either ineffectual or perilous. This means that it must be intimately tied in with the top policy-makers of government, including the President and the National Security Council, but it also must be closely allied with the lower levels of government at which foreign policy is also made.[9]

A Nonofficial Instrument of Foreign Policy

Although there is some liaison between RFE and Washington, there is nothing comparable to what Barrett feels is desirable—indeed, necessary. Perhaps during the first decade of the cold war close liaison was not necessary. The issue between East and West was closely drawn; there was little room for maneuver on either side. But since the Geneva conventions in 1955 and the Twentieth Party Congress in 1956, Soviet policy has become more flexible and more imaginative. It should therefore be met with a more flexible and agile American policy, which would increase the demand for more coordination among the various instruments. During the early years of the cold war there was only a limited number of propaganda responses that could be made to the Soviet Union's moves. Even without a great deal of active coordination RFE and VOA would not be far apart on basic propaganda lines. But following the Twentieth Congress there were more alternatives and thus a greater possibility of diverging if not conflicting lines. Any one might be acceptable, but several pursued simultaneously by two American stations could be self-defeating.

As regards the fundamental problem of integrating and coordinating the propaganda agencies with basic foreign policy, this author feels that the root of the problem lies in the basic policy formulating structure of the American government. In the present state of this structure, coordination with even the official propaganda agency is difficult—at times impossible. Consider the time of the Indochina crisis in the spring of 1954. In March Secretary Dulles warned of the threat to the free world if Indochina fell. In the middle of April the Vice President said that American troops would have to be sent to Indochina if the French withdrew. Three days later Mr. Dulles doubted that American troops would have to be sent. The last day of April the President said that Communist conquest of the area was unacceptable to the United States. This statement was widely interpreted to mean that he favored American intervention. On May 11 Mr. Dulles commented that Indochina was important but not essential to the preservation of southeast Asia, and the pendulum swung back to the side of nonintervention. As long as the potential for this kind of policy formulation exists, efforts to achieve coordination between any information agency and the top policy-makers will be useless because the best coordination can only echo the confusion that is present in Washington.

It would seem to this author that a private organization can be a very effective supplement to the official information agency during a period of cold war if—and the qualification is important—if it is astutely operated. There have been a number of criticisms of RFE, however, which claim that its operations have been something less than astute. The most carefully analyzed and reasoned criticisms were written by C. L. Sulzberger in the spring of 1956, shortly after a tour of the satellite states.[10] Three points raised by Sulzberger must be discussed in detail.

A number of people have expressed concern over the possibility that the exiles broadcasting over RFE are out of touch with the people and conditions in their homelands, and thus their broadcasts are meaningless if not downright harmful. Sulzberger reported: "From Poland to the Danube Valley listeners complain that *émigrés* working for American radio stations have lost touch with changing local conditions. A Bulgarian anti-Communist protests: 'They are like all *émigré* movements. They are unaware of some changes that we accept with pleasure while opposing the regime—such things as free medical care. Many people think the *émigrés* enjoy a better life abroad than is actually the case. Nevertheless, unfortunately, they resent it. Such is human nature.'"

The findings of this study would suggest that this charge has been greatly exaggerated. This writer has talked to no exile in RFE who thought it possible to go back to the "good old days." Furthermore, most of them seem aware of the tremendous changes that have taken place in their homelands in the past decade—some of these innovations like social security, welfare legislation, and opportunities for social advancement are actually welcomed and looked upon as accomplishments. The response of the Voice of Free Poland to Gomulka's "palace revolution," discussed in the last chapter, was hardly the response of individuals who were out of touch with what was happening in Poland.

And RFE goes to considerable effort to see that the best, the most, and the latest information is made available to its writers and policy people. Hundreds of newspapers and periodicals, and thousands of interview reports, plus the monitoring of satellite and Soviet radio, provide as detailed and accurate a picture of developments behind the Iron Curtain as is possible. Audience Analysis and other units are beginning to prepare expert analyses of this information.[11] Indeed, no less able an expert on the satellite states than Professor Hugh Seton-Watson has rated RFE as the most valuable source of information on these nations available in the western world.[12]

Finally, when the directors of RFE have evidence that an exile writer or editor is out of touch with developments in his homeland, he is dismissed. For instance, some personnel on the Hungarian desk were dismissed in 1957 when it was discovered that their views on developments in Hungary were quite different from those held by a majority of Hungarians as indicated by the vast number of refugees that escaped in late 1956.

A second charge made about RFE is that it broadcasts "'intelligence' information that is entirely inaccurate or ridiculously late . . . Much that [RFE and VOA] broadcasts no longer has any bearing on reality."[13] This too appears to be an exaggeration. The International Research Associates' study of the 1956 Hungarian refugees indicates that the Hungarians have considerable faith in the trustworthiness of western radio.[14] Radio Free Europe, however, does not rank as high as the BBC or VOA. In part, the reason for this is that RFE has set for itself a more difficult task. It tries to provide a complete home news coverage. Without normal sources of information, this is exceedingly difficult. Inaccuracies are bound to creep in. However, the larger listening audience that RFE commands, as revealed by the International Research Associates, suggests that the audiences in Hungary wanted this kind of news coverage even though they recognized that it involved some inaccuracies.

It should also be pointed out that if the comments of M. Ben and *Zycie Literackie* on RFE's role during the crisis days in Poland in October 1956, are accurate, the people of Poland—Communists and non-Communists—must have considerable faith in the truthfulness of RFE's news reports and commentaries.

The accusation that "ridiculously late" information is broadcast must be dealt with on different grounds. The matter of timeliness is relative. Information is late if one has already heard it; it is not necessarily late if it was unknown, even though the particular events in question may have occurred at some time in the past. In this regard some of the research done by Bauer and Gleicher on communication in the Soviet Union is relevant. These men report that nonofficial sources of information perform for the urban intelligentsia a function entirely different from that for workers and peasants. For the intelligentsia they act as a *supplement* for the official sources, providing this audience with information not officially available and affording a check on the accuracy of that which is available. For the workers and peasants the nonofficial sources serve as a substitute for the official media.[15] This research suggests that information that may be "ridiculously late" for a member of the intelligentsia would actually be welcomed by workers and peasants. For example, Harrison Salisbury, in June 1956, reported in the *New York Times* that Czech students had presented the government with a series of demands "among the most sweeping to be submitted to a Communist government in recent years. The demands could hardly be granted without radical revisions of the whole basis of Communist rule in Czechoslovakia."[16] The resolutions were apparently drafted between April 24 and May 10. Although they were never published in Czechoslovakia, they were circulated rather widely by hand, according to Salisbury. Radio Free Europe received a copy in June and broadcast the demands. For anyone who had seen the resolutions in April or May, this information may have been "ridiculously late." But for millions of others, it might have been a welcome addition to their knowledge of events in their own country.

Because of the fact that Sulzberger's criticism that RFE broadcasts both late and inaccurate news was a direct quote from an "American envoy in the area," we interviewed a number of officials in the Office of Eastern European Affairs in the Department of State to determine how frequent this kind of criticism is. The reply from all those interviewed was that it is rare. In fact, only one official could recall specific reports that contained such a charge.[17]

The most serious charge that has been made against RFE is that it has incited its listeners to suicidal action. In a number of places in this study we have pointed out that such broadcasts are strictly against RFE's policy and that an examination of scripts shows that this charge is simply not true in any immediate sense. But in its most devastating form the charge is not a direct one. It is not based on an analysis of RFE's scripts or policy guidances. It proceeds from the simple logic that if vast efforts are put into a propaganda operation and thousands of hours a week are broadcast to the countries behind the Iron Curtain, the listener might easily and not unreasonably believe that stronger action is coming, and will come, if trouble starts. This argument is stated in powerful terms through the lips of a Hungarian refugee quoted in James Michener's moving portrayal of the Hungarian uprising, *The Bridge at Andau*. One passage is worth quoting at length:

Ferenc Kobol was a twenty-six year old who had experienced much and who had studied revolution so deeply that he saw no need to spare my feelings. He said, "Of course Hungarians are bitter about the lack of interest you Americans showed in our struggle for freedom. For years now, as part of your battle with communism for the possession of men's minds, you have been giving us hope and assurance. You have been saying to us, 'You are not forgotten. America's ultimate aim is to help you win your freedom. To achieve this we will support you to the best of our ability.'

"America spent millions of dollars and every known psychological trick to bring this message to us behind the iron curtain. Your Voice of America broadcast fifty hours a day of freedom programs. You used seventy frequencies and sometimes I would hear you from Tangiers or Munich or Salonika. I can remember the thrill we got when we heard that you were outfitting one of your Coast Guard cutters, the *Courier*, to dodge jamming stations. You said the *Courier* 'would punch deeper holes in the iron curtain.'

"Then you set up Radio Free Europe in 1950 and you got right down to the business of freedom. You had eleven separate stations which broadcast one thousand hours of encouragement a week from Frankfurt, Munich and Lisbon. RFE told us many times, 'Our purpose is to keep opposition to communism alive among the people of the slave states behind the iron curtain. We want to help such people gradually to make themselves strong enough to throw off the Soviet yoke.'

"How did you help us to grow strong? You constantly reassured us that we were not forgotten by the West. You said that the fact that so many American citizens supported RFE proved that your nation was with us. We believed you.

"Next, to make your message even more clear, you began to launch balloons to fly over our country bearing leaflets and aluminum medals. I got one with a Liberty Bell on it and the legend 'Hungarians for Freedom—All the Free World for the Hungarians'.

"These balloons were very important to our psychological reactions. I remember thinking at the time, 'At last something tangible. Something more than words. If America could reach us with these aluminum medals, why couldn't they reach us with parachute supplies if a revolution started. Obviously, America intends to help us.'

"In 1952 all of your radio stations broadcast over and over the promises made in your election campaign. We were told that America was to roll back the iron curtain. You would stimulate a desire for freedom among the eight hundred million under communist domination. We were assured many times that your President would find ways to make the Russians want peace. The speeches of your leaders were quoted to us day after day . . .

"Then what happened? When the Germans in East Berlin rioted against the Russians, your stations told us each detail. This year when the Poles rioted against the Russians in Poznan, we were again fed the full propaganda of freedom. Should we be blamed for believing what we heard? You must put yourself in our place. We had no honest newspapers, no honest radio stations of our own. We could rely only upon what you told us, and you told us to love freedom . . .

"Words like 'freedom', 'struggle for national honor', 'roll-back', and 'liberation' have meanings. They stand for something. Believe me when I say that you cannot tell Hungarians or Bulgarians and Poles every day for six years to love liberty and then sit back philosophically and say, 'But the Hungarians and Bulgarians and Poles mustn't do anything about liberty. They must remember that we're only using words.' Such words, to a man in chains, are not merely words. They are the weapons whereby he can break chains . . .

"If America wants to flood Eastern and Central Europe with these words, it must acknowledge ultimate responsibility for them. Otherwise you are inciting nations to commit suicide." [18]

To any American these are sobering paragraphs. But they are not primarily addressed to RFE; they are an indictment of the United States government and its foreign policy. When the President of the United States solemnly announces that "it is a major goal of the United States policy to achieve peaceful liberation of the captive peoples," does he not imply that action will be taken to that end? Does he not imply that at a minimum a plan of action is being devised? The switch in United States foreign policy from "containment" to "liberation" precipitated considerable criticism both at home and abroad. Most of it revolved around the charge that the new policy involved unnecessary risk. But this was not its major drawback. Even that prime apostle of liberation who prides himself on having learned to go to the "brink of war" will practice his art only when he feels that the preservation of the peace is at stake. There never was any responsible talk about going to the precipice in order to free the satellites. However, this is not to say that the "liberation policy" is immune to criticism. But the weakness is not that its strategy is too dangerous, for it never had a strategy. That precisely is its error. A goal without a strategy constitutes the bankruptcy of policy. "Peaceful liberation" was such a goal.

A strategy is a plan of action to achieve a given goal (or goals) involving the integrated use of all available instruments and based on a realistic assessment of the situation. It is important to recognize that major foreign-policy goals cannot be achieved by the use of a single instrument of statecraft, or by various instruments employed independently of one another. Goals demand strategies—good strategies if possible, but bad strategies are better than none. When Mr. Dulles called for a "psychological war for liberation," the weapon at hand was a sort of mechanical reincarnation of Joshua's trumpet, engaged in trying to bring the Iron Curtain tumbling down with the amplified din of righteous invective. As long as it worked singly, it was doomed to inconsequence; until some strategy of liberation was developed, it was doomed to work singly.

No one was more aware of the frightful inadequacies of the liberation policy than were the people at RFE. By the end of 1953 they knew that "punching holes in the iron curtain" through which "truth" could be poured would not lead to liberation. It was at this time that a rigorous analysis of the situation in the satellites led to the concept of liberation as the result of the workings of a "confluence of forces." This concept formed a foundation upon which a strategy of liberation could be developed. It suggested the various roles of the military, economic, diplomatic, and propaganda instruments of statecraft. That the concept was a realistic one was proved in Poland in the fall of 1956 when a "proper confluence" of the "internal" and "orbital" forces led to a measure of freedom in Poland. Radio Free Europe helped to provide for this proper confluence by nurturing the "internal" force through the years, and in the crucial moment used all its influence to see that the "internal" force and the "orbital" force worked together for a given limited end rather than destroying each other.

In the case of Hungary one might argue that operations based on the same concept led to tragedy. However, if one compares the events in Hungary with those in Poland from RFE's frame of reference, one of the crucial differences is in the condition of the "external" force. Just as events in eastern Europe were reaching a climax, the British and French felt compelled to pursue an independent course in an attempt to secure vital interests that were being neglected by United States policy. When the Hungarians made their move, the Western Alliance could present no common front. The "external" force was shattered. Until the archives of the Kremlin are opened, one cannot support the argument that it was the British and French use of force in the Suez crisis that led the Russians to use force in Hungary, although skilled analysts of Soviet policy have said that it was an important factor.[19] But one can imagine that if the West had presented the Soviet Union with a united front and had used skill and resourcefulness in diplomatic negotiations with the Russians at that crucial period, the outcome of the Hungarian uprising might have been different.

And the United States must share some of the responsibility for the hasty, ill-conceived, and foolhardy French and British action in the Middle East. One of the major responsibilities of the leader of an alliance is to provide a policy that meets the minimum security requirements of its allies. In the Middle East the United States failed miserably to meet this requirement and the French and British felt compelled to pursue an independent course of action in an attempt to secure vital security interests that were being neglected by United States policy.

United States action after the revolution broke out also appears to have been based on the most superficial analysis of the drama that was taking place in eastern Europe. Our major move (outside the UN) was to offer the Poles and Hungarians economic aid—a policy based on the ludicrous assumption that the Poles and the Hungarians needed more motivation to break away from the Russians. This is not to say that such an offer should not have been made or that economic aid at some time should not actually be given. But while the revolution was still in progress it could do little to help the Hungarians because it could be used by the Russians as evidence that they had to intervene to prevent American "economic imperialism" (which apparently they still fear) from getting any foothold in eastern Europe.

Most of the post-mortems since the Hungarian revolution have conceded that there was little the United States could have done. The

Hungarians needed military aid, and if the United States would have supplied it, World War III with all its atomic horrors would have broken out. It is difficult to imagine that American troops could have faced Russian troops in Hungary without a general war occurring. The weakness of American policy was not that it failed to send military aid, but that it failed to exhaust the possibilities of the nonmilitary action that might have been taken.

The Soviet Union could not have yielded to Hungarian demands without suffering a severe blow to its power position in eastern Europe. An acute American policy would have been based on a recognition of that fact and sought to find some diplomatic action that might have made the Kremlin more prone to accept the loss. Would it not have been wise to have re-evaluated our entire German policy to see if there were some concession in that part of Europe that we could have made on the condition that the Soviets evacuate Hungary? Would it have strengthened the United States' position in Europe vis-à-vis the Russians to have negotiated for a neutralized, re-united Germany on the Austrian model in exchange for a neutral Hungary and Poland? Would it have been worth trading twelve German divisions (which in any case seem hard to get) for Soviet withdrawal from Hungary?

The answer to these questions may be yes or no. But the sad fact of the matter is that they seem never to have been asked. The United States government, which had talked openly of liberation and had through its words and actions indicated that the captive peoples should maintain faith and hope in liberation, had not the semblance of a policy even tentatively outlined to deal with a crisis such as the Hungarian uprising.

It is the considered opinion of this writer that the policy analysts at RFE have not been unaware of events and changes behind the Iron Curtain (as some of its critics maintain) but that they have been more aware of developments, more skilled and sophisticated in their analysis, and more diligent in the development of strategies than those responsible for the official policy of the United States government. But this conclusion itself raises some questions about the very existence of RFE. Is it wise to have a private organization, which, in the absence of an official strategy, develops one of its own—no matter how astute that strategy may be? One could certainly argue that it might be more effective to limit a private network to straight news and entertainment in an attempt to maintain a listening audience in the satellites until some kind of official strategy was worked out. Or one might alternatively argue that it would be wiser to direct the time, money, and effort that goes into RFE into improving the official American foreign policy effort.

There is one other point that might be made. The well-known expert on propoganda, Leonard Doob, while recognizing that there are "important momentary advantages" that accrue to a private agency, feels there is one notable disadvantage which is all-important.[20]

But such a station has one tremendous disadvantage which in my opinion is more important than all the advantages which I can think of; even though it is privately owned and even though directly or indirectly it emphasizes this fact in its broadcasts, its listeners are likely not to make the fine distinction. It has something to do with America, therefore it is American, which means the American government. I suspect, therefore, that Radio Free Europe for many or most listeners is not distinguished from the Voice of America; hence government should be in control.[21]

Doob is making a strong argument. Certainly, a number of listeners do not differentiate between a private and a public broadcasting effort.[22] If RFE had indeed promised the Hungarians that the United States would intercede in any uprising, it is doubtful whether in the excitement of the situation many would have reasoned that the offer came from a completely nonofficial source. Radio Free Europe potentially could commit the United States to a position that it would not want to support, making the government appear inconsistent and thereby causing it to lose considerable prestige abroad.

The argument for democratic parliamentary control of political instruments has never been made in terms of efficiency. In fact, efficiency may be sacrificed to the end of gaining responsibility to the public. The democrat has always been suspicious of concentrations of power with no formalized lines of control to the people. If we assume that RFE is effective among its audiences, then we must assume that it has power power that can (or could in the future) affect the vital interests of the United States in these areas. What are the lines of accountability? At best, they are hazy. The argument that since it is supported by public contributions, it is responsible to the public is fallacious for two reasons. First, the "franchise" for the voters is financial. Secondly, in a large democracy the people exercise control through an intermediary body consisting of their elected representatives who may be removed from office. No such mechanism exists or could exist in the Free Europe Committee.

This does not mean that RFE is an "irresponsible" organization. But it is responsible, not because of institutional lines of control, but because of the self-imposed responsibility and discipline of the individuals who hold positions of authority. There are two secrets to the success of this kind of responsibility: (a) the employment of individuals who have a "built-in" sense of responsibility and an awareness that they are operating an instrument that could have a grave impact on the position of the United States in eastern Europe; (b) the absence of any powerful interest groups, with large sums available, that have a special interest in the area. Both factors are present in the case of RFE. But this does not mean that any private agency would operate with the responsibility of RFE. For instance, if some private group began broadcasting to the Middle East, it is difficult to imagine American oil interests not being involved and to conceive of a situation in which considerable pressures would build up to support a policy different from that of the government.

Any discussion of RFE as an unofficial instrument of American foreign policy must recognize that it is an embodiment of the American tradition of voluntarism applied to foreign affairs in a period of history in which international events have come to affect deeply the personal lives of millions of Americans. Mr. Grew and his associates are part of the long line of American citizens who have taken upon their own shoulders responsibilities that in most societies are left strictly to the government. It is a tradition that has produced both good and ill—both its Robert Morrises and its John Browns. It is hoped that this book will enable the reader to decide to which part of this tradition Radio Free Europe and the Free Europe Committee belong.

APPENDIX, NOTES, AND INDEX

Appendix

A MESSAGE OF THE CZECHOSLOVAK PEOPLE: One of a Series of Comprehensive Reports Designed to Stimulate Thought and Supplement the People's Opposition Press. (Prepared by the Czechoslovak Desk of the Free Europe Press and dropped by balloon in Czechoslovakia in the spring of 1956.)

KDY TO SKONCI? (HOW LONG WILL THIS GO ON?)

This is the question people ask themselves not only in our country but in the free world as well.

People in the free world keep asking themselves where the end is to international tension and insecurity, to the armaments race, and all the difficulties flowing from the present anomalous state of world affairs.

To Czechs and Slovaks the question about the *end of all this* is a thousand times more burning. When do we cease to be a Soviet colony? When will we be able to choose a government of our liking in free elections? When will we be able to think, talk, work, and manage our affairs the way we want to? When?

Let us say straight away that nobody can answer that question. Yet we all feel that this cannot go on forever. We feel it as powerfully and certainly as we felt during the darkest hours of the war, when Germany was winning on all fronts, and we knew that Hitler would ultimately be defeated and that the forces of freedom would prevail. At that time too, we did not know when the occupation and the reign of terror would end—we only knew that the end would and had to come.

But faith and feeling alone would have helped neither ourselves nor the Allies, without reason, effort, and struggle. This is equally valid today. The free world already knows that Communism will not retreat to the borders of Russia by itself; the free world is aware that even if there should be no war, it must engage in contest with Soviet imperialism on other fronts—political, economic, cultural. The free world must, in the words of President Eisenhower, fight out the most important battle of all: the battle for the human soul.

We, and with us all the other captive nations, know equally well that freedom is not a ripe pear that will simply fall into our laps. True, there are people among us who comfort themselves with old wives' tales about some powder that would, in no time at all, put all the Commies to sleep, or with stories like those about the Danish troops supposedly on the march to Czechoslovakia to carry out free elections. Such stories simply help the regime's purposes. The regime is not afraid of stories; stories won't harm it. The regime would be only too happy if its opponents were to play the Sleeping Beauty who does nothing but slumber and wait for some prince from the West to come, wake her up and free her.

Fortunately, there are few such Sleeping Beauties in our country. Fortunately we Czechs and Slovaks are a sensible and realistic people. Therefore, we know that things won't come the easy way. We know that we will have to rely on our brains, survey the situation carefully, choose our own sector in the great struggle between the two

217

worlds, and in that sector do all that we can. No good will come of guessing and prophesying *when it will end*. But it will do us a great deal of good if we do some thinking about what must happen—in the world and in our country—*to bring this end about* as soon as possible.

Before we survey our own Czechoslovak sector, let us first take a look at the developments on the international scene.

The "Spirit of Geneva"

No wonder many people were confused by all that went on in the world before Geneva, at Geneva, and afterward. Could anyone have imagined as recently as 1954, that the Moscow leaders would come to lay their repentant apologies at Tito's feet? People didn't believe their eyes when they saw pictures of Eisenhower, Bulganin, Eden, and Faure sitting sociably on a Geneva lawn, like old friends getting together on a Sunday afternoon. And the Red Army pulling out of Austria! And Chancellor Adenauer's trip to Moscow! And Khrushchev's and Bulganin's propaganda stunts in Asia! What was the meaning of all that? What new game was being played in the world? Who has hoodwinked whom? Which is the winning and which is the losing side? And, above all: what does all this mean to us? Is the new international situation favorable to the Czechoslovak struggle for freedom—or is it unfavorable? Let us try to draw at least a rough balance sheet.

First comes the question of how the Geneva business actually came about. Obviously this could not happen overnight. To bring Geneva about, it was necessary for a whole series of events, in the international situation, to change gradually. Among such events were, for instance, the wars in Korea and Vietnam, Stalin's death, the formation of the Atlantic Alliance, and many other such events. Only future historians, viewing these events from an adequate distance in time, will be in a position to say which of them contributed most. But it can already be said with certainty that the sum total of these events caused two basic changes: a change in the balance of power between West and East, and a change in the attitude toward war as a method of solving international conflicts.

Shifts in the Balance of Power

We Czechs and Slovaks remember only too well how the western democracies were deceived by the Soviets at Teheran and Yalta, and how unwise was western haste to disarm after the war. We have experienced on our own skins how the Soviets took advantage of this error. Churchill was certainly right in saying that, in those postwar years, only the American monopoly in atomic weapons deterred the Soviets from further conquests.

Today the situation is substantially different. Under the shield of its atomic superiority, the West built the so-called North Atlantic Treaty Organization (NATO) which at present has immediately available to it 48 divisions plus, of course, the overseas armies of its member countries. NATO military bases stretch from Norway across Great Britain, France, Germany, Italy, and North Africa, as far as Turkey. Turkey is also the hinge of two extensions of this defense system into the Middle-Eastern area: the Balkan Pact (Turkey, Greece, Yugoslavia), and METO (Turkey, Iran, Iraq, Pakistan and Great Britain). In the rear of this semicircular defense line, there are air bases extending from Greenland across Iceland, Spain, North Africa, and reaching into the Middle East and the Far East as far as Pakistan and Japan. They are complemented by additional bases on the North American continent, from which it is possible to reach Soviet centers by air across the North Pole. Thus, the Soviet power sphere, penetrating deep into central Europe, is enclosed in a horseshoe forged of the western "positions of strength." It is true that the Red Army is still the largest land force in the world. The Soviets could perhaps try something like the Japanese did in the last war; that is, try to paralyze the principal defense and production centers in western

Europe and the United States by a surprise atomic attack. But Moscow knows very well that such an attack against western centers would meet with immediate and greater retaliation from the NATO air bases. Moreover, western Europe is now protected by highly mobile and well-equipped NATO troops, so that the Red Army has long ceased to be the "steamroller" which could not be stopped before reaching the Atlantic coast.

This shift in relative military strength was further accentuated by a number of changes within both eastern and western blocs and these internal developments, political and economic, have also influenced the balance of power, a subject we will discuss later in much greater detail.

But to avoid wishful thinking, we must realize one thing clearly: it would be foolish to believe that Soviet strength is disintegrating, and that it would be enough for the West merely to pound the table to make the Soviets retreat hastily to their prewar frontiers. On the other hand, however, there is little doubt that the postwar thrust of the Soviets into Europe has now lost virtually all of its momentum, and that, in fact, Moscow can hardly cherish any hopes of pushing further into Europe. Another question now comes to the fore: how to push Moscow back.

The other and historically most important change has been brought about by the atomic and hydrogen bombs.

In our country and elsewhere under Soviet domination, there are people, who, with understandable impatience, are prompted to say: "Rather an end with horror, than horrors without end." Let us put aside the question of whether anyone would be interested in liberation by war. Those who dream of it apparently have no idea of just what modern atomic warfare really means. But no matter what these opinions are, the fact is that liberation by war is for the time being completely out of the question.

The Soviet Union will not start a war, because it cannot hope for a victory. The Western Allies will not start it as a matter of ethics and common sense. True, one cannot entirely rule out the possibility that the Soviets could maneuver themselves into a war, whether through their own fault (as nearly happened during the Berlin blockade in 1948), or because of their allies (the most likely case would be Red China). Events so far seem to indicate that the Soviets are well aware that they have little to gain by such a war. Until now they have always known how to stop in time, and even if they love to stir up minor local conflicts—as, for instance, between Egypt and Israel—they watch carefully to keep the conflict from spreading too far, and so being drawn into it.

The Cold Peace

Thus, while on one side both camps—West and East—go on arming themselves, on the other side their armaments in a sense cancel each other out. Stock-piling of atomic weapons makes armed world conflict less and less probable. Does this mean that West and East entrench themselves in their present positions and will remain so for ages? Is the so-called "cold war" also drawing to an end and is the cause of our freedom now permanently buried, as Communist propaganda has attempted to assert by referring to the so-called "Geneva spirit"?

No fear. It is true that to count on war would not be realistic. It would be still less realistic to believe that things can stop where they are now. The present state of affairs is a source of constant tension: Germany divided into two parts; the Soviet Union controlling central Europe like a colony; the Iron and Bamboo Curtains; all this cannot remain permanently fixed. Too many forces are working for change. That there is change without war is shown by the case of Yugoslavia, which threw off Soviet control without causing war, or the example of Austria, from which the Red Army pulled out without firing a shot.

If, therefore, someone asks how the "Geneva spirit" and the Geneva talks were to be explained, the answer is: "Cold war conducted by different means." The Great Powers do not want to, and cannot, achieve their goals by war. How then, do they want to achieve their goals? By diplomatic negotiations. But also by winning new allies. And by economic penetration. And by consolidation at home. And by ideological influence. In short, by all the peaceful means they have at their disposal. It is a struggle for world public opinion, a struggle for a "position of strength"—both moral and material— whose superiority would in the end become unquestionable and decisive.

The New Soviet Tactics

Stalin had a *reputation* for being a realist. However, his present collective heirs proved that they *are* realists. By his brutal provocations—the Berlin blockade, the Korean war—Stalin brought the Western Allies closer together. By insistence on matters of prestige, Stalin lost Tito's Yugoslavia. By stressing his "dogmatic infallibility," Stalin caused serious economic difficulties at home—Soviet bloc agriculture will need a long time to recover from them—and by his stubborn obstinacy abroad (in Austria's case, in the attitude toward West Germany, and elsewhere), he undermined the effects of Communist "peace" propaganda. When he died, he left to his heirs discontent at home and distrust in the world. Further conquest would have meant war, with the Soviet Union losing.

His heirs, therefore, set out to review Stalinist tactics. With no regard for prestige, they accepted Yugoslavia's independence, in order to be able before the world to use their new relationship toward Tito as a "proof" of their tolerance. Stalin's heirs swallowed all the Stalinist regime ever said of the "imperialist lackey" Chancellor Adenauer, and then invited him to Moscow. To show him, and through him the entire world, how magnanimous they could be, they prepared the ground by evacuating Austria. No sooner had they displayed for the West-German eyes the attractive picture of German reunification, than they also invited their East-German protégés. They gave East Germany "sovereignty" and let it be known to Bonn that the road to German unity leads through negotiations with their East-German puppets. Stalin's heirs began to radiate smiles, give banquets, assist western diplomats in berry picking, and give them friendly boat rides. They came to Geneva: first Bulganin, who quickly agreed with Eisenhower, Eden, and Faure that it was necessary to unify Germany, to subject armaments to international control, and to extend relations between West and East. After Bulganin came Molotov, and it was discovered that the only Germany whose unification Moscow was willing to accept was a Communist Germany. It was revealed that the only armament control Moscow was willing to submit to was ineffective control; that the only extension of relations Moscow was interested in was extension of economic contacts, more precisely, easing of exports of strategic materials from the West to the Soviet Union.

To sum up, Stalin's heirs decided that they must back out of their blind alley. They resigned themselves to the fact that if they wanted to move ahead they had to retreat first, change their tactics here and there, and open new fronts; in short, as it is called in diplomatic language, bring about a fluid situation, or as it is known in plain Czech, get things moving. From their point of view, it is a high and dangerous gamble. However, viewed with realistic eyes, under present circumstances, it is the only way which could bring them close to realization of their goals.

How Does the West React?

Western statesmen are certain that though Soviet maneuvers are causing confusion here and there, the new "fluid" situation will ultimately prove to the advantage of the West, provided of course that the West can turn it to its own full advantage.

Let us look at the situation as it is today. In Europe, Moscow's immediate aim is to break up, or at least weaken, the North Atlantic Alliance and to prevent its being strengthened by a West-German army. In this Moscow has failed. The Soviets were left with nothing but hope that this situation may change when Chancellor Adenauer departs from the political scene, and anticipate that West-German politicians will then show more willingness to negotiate with the East-German Communists, thus voluntarily putting their heads into the Soviet noose. However, let us not attempt to predict the future. The facts so far indicate that even if there is occasional friction among the Western Allies—such as in the case of the Saar, for example—NATO is stronger now than ever before. Against the Soviet birds in the bush, the West has a few in its hands; the Soviets are out of Austria and can return there only by war; in Germany, both the Christian Democratic government majority and the Social Democratic opposition are willing to negotiate with Moscow on the basis of full equality—but refuses to negotiate with the East-German Communists.

In Africa and Asia, the lines are not as clearly drawn as in Europe. In Africa, the Soviets are trying to utilize the discontent among the Arab population; in Asia, the military advances of Red China, whom the Soviets used as a battering ram in promoting the objectives of their Asian policy, have at least temporarily been checked. The Western Allies have established in Asia a counterpart of the Atlantic Alliance— the so-called SEATO—but in a number of countries there is still parallel penetration by both Communist and western influences (Indonesia, Burma, India).

How much importance Moscow attaches to this area was shown by the Khrushchev-Bulganin trip in November and December of last year to India, Burma, and Afghanistan—three countries which, in varying degrees, have been recipients of western aid, but which are not linked to the West by any formal alliance. Both travelers from Moscow bent over backward to influence the neutrality of these countries, and missed no opportunity on Asian soil to abuse the West, and revive the memories of old colonial injustice. Moreover, by offering Soviet economic and technical help, they attempted to present the Soviet Union as a world power whose economic potential can substantially contribute toward the building up of underdeveloped Asian countries.

Soviet promises scored initial propaganda success. But for how long? The West has already proved by deed—the Marshall Plan in Europe and the Colombo Plan in Asia— that it is not only in a position to help, but that it actually makes help available on a tremendous scale. Moscow has yet to furnish such evidence. Its propaganda success will shortly be reduced to nothing if the Soviets fail to fulfill, or only fulfill to small extent, the promises so freely made by both traveling salesmen from Moscow while in Asia.

Further Prospects

As we can see, the picture of the East-West contest is not quite black or white for either side. Yet the West welcomes the new Soviet tactics. Why?

First, a state of flux is more hopeful than a static situation. Stalinism meant a period of entrenchment. Abandonment of this Stalinist policy, and its replacement by flexible tactics, inaugurated maneuvering in which the western "position of strength" can be brought to bear by means *other* than war. It has not yet been brought to bear in our favor, and we do not know when it will be, but we do know that it has been brought to bear in the case of Austria, and Austria is now free.

Second, the "Geneva spirit" is now turning against those who wished to misuse it. Although western alertness did slacken here and there as a result of the Soviet smiles offensive, the basic attitude of the West has not changed. The West continues to be aware that the Soviets cannot be trusted and that the free world must go ahead in building its positions of strength. When the formal speeches were over and the actual negotiations began, the Soviets at Geneva and subsequent to Geneva were forced to show their cards and demonstrate that, in reality, agreement was not what they wanted. In the struggle for world public opinion, such a display of Soviet obstinacy unquestionably scored one point in favor of the West: it opened the eyes of those still inclined to take Soviet smiles at face value.

Third, we may safely assume that on the basis of the given conditions, western preponderance will continue to increase. It is not merely a question of relative military power; in view of the atomic stalemate, this is now less important than before. The question is also how moral, social, and economic forces look inside each camp; where are people more satisfied and consequently willing to work harder and fight for their way of life? In which camp do people produce more and better? And where is there a more equitable distribution of national wealth? In which world can people do more independent thinking, as a consequence of which they forge ahead in knowledge, power, and morality?

Western Strength and Soviet Weakness

The strength of the free world derives from its belief in the value of the human individual created in the image of God. From this belief flows respect for human personality, human freedom and equality. These foundations lend the free society a strength which makes it immeasurably superior to any totalitarian system.

This superiority makes itself felt incessantly in actual life. So, for instance, according to Communist prophecies, the free world's economic system should have fallen apart long ago: the western proletariat should long ago have settled its accounts with other classes by means of a victorious revolution; the final conflict, as the *Internationale* sings about it, should have been fought and won. In reality, however, the free world has recovered from war damages more rapidly and more thoroughly than the Soviets. The old-style, exploiting capitalism has either vanished from the modern democracies, or is in process of liquidation. It has not, however, been replaced by Communism, but by a system combining social responsibility with private initiative, in which workers have a thousand times more to say than in the "People's Democracies," not to mention the difference in workers' standards of living. In North America and western Europe, people never have lived so well as they live now. Although the free world had to provide itself with adequate armaments to protect itself against the threat of Soviet aggression, it did not have to take anything from its peoples that makes life more gratifying. Why is that so?

It is so because free people, who have governments of their choice, work more creatively in everyday life. Under the Soviet system the party knows everything; the individual, in the party's opinion, knows nothing and is therefore considered generally incapable. He doesn't know what he likes, what his taste is and what his enjoyments should be. Over and over, Soviet planning makes cramped efforts to predict and control the infinite variety of life down to the minutest detail, and over and over again, it fails. In the end, people in the West find it difficult, for instance, to choose kitchen utensils from among a multitude of various types, while in our country people find it difficult to get any kitchen utensils at all. An American worker annually produces four and a half times more than a worker in the Soviet Union. The free world turns over its agricultural surpluses to the Asiatic nations free of charge, while Soviet agriculture suffers from a permanent and incurable crisis and chaos. In short, in the contest as to which can offer mankind more progress, more spiritual and material values, more happiness and more enjoyment, the livelier and more vigorous democracies are winning over the sterile, ineffective, and dull Communist reality. This is best demonstrated by youth, which refuses to accept Communism as its philosophy in life.

But there is yet another important factor which has already made a substantial contribution toward building up the western "position of strength," and which can rightly be expected to continue to do so; the peoples behind the Iron Curtain. Czechs and Slovaks, Poles, Hungarians, and other neighbors in central and eastern Europe, are described by the Soviets as their "allies," but what kind of allies is known not only to us but also to the West and to Moscow. As the late quisling Moravec promised a thousand-year allegiance to the Greater German Reich, so do Zapotocky and Siroky today promise their "forever with the Soviet Union." Both promises have just about the same value.

The Soviet Union has millions of such "allies," allies under bayonets; such allies are poor assets as workers for their masters, and a still poorer asset as fighters for them. It would not be advisable for the Communists to put weapons into the hands of such allies.

Let us exclude the people of the Soviet Union: it is enough to look at our country and the neighboring captive nations. In our country, the Communists have been in power for eight years, in others a year or two longer. What position have they achieved with the people? They represent a thin layer even where they used to enjoy wide support among the people, and they are faced with the millions of the People's Opposition. There will be much to say about the function and possibilities of this opposition in another place, but for the present let us bear in mind that in the over-all balance of forces, this home opposition plays a key role.

The Belgrade Spirit

Khrushchev's and Bulganin's trip to Belgrade in June of last year was a part of the Soviet plan to thaw the international situation, which had been frozen since the Stalin era. Tito's successful break was intolerable to Moscow and Moscow therefore resolved that since Yugoslav independence could not be suppressed, it would be better to make a right-about-face, and accept the fact with a friendly countenance.

Thus, the Soviet leader's journey of repentance to Belgrade, and the diplomatic reconciliation of Soviet and Yugoslav Communism, came about. The price Moscow had to pay for that reconciliation was not small: not only was it compelled to recognize Tito's regime as ideologically acceptable, but moreover the Soviets had to join in a statement that not only Yugoslavia, but every other country, had the right to choose its own road to socialism, depending on that country's specific national conditions. Such a declaration is a time bomb under each of the satellite regimes. It is true that Tito won his independence from Moscow by his fight for Yugoslav independence against the Nazis during the war, and that he did so by force of his own arms, on his own Yugoslav soil, at a time when the Gottwalds, Bieruts, and Rakosis were eating caviar and drinking vodka in Moscow hotels. Perhaps this is a fact that the present Moscow puppets do not clearly realize, but what they certainly do realize is how much easier Tito's life is now, because he is no longer a puppet and there is no permanent threat of liquidation hovering over his head. Marshal Tito's existence as master in his own country, rather than as someone else's serf, must act on the satellite leaders, high and low, as a perpetual temptation.

But the Belgrade cuckoo's egg in the Communist nest is being felt even more intensely in still another direction: the spirit of the Belgrade Declaration, of the right to choose one's own road to socialism, is a powerful current, among other powerful currents strong among the captive people, where people want to manage their affairs in their own way: in short, where the people would go their own road.

During Stalin's lifetime and after his death, Moscow attempted in vain to eradicate this desire, but neither terror nor promises helped, and the Belgrade statement is a candid admission of the failure of Moscow's intentions to sovietize eastern and central Europe. It shows that the Soviet rulers were forced to state, though unwillingly and insincerely, a principle which forms a part of a historical trend.

Moscow's lack of good will and sincerity will not jeopardize this trend. The satellite regimes in our country, in Poland, and in Hungary were compelled to grant a number of concessions on this "own road." The Belgrade spirit, confirmed during the Brioni meeting of Tito and U.S. Secretary of State Dulles, is another powerful force in the struggle against Soviet imperialism, the more powerful since it undermines the foundations of Soviet power and ideology in the captive countries: it grants even Communists the right to demand greater independence and to try to break Moscow's domination.

Are We on the International Agenda?

When the Russians pulled out of Austria, and Geneva drew nearer, many people began to entertain hopes that the Western Powers would, among other things, bring our cause into the negotiations, and that Prague and Bratislava would soon become as free as Vienna is now. When such hopes fail to materialize, there is usually disappointment and depression. This is understandable. People then ask: "And what about us—what's going to be with us? What are the people in the West waiting for? Why don't they negotiate about us, too?"

Why? Because only those questions could be put on the Geneva agenda which offered at least some prospect of East-West agreement. President Eisenhower came to the first Geneva Conference with a number of problems which he said were necessary to solve if real power was to be achieved, and among those issues the problem of our freedom appeared in a prominent place. Of all those problems, only three actually were placed on the Geneva Conference agenda. They were: (1) unification of Germany and measures to achieve European security, (2) armaments control, and (3) extension of East-West contacts. The others were deferred because the Soviets flatly refused to discuss them. They were *deferred*, but not abandoned. Since that time western spokesmen have been emphasizing that solutions must also be found for the other problems which have not yet appeared on the Geneva agenda, primarily the problem of the captive countries of central and eastern Europe.

In other words, it appears that while the situation has already become ripe enough for liberation of Austria, it has not yet become ripe enough for liberation of East Germany. As far as our liberation is concerned, the situation is only beginning to take shape. That this situation has improved demonstrates not only western attempts to "put us on the agenda," but above all the fact that, for the first time, world public opinion has become fully aware of the problem of the captive countries. Even in places where long ago various neutralists and pusillanimous cowards shut their eyes in the face of this "inconvenient" problem, it is now understood that in the interest of world peace, this is an *abnormal* situation, for which a solution must be sought and found. This opinion not only prevails in America and western Europe. A year ago it reverberated from as far as the Bandung Conference of Asiatic and African nations, and recently again from Yugoslavia, where Dulles and Tito expressed their mutual agreement on this point.

In this sense, therefore, we do constitute a part of the international agenda. But before we can achieve actual negotiations, it is necessary that still greater changes in the balance of power come about, that world events come even more into a state of flux. This is perhaps a bitter pill, but it would make little sense to comfort ourselves with illusions. The regime, however, has had to swallow a much bitterer pill. No matter how radiant Bulganin's smiles, no matter how many times Zapotocky and Siroky vowed eternal allegiance to the Soviet Union and nobody else, and swore that we do not desire anything but to remain in our present state; in the free world from Norway to as far as Australia, and from Washington to Ceylon, the conviction is growing that if there is to be peace in the world, our country and our neighbor countries must also regain their freedom.

Our Strength Is In Our Resistance

Speaking of the international agenda and how to get on it—to bring our Czechoslovak problem into the foreground so that its solution cannot be continually postponed—let us add a few plain words on this subject. Free peoples have a moral obligation to help those who have been deprived of their freedom. That is correct. Genuine peace must be based on justice and not on lawlessness: nothing could be truer than that. It has also been said that truth prevails.

Yes, truth does prevail. However, as Jan Masaryk added: "But it's a tough job." An old Russian proverb says that if truth is to prevail, it must have teeth. Who will give it teeth? In the first place, we Czechs and Slovaks.

But how? In the same way as we have done so far, only more so. If we should let ourselves be ensnared by Communism and inwardly succumb to the Soviets, if we should allow ourselves to become obedient serfs, then the free world would feel no moral obligation to us. Then the injustice being done us would not endanger anyone's peace and would not disturb anyone's sleep. Together with our neighbors, we have become an international problem primarily because we have not resigned ourselves and therefore we Czechs and Slovaks create tensions not only in the international conscience, but also in international relations. Where millions of people resist foreign domination, one can see little peace: there can be only tension, and this tension is conveyed throughout the whole world.

It is true that Tito would not have been able to achieve and preserve his independence from Moscow without the support he received in the form of effective western aid. It is equally true that the Soviet withdrawal from Austria was to a large extent the result of the international situation. But no one would have lifted a finger for either Yugoslavia or Austria, had not the Austrian and Yugoslav peoples demonstrated clearly, by a series of politically important actions, that they were determined to rid themselves of Soviet domination. Only in this way did they succeed in mobilizing the decisive aid of the free world.

In other words, *our strength is not in our suffering: it is in our resistance.* This does not mean that people in the world would not feel sorry for us, and that they would not with sincere disgust condemn the methods by which the regime oppresses us. But pity alone would not help. If we have entered the realm of international debate, and if we have gotten on the agenda of controversial items, it is not because someone felt sorry for us. It is because after the currency reform the workers in our country walked out into the streets and shook the regime's foundations. It is because in Hungary the peasants dissolved one half of the collectives. It is because in Poland the people forced the removal of at least some of the outward signs of the Soviet masters. It is because we have not given up our Christian and western traditions, and because we keep fighting for them. Our spokesmen abroad would not be able to achieve much if they told our American, British, and other friends only what the regime in our country does to the people. Our friends are even more interested in knowing what the people do to the regime. This, much more than pity, will strengthen their desire to help us. No Eisenhower and no Eden will ever get us on a conference agenda if we fail to remind the whole world—including the Soviets—of ourselves again and again as a burning international issue.

At the root of all this is a truth which we must bear in mind at all times: free mankind has indeed a moral obligation to fight for Czechoslovak freedom. But in the first place we, Czechs and Slovaks, have this obligation to ourselves.

The Confluence of Forces

Now let us see in what forms and by which methods we Czechs and Slovaks can wage this struggle today.

How can we rid ourselves of the present regime without war?

In theory, for example, it is possible that one of the present regime people might carry out a successful Titoist coup, a "palace revolution." Such independence from Moscow might possibly become the first step toward democracy. The joint Soviet-Yugoslav declaration that each nation has a right to choose "its own road to socialism" can provide handy justification for a potential Czechoslovak Tito. Whether some as yet unknown Czechoslovak "Tito" would want to use, and would be in a position to use, this justification depends on the confluence of a number of unknown circumstances. Only someone in the highest ruling circle, or near it, can have some notion of what those circumstances might be.

Then, there is another theoretical possibility that the present regime might be swept out with one stroke by a sudden popular rising. No doubt the idea of such a revolution has great appeal among us, because there is not a single group in our society—with the exception of a thin layer of party leaders and bureaucrats—that would not want to see the regime go. But it is hard to imagine that such an uprising in a totalitarian state, involving the establishment and coordination of underground cells on a national scale, with adequate finances, equipment, training, supplies, etc., could be provided in the absence of outside support. And outside support on a national scale is simply not to be thought of in time of peace.

Finally, there are still other possibilities, such as, for instance, free elections under international control, or disintegration of the regime by factional struggle—or possibly as a corollary to gradual disintegration of the Soviet power—or perhaps other alternatives which at present no one can foresee. It is difficult to imagine that this internal process could take place independently of the international situation. The growing strength of the West in itself represents a pressure capable of substantially accelerating these internal developments. In its final stages a favorable international situation would, of course, represent the indispensable prerequisite permitting the people to deal with the regime without intervention from Moscow.

In any case, much depends on the concurrent domestic, internal element of this effort. Much depends on the people and the vigor of their resistance, on their morale, their consciousness and courage.

The Police Regime Has its Limits

In an environment of totalitarian rule enforced by police, the People's Opposition meets with a number of serious obstacles. But the experience in our country shows that no regime of our time is or can be all-powerful. People are educated; they can read and think. Thanks to radio and other modern means of communication, such as, for example, the balloons carrying the printed word, no Iron Curtain is impenetrable. The regime may send tens of thousands of workers and peasants to its concentration camps but it cannot shut them all up any more than it can post a policeman behind each citizen. The regime still needs the people: it needs their work, and, if possible, their good will.

How vulnerable the regime is was demonstrated to us most clearly in 1953, after the currency reform. At that time the gentlemen in the Castle and at the Powder Tower went somewhat weak in the knees, while minor functionaries flushed party cards and emblems down the toilet. The regime suddenly realized that it could not go on by force alone. In order to calm the waves which rose against it, the regime began to make concessions. It began to cut prices and produce more consumer goods, to increase wages for the worker, to boost bulk and purchase prices for the farmers, to lower quotas and make it less difficult to quit a collective farm.

The regime retreated where it felt the strongest pressures, where the demands of the People's Opposition were put forward most vigorously. There is a large number of such demands in our country. The Ten Demands, printed on leaflets in the West, which went to Czechoslovakia in May 1954, represent only a small part of the long list of demands. But precisely because those Ten Demands spoke for all the other, in millions of copies, they developed a symbol of the people's resistance.

Pressing for Popular Demands

To what extent have the people's demands been fulfilled? None has been realized one hundred per cent. In some places, the regime increased its pressure; in others, the

People's Opposition succeeded in enforcing its amendments. From statistical data, we can see that money wages are slowly increasing, and that the people have wrested certain improvements in the living standard from the regime, though not a general and satisfactory increase. On the other hand, the regime continues its attempts to cut wages by means of the "khozrazchot" and other "socialist" achievements. The number of agricultural cooperatives generally declined (by 8 per cent in UACs of Types 3 and 4 between June 1953 and June 1955), and this is a great success for our farmers. But the collectivization drive has not yet subsided, nor has the persecution of independent farmers and cooperative members in the courts ceased. Retail prices of some commodities were reduced several times, but there are as many complaints as ever about the shortage of some items, and in general about their quality. Workers' efforts towards democratization of the trade unions have not met with success. The ROH continues to be an organ of State control, a yellow-dog union, not a spokesman for the workers. But there was a loosening of the chains which bound the worker to his job (therefore, the regime sounds the alarm against labor turnover), and on the whole it can be said that the workers have discovered viable methods of preserving and possibly even of increasing their quota of spare time. The most effective of these methods is absenteeism.

On the social fronts where the regime encounters the people—in all the walks of our daily life—there is not and cannot be peace or armistice. Each pressure necessarily evokes its counterpressure; each action is followed by its reaction. If, in a factory, the workers manage to soften their norms, after a while the time-checkers come and begin to stiffen them again. If, in a village, the regime manages to herd the farmers into a collective, later it appears that on the private plots the crops are excellent while the collective fields are full of weeds. Each of us in his own environment can see best how this quiet but obstinate struggle goes on.

By now, we already know that the power of the police has its limits. We talk more openly; we are not afraid to show what we think of the people who rule us. Having enforced satisfaction of a number of our demands, we have increased our self-confidence and deflated the self-confidence of the regime. Each shop where the workers managed to win this or that improvement, each collective dissolved by the will of its members, becomes visible and tangible proof that even in a police state there are ways and means to act, and that those who lament: "What can one do?" are wrong. Something can be done, and what cannot be done today may possibly be done tomorrow.

By realizing more clearly that each concession yielded by the regime means not only a bit more material improvement, but also a bit more freedom, one step on the road toward full freedom, we have already formulated our political program. This is a program which suits everyone except the regime; a program which everyone understands, including the regime, which can do little about it; a program for which everyone can do something, and the regime cannot prevent it because it needs the workers and farmers more than they need it. And so the little drops of personal actions unite into the current of the People's Opposition which persistently undermines the regime's foundations. Everyone does something to weaken the regime, and in millions of men and women a feeling of solidarity grows, the indispensable unity of an effective opposition movement: the People's Opposition.

The name "People's Opposition" was given spontaneously in the free world. Even from abroad one could not fail to note that during the past few years, the people are learning to live with Communism, how to oppose it with their stubborn resistance, wrest concessions from it, and weaken it. This opposition is unorganized but widespread. It is not revolutionary in character; sometimes it is active, other times only passive. It is so evident that the regime devotes much of its written and spoken propaganda to criticizing and attacking it: denouncing workers who violate State discipline, farmers who do not want to join the UAC, young people who are supposedly not active enough, and so on and so forth. Everyone knows these regime laments. As the

Communists would put it, such resistance has a mass character. It is not and it cannot be merely individual resistance. It is the resistance of an overwhelming majority of the people in opposition against the regime. And that is how it got its name.

The regime call the People's Opposition an opposition of spies and traitors. But the miner who opposes norms, "socialist" competition, yellow-dog State unions, and low wages, knows that he is no spy or traitor. The same is true of the farmer or apprentice clerk opposing the regime, which deprived them of both liberty and a decent standard of living. The regime's vituperation has only strengthened their awareness that they are not alone in their resistance, that they are part of something bigger. In other words, the regime itself has helped to popularize the name of the People's Opposition.

No one would boast aloud that he considers himself a part of the People's Opposition unless he was an *agent provocateur*. Nor is the People's Opposition anything like a political party: it issues no cards, has no regard for years of service or "merits," and does not organize underground or illegal groups. What, then, is the People's Opposition? It is a name for the movement of the Czech and Slovak people, for a community of millions of Czechoslovak men and women united in a common hatred of their Soviet masters, and their Prague and Bratislava puppets, and equally united in their desire for independence, freedom, justice, and democratic government. In quotes, the "People's Opposition" is a mere slogan. But the People's Opposition is a community of individuals and social groups conscious of what they want and of what they reject; it is a reality, the most terrifying for the regime and the party because it is invisible, intangible, a force that can move mountains, a feeling in a man's bones—a fact.

What Does the People's Opposition Consist of?

We have said that the People's Opposition is the movement of the nation against the regime. It is a conscious striving toward definite aims. In addition to their common interest, each of its component parts has interests of its own, and has its own possibilities for action. Some have better possibilities, some lesser ones.

Among these component parts, the workers occupy a strategic position. In the last fifteen years, Czechoslovak workers have undergone a series of trials which, to some extent, broke their consciousness and confused their political outlook. Today, the workers are recovering their morale. They are beginning to overcome the demoralization into which they were thrown first by the war and the years following the end of the war, then by their role in the Communist coup of 1948, and finally by the defeats suffered through their betrayal by trade-union leaders and the ruthlessness of their present state-capitalist exploiters. The workers have begun to realize their potentialities, and by seeking both individual and collective ways aimed at systematic defense of their interests, they are undermining the regime's foundations. The strategic advantage of the workers' opposition lies in the fact that the regime cannot exist without labor, and that the large workers' collectives in the factories are a natural basis for facilitating the growth and intensification of collective consciousness among employees. The result is that workers' collectives transform themselves into social collectives, and from time to time have already emerged as fighting collectives.

Hand in hand with the revival of the workers' movement goes the farmers' resistance against regime interference. The struggle continues both on privately-owned farms and inside the agricultural cooperatives. Farmers are exposed to different kinds of pressures from those which the regime exerts against the workers. The character of the farmers' way of life, their indomitable desire for independence, their spiritual relationship to the soil inherited from their ancestors (to them the earth is not merely a means of production), their dispersion: all these tend to influence the mode of the farmers' resistance. If we add up the various expressions of this farmers' resistance from nonfulfillment of delivery quotas to the dissolution of collectives, we realize the strength this total represents and the difficulties the regime faces from it.

Around these two principal foci of the People's Opposition are grouped the other components. In part, they overlap with those of the workers and farmers; in part, they consist of individual ways of fighting the regime, each group in its own field and by its own method. In this sense the ranks of the People's Opposition include every member of the SNB who remembers his Schweik during duty hours and does not hear and see what he doesn't have to. In this sense the People's Opposition includes every teacher who, despite controls and regulations, manages to tell the children a bit of the truth, a bit of the national tradition. In this sense, the People's Opposition includes every official, every National Committee member, every employee of the bulk-purchasing apparatus, every foreman who manages to make it easier for workers or citizens in general, who attempts to satisfy their interests, and who fails to comply with the regime's directives or does so only halfway.

The People's Opposition includes thousands of Communists too—those among them who for one reason or another joined the party a long time ago, who by now have become disillusioned, and who are presently on the side of the people. It also includes party functionaries, and even party dignitaries, inasmuch as they realize that it is in their interest to seek a way out—a way that leads back to the people and to joining the people's struggle against Soviet exploitation, to which they can contribute ways and means of their own.

In other words, the People's Opposition includes everyone who has a certain resolve, and who is capable of translating that resolve, in one way or another, into action. We can all contribute something to the goals of the People's Opposition. Some of us can do more, others less. No one can sit in judgment on our personal contribution; that must depend on each person's conscience and on his opportunities to contribute.

The Prerequisites

What are the prospects that the People's Opposition will continue to grow and achieve more and better results? Will it manage to build protective walls against the regime's onslaught and, moreover, enforce satisfaction of further demands, forcing the regime to retreat more and more? No one can give guarantees. Everything depends on our consciousness, on our ingenuity, perseverance, and courage.

However, there are certain prerequisites which can contribute to further consolidation and growth of the People's Opposition. In the first place, there is the need for increasing the extent to which people can exchange information, above all, information regarding the experiences derived from their own opposition actions. The regime has been striving to keep factories, towns, villages, and regions in isolation from one another. It is necessary to break this isolation. More than whispered propaganda, the People's Opposition needs a whispered information service.

Then there is the need to strengthen the feeling of solidarity between the various strata of people. If your neighbor is abused it concerns not only your neighbor but you as well, because your turn will be next. If a student, a writer, an official is attacked, it concerns the workers. If a worker is having a rough time, it concerns everyone else. It is imperative to break the old prejudices which force of habit still keeps alive, or which are deliberately kept alive by the regime: workers' prejudices about members of the middle class, middle-class and farmers' prejudices about the workers, the prejudices of the intelligentsia and the prejudices about the intelligentsia. And in particular, it is necessary that members of one sector of society resist the regime's efforts to mobilize them for actions weakening the resistance of, or damaging, other sectors. A typical example is the use of the labor brigades.

Further, it is necessary that we all become more aware of what is called the "law of great numbers," and that in practice we apply it more frequently. If one farmer quits his UAC, he is exposed to greater dangers than if all the members of the UAC do the same thing at the same time. The law of great numbers states that the risk of persecution declines proportionately with the increasing number of people who participate in the act of opposition.

229

And finally it is necessary that not only some but all understand the People's Opposition strategy. It is necessary that we remain aware of the regime's vulnerability. We must know its weak spots so that we can take advantage of them. In doing so—each bringing his own little contribution in his own field—it is necessary to know that the sum total of all these little contributions will result in a vast pressure forcing the regime into one concession after another, driving it from uncertainty to weakness, along the road at the end of which our freedom lies.

What Can We Achieve?

To this question everyone can give his own answer. What can the People's Opposition achieve? The worker will drive the factory management into a corner; a collective farm in this or another village will be dissolved; an official will lose some important paper. So what? All this will not be sufficient to push the regime over. How, then, does it make sense with respect to the final goal: the removal of the regime?

In other words, it is a question of whether the People's Opposition will end in the management offices, at the National Committee, at the organs of State Control, in this or that ministry. Can it reach higher up? Can it have some effect there and weaken the regime?

It can and in fact does reach that high, going along two avenues: first, the People's Opposition sharpens the factional struggles inside the party and thereby causes internal crises which are the characteristic of totalitarian regimes. Secondly, it undermines the strongholds and foundations of the regime, reducing its mobility for action, thereby paralyzing not only the operation of state power but also the determination of those who wish to impose it from above.

So far as the factional struggle within the party leadership is concerned, this is a well-known phenomenon. During Slansky's trial we saw the lengths to which this struggle could go. In neighboring Hungary we saw something similar though not so bloody. The basis for such factional strife is the naked struggle for power. Of course, the contestants for positions of power disguise their personal ambitions with ideological masks. Allegedly they do not fight for positions in the Politburo or in the government, but for this or that tactical concept, this or that solution to a particular problem. A typical area for factional struggle is the dispute about whether the regime should counter the People's Opposition by tactical concessions, or by harsh means. The stronger the People's Opposition, the sharper this dispute becomes, until at last it results in a permanent regime crisis, at first in a limited field (in Czechoslovakia, for instance, there is such permanent crisis in the problem of what to do about the farmers' resistance). Later it spreads through the entire domain of State policy. As a consequence, the regime becomes nervous, it begins to improvise, issues contradictory orders (our farm sector is again a typical example), creates confusion among the lower echelons, and by all this facilitates the further ripening and strengthening of the opposition forces.

The other lever reaching up among the leadership is the immediate pressure of the People's Opposition on middle and lower functionaries. There are great numbers of functionaries and thousands are certainly unreliable from the regime's point of view. How many of them are members of the People's Opposition? We don't know but neither does the regime, and this uncertainty is a great headache for the regime. Careerists who still remain loyal to the regime are confused by the helplessness of the party and the regime, because they can see that both party and regime are unable to solve their problems. They are confused by the zigzags in the party's line. They hear of the factional struggles rocking the party's leadership, and they worry about what will happen if this or that faction prevails. What will happen? A purge.

On top of all this, the functionaries are exposed to direct popular pressure and they are exposed to it all the time. Zapotocky and Siroky are in a more favorable situation. They are well-cushioned against the possibilities that some citizen may reach them with his complaints and dissatisfactions. The people see them only from the speaker's platform and over the heads of the police line. The activist in the workshop and employee of the bulk-purchasing apparatus in the village are much worse off. They hear much more of the dissatisfaction and they have no SNB members to shield them from the hatred of their neighbors and co-workers. In this way a feeling of solidarity between workers and members of the people's militia arises, or between members of the National Committees and their village neighbors. The regime knows about it, complains of "lukewarm" functionaries, of the "susceptibility to elemental moods," of their "endeavors to be popular with everybody." But it does not know any cure for these things.

True, all this would not amount to much as long as it remained only a matter of individual examples. Each component of the opposition forces would be weak and ineffective were there not whole battalions of them operating all over the country and in all walks of life. The strength of the People's Opposition is in its numbers and in its anonymity, and the value of the actions undertaken by its members is in the sum total of these actions. An individual cannot visualize the sum total: he sees only what goes on around him. But the party bosses at the Powder Tower see the totals before their eyes when their subordinates put before them the statistical data about coal output, labor time lost, unfulfilled deliveries. Then they get reports on the mood of the people, they see that the People's Opposition is no mere slogan. They realize that even pinpricks can kill, if there are millions of them.

The forces and methods of the People's Opposition will not remove the regime with one stroke, but each blow prepares the ground for the blow which will be the last.

Conclusion

We cannot persuade the free world to guarantee us a date on the calendar when the situation will be ripe for the regime's fall. We cannot predict when, under our pressure and under the pressure of the West, the change will take place which will put an end to the present untenable state of affairs. We can, however, do something to speed up the arrival of that date by strengthening and deepening our opposition. In modern times not only people, but problems move faster. In the Middle Ages it took several centuries to solve any of the substantial problems facing mankind. After the French Revolution a hundred years was enough. After World War I, the black horror precipitated by Fascism matured and was overcome within decades. Since World War II, the pace of history has been speeded up even further, and where not so long ago, people thought in terms of decades, today they think in terms of mere years.

We cannot command western strategy and organize the forces of the West, but on our Czechoslovak home front we ourselves and no one else are the decisive factor. This is *our* sector of the battle line. On this front we fight our own battles and do so without regard to whether the diplomats in the outside world are for the moment exchanging smiles or frowns. Cold war tactics may be as variable as April weather, but the basic nature, strategy, and aims remain unchanged. They remain unchanged for the free world and they haven't changed for us.

Much *has* changed in our country and around us during the last few years, and much will change still. We will need patience and coldbloodedness, a great deal of common sense, and a great deal of courage. We will not wait for instructions and commands, which no one from outside can give us. We will go on, each in his own way and each in his own place, with the steadfast opposition of decent people to a hateful and oppressive regime. And this People's Opposition cannot be stifled or invalidated by the regime. It is here to stay until that time when the opposition of the people becomes the government of the people.

Notes

Introduction

[1] See Harold D. Lasswell, "Psychological Policy Research and Total Strategy," *Public Opinion Quarterly*, vol. 16, no. 4 (Winter 1952–53), pp. 491–500, and Daniel Lerner, *Sykewar: Psychological Warfare against Germany, D-Day to VE-Day* (New York, 1949).

[2] Free Europe Committee, Inc., *President's Report for the Year 1954*, p. 3.

[3] W. Philips Davison and Alexander L. George, "An Outline for the Study of International Political Communications," *Public Opinion Quarterly*, vol. 16, no. 4 (Winter 1952–53), p. 508.

[4] This formula is well known in propaganda research. "As developed in the past few years, the scientific study of communication centers around the four successive phases of any act of communication: In what channels do communications take place? Who communicates? What is communicated? Who is affected by the communication, and how?" B. L. Smith, H. D. Lasswell, and R. D. Casey, *Propaganda, Communication and Public Opinion: A Comprehensive Reference Guide* (Princeton, 1946), p. 3. "Control, content, audience, and effect analysis can be considered as answers to the four-pronged question: 'Who is saying what to whom, and with what effect in the mass media?'" Paul F. Lazarsfeld, "Audience Research in the Movie Field," *Annals of the American Academy of Political and Social Science* (Nov. 1947), p. 160. Daniel Lerner's study of "psychological warfare" in Europe during World War II is organized around this formula. (See note 1 above for complete citation.)

[5] See Bernard Berelson, *Content Analysis in Communications Research* (Glencoe, Ill., 1952).

[6] Marie Jahoda and Joseph T. Klapper, "From Social Bookkeeping to Social Research," *Public Opinion Quarterly*, vol. 16, no. 4 (Winter 1952–53), pp. 623–30.

[7] Davison and George, *op. cit.*, p. 502.

[8] *Department of State Bulletin*, vol. XXX, no. 780 (June 7, 1954), p. 881.

[9] *Department of State Bulletin*, vol. XXXII, no. 810 (Jan. 3, 1955), pp. 14–15. Emphasis added.

Chapter 1. The Origins of Radio Free Europe

[1] The name of the organization has been changed twice; first to the National Committee for a Free Europe and later to the Free Europe Committee—the name used throughout this study.

[2] Letter from Joseph C. Grew to George Kennan, Oct. 28, 1954.

[3] Letter from George Kennan to Joseph C. Grew, Nov. 4, 1954.

[4] Letter from Joseph C. Grew to George Kennan, Oct. 28, 1954.

[5] Joseph C. Grew, "Chronicle of the Free Europe Committee" (typescript, n.d.), p. 2.

[6] Joseph C. Grew in interview, Nov. 12, 1955.

[7] Joseph C. Grew, "Chronicle of the Free Europe Committee" (typescript, n.d.), p. 3.

Notes

[8] In addition to Mr. Grew and Mr. Poole, the original Committee consisted of Frank Altschul, Hamilton Fish Armstrong, A. A. Berle, Jr., Francis Biddle, Robert Woods Bliss, James B. Carey, Hugh A. Drum, Allen W. Dulles, Dwight D. Eisenhower, Mark F. Ethridge, William Green, Charles R. Hook, Arthur Bliss Lane, Henry R. Luce, Arthur W. Page, Charles M. Spofford, Charles P. Taft, DeWitt Wallace, Matthew Woll, James A. Farley.

[9] National Committee for a Free Europe, Inc., "Portion of Introductory Statement to the Press by Joseph C. Grew," June 1, 1949 (mimeographed), pp. 1–2.

[10] *Ibid.*, p. 2.

[11] *Ibid.*, p. 3. Already at this early stage the program began to expand beyond what Mr. Kennan had envisioned just a few months before. Thinking back on these events after five years, he recalls that he had conceived of a private organization dealing with exiles and refugees from the captive countries that would take the form and perform the functions of the East European Fund, which was later established under his direction to deal with Russian refugees. This organization has helped refugees and exiles from the Soviet Union find suitable employment, has supplied them with psychological and physical comfort, and has helped a non-Bolshevik press to publish pertinent work on the Soviet Union, much of which had to be translated from the Russian. It has never carried on any work outside our shores, nor has it been in any sense an instrument of "psychological warfare." (George Kennan in interview, Nov. 28, 1955.)

[12] National Committee for a Free Europe, Inc., "Portion of Introductory Statement to the Press by Joseph C. Grew," June 1, 1949 (mimeographed), pp. 3–4. The four immediate goals of the Committee were presented in abbreviated form in a formal press release: ". . . the Committee will assist these leaders (1) to maintain themselves in useful occupation during their enforced stay in the United States; (2) to come to know the people of the United States and to understand their spirit and aims; (3) to engage in efforts by radio, press and other means to keep alive in their fellow citizens in Europe the ideals of individual and national freedom; (4) to establish effective means of cooperation with like-minded European leaders in the United States, and to coordinate their plans with those of similar leaders abroad."

[13] National Committee for a Free Europe, Inc., "Portion of Introductory Statement to the Press by Joseph C. Grew," June 1, 1949 (mimeographed), pp. 1–2.

[14] These divisions, projects, and programs of the Free Europe Committee have undergone a number of changes in the past six years. The details are not important to this study, but the interested reader can trace them in the annual *President's Reports* of the Free Europe Committee. However, a word should be said about the Crusade for Freedom. This was originally established as a division of the Free Europe Committee to carry on its public relations and conduct a national campaign for funds. In October of 1950 it was incorporated as a separate organization. In 1953 it was felt that the Crusade could better carry on its work if it was associated with the American Heritage Foundation. This relationship was maintained until July 2, 1955, when the Crusade again became independent.

[15] The goals of Radio Free Europe will be treated in detail in Chapter 2.

[16] Lucius D. Clay, "Origins of Radio Free Europe and Crusade for Freedom" (mimeographed, n.d.), p. 2.

[17] *Ibid.*

[18] National Committee for a Free Europe, Inc., *President's Report for the Year 1952*, Jan. 1953, pp. 3–4.

[19] John Dunning in interview, Nov. 1, 1955.

[20] Free Europe Committee, Inc., *President's Report for the Year 1954*, n.d., pp. 4–5.

Chapter 2. Basic Purposes and Policies

[1] The pattern of Communist takeover is well documented. See, for example, Dana A. Schmidt, *The Anatomy of a Satellite* (Boston, 1952).

² For a discussion of the Soviet propaganda apparatus and the social purposes of propaganda in the Soviet system, see Alex Inkeles, *Public Opinion in Soviet Russia, A Study in Mass Persuasion* (Cambridge, Mass., 1950). Some very interesting speculation on the social function of terror in the Soviet Union is contained in Barrington Moore, *Terror and Progress USSR* (Cambridge, Mass., 1954).

³ The term "policy" will be used throughout this study to refer to the basic goals of an organization plus the strategies that have been developed to reach these goals.

⁴ *Radio Free Europe Policy Handbook* (unpaginated, n.d.).

⁵ Memo from W. J. C. Egan to RFE Personnel Concerned, March 27, 1957, p. 2.

⁶ *Radio Free Europe Policy Handbook.*

⁷ Summary of Accomplishments and Findings, RFE Staff Conference, Jan. 3–5, 1957, p. 1.

⁸ Memo from W. J. C. Egan to RFE Personnel Concerned, March 27, 1957, p. 2.

⁹ *Radio Free Europe Policy Handbook.* This post-liberation policy of RFE has two important corollaries. First, RFE does not take sides in any of the territorial disputes which are latent in eastern Europe. If one supports a United Europe, these issues are meaningless, because all countries will become part of one large nation. Secondly, the position that certain peoples have "eternal enemies" among other peoples is not tolerated. There is no place on any of RFE's programs for the idea that the Poles and the Germans and the Hungarians and the Russians will be enemies for all time.

¹⁰ Special Guidance for Broadcasts on Liberation, Sept. 2, 1952.

¹¹ Special Guidance No. 20 (July 8, 1954), p. 1. It is interesting to compare the statement here with that found in Lerner, *op. cit.*, p. 26.

¹² *Ibid.*, p. 198.

¹³ For most of the exiles, but particularly the Czechs and the Poles, Munich is such an unattractive environment that, almost in a physical sense, one can say that a "little Poland" or a "little Czechoslovakia" is a reality. Many of the exiles had wartime experiences that understandably cannot be forgotten, and want to have no contacts with the Germans.

¹⁴ Interview with R. S. Nathan, Nov. 17, 1955.

Chapter 3. Organization, Personnel, and Setting

¹ Before the New York Director took an active part in developing propaganda policy, guidances went directly from their originator in New York to the political adviser in Munich along what might be called a "technical chain of command."

² Interview with R. S. Nathan, Nov. 17, 1955.

³ R. S. Snyder, H. W. Bruck, and B. Sapin, *Decision-Making as an Approach to the Study of International Politics*, Foreign Policy Analysis Project: Foreign Policy Analysis Series No. 3 (Organizational Behavior Section, Princeton University, June 1954), p. 72.

⁴ The biographical sketch of Mr. Bell was prepared by him especially for this study. Hence the use of the first person singular. The other sketches were prepared primarily for other purposes and use the third person singular.

⁵ Mr. Michie retired from RFE on Aug. 1, 1957.

⁶ Jiri Broada, "A Close-up View of Radio Free Europe," *Facts Forum News*, Vol. v, No. 1 (Jan. 1956), p. 11. This was the first of three articles attacking RFE, published in consecutive issues.

⁷ It is interesting that some of the right-wing American criticisms of RFE seem to mimic the *Sudetendeutsch* line.

⁸ *Welt Am Sonntag*, March 29, 1953.

⁹ *Ibid.*

¹⁰ Quoted in the *Heilbronner Stimme*, Jan. 16, 1953.

¹¹ *Welt Am Sonntag*, March 29, 1953.

Notes

Chapter 4. Policy Formulation and Programing

[1] In Central Production we also find such centralized facilities as the Tape Library and the Music Library, which serve all the desks.

[2] The rapid growth of RFE-Munich could have contributed greatly to the housing problem in war-torn Munich. In 1951 RFE approached several large German insurance companies, explained to them the American practice of insurance companies building housing projects, and asked if they would be interested in such a project financed by the Free Europe Committee. Most of RFE's non-German personnel are housed in such apartments today.

[3] See "1956 Program Concept for the Voice of Free Poland" (mimeographed, n.d.).

[4] *Ibid.*, p. 5.

[5] *Ibid.*, p. 6.

[6] *Ibid.*, p. 8.

Chapter 5. The Voices of Radio Free Europe

[1] Of course some writers "voice" their own commentaries while others, who are formally in the production section, write their own shows as well as produce and act in them.

[2] Each desk differs slightly in this regard. The Hungarian desk, for instance, has a program editor and two group editors who occupy positions between the desk chief and the senior editors. For purposes of generalization these are included in the discussion of senior editor-writers. It must be remembered that the desks are going to differ because (a) of the different skills available; (b) the desk chiefs differ in their approach to the managerial function; (c) unique problems are involved because of the differing natures of the targets.

[3] The operation of the Central Newsroom will be examined in the following chapter.

[4] No English translation of this script written in New York is available.

[5] "Polish Target No. 9—Campaign on Progressive Catholics," Aug. 2, 1955, p. 1.

[6] *Ibid.*, p. 1. The analysis of Lenin's position was taken largely from *Socialism and Religion*, vol. x of Lenin's works.

[7] *Ibid.*, p. 3.

[8] *Ibid.*, pp. 4–5.

[9] *Ibid.*, p. 5. (Quoting from B. Piasecki, *Zagadnienia Istotne* (Essential Problems), p. 200).

[10] *Ibid.*, p. 8.

Chapter 6. News, Information, and Research

[1] The *Hellschreiber* is little known outside of Europe. It is a simple form of facsimile machine that can perhaps be looked upon as one of the forerunners of radio teletype. It is a long-distance, slow-speed transmitting and receiving system that can be used on short, medium, and long wave. In use, the *Hellschreiber* is connected in place of the loud-speaker to the output of a communications receiver. Special signals activate the reproducing head located in the recorder unit. Narrow paper tape passes between the head and a rotating inked drum. Various combinations of pulses produce printed letters on the moving tape. Thus, complete words are spelled out along the length of the paper strip.

[2] In addition to providing the technical facilities for monitoring, the Schleissheim station receives the daily hour and a half of feature material from New York and sends it in to Munich where it is recorded for later broadcast. It also receives Morse code radio telegraph signals from RARET, Lisbon, with cue instructions to the RFE relay transmitters in Germany. The wave length of these transmitters is then adjusted to avoid "jamming" and to ensure optimum propagation conditions. These signals are sent over telephone lines to a radio dispatcher at the RFE transmitters. This whole problem of the Lisbon relay will be discussed below.

[3] AP and UP will not sell their services to RFE because they regard it as a "propaganda agency."

[4] The teletype copy is received with a carbon backing so that up to 100 duplicates can be made directly from the original.

[5] This organizational structure is partially due to circumstances. Before the present building was completed, the evaluation units were in a separate building from the program desks. But the editors needed access to material much faster than was possible if they went to another building. Thus there developed as an integral part of programing the research and library service. After the present building was occupied, the research and library service was brought into the evaluation section but retained much of its internal structure as well as its chief.

[6] Martha Schmidt in interview, Jan. 20, 1956.

Chapter 7. Breaking Through the Jammers

[1] These figures become more meaningful to the layman when it is pointed out that the largest broadcast transmitter in the United States is 50 kw.

[2] Diversity receivers (containing up to 302 radio tubes) are used to pick up the relay in Lisbon. Each receiver is connected to independent antennas located in different places. The set automatically chooses the one which is receiving the best signal.

[3] In the thirties, however, the Austrian government undertook to disrupt German broadcasts directed against the Dollfuss administration.

[4] Edward W. Barrett, *Truth Is Our Weapon* (New York, 1953), p. 166.

[5] *Ibid.*, p. 167.

[6] "Jamming: The Retort Discourteous" (dittoed, n.d.), p. 2.

[7] *Ibid.*, p. 2.

[8] The angle of incidence, in turn, is determined by the antenna design and to some extent by the wave length used.

[9] "Jamming: The Retort Discourteous," *op. cit.*, p. 2.

[10] RFE engineer in interview, April 24, 1956.

[11] *Ibid.*

[12] Within the practical technical limits of construction, it is possible to increase the amount of signal available to the listener. Power, however, has to be doubled or quadrupled for effective increase. Increasing a 50,000 watt transmitter to 75,000 watts would thus not be efficient, whereas an increase to 100,000 watts would be a minimum required to make the effort worthwhile, and a tangible increase would be up to 250,000 or 500,000 watts. In technical jargon this is seven decibels. (Three decibels represent perceptible power doubling.) Short-wave transmitters of 250,000 to 500,000 watts would produce usable short-wave programs under almost all conditions of interference and jamming. (RFE engineer in interview, April 24, 1956.)

Chapter 8. The Effectiveness of Radio Free Europe

[1] Davison and George, *op. cit.*, pp. 509–10.

[2] "RFE is such a large and complex operation no practicable outside machinery could possibly collect all the raw material necessary for an evaluation . . ." Wilbur Schramm, "An Estimate of the Effectiveness of Radio Free Europe," Sept. 1, 1955, p. 6. (This report was apparently one of a series prepared for the Operations Coordinating Board.)

[3] Exactly what is meant by regime and audience response will be explained below.

[4] For a discussion of one of these memoranda, see Chapter 11.

[5] Robert Sorenson in interview, April 12, 1956.

[6] *Ibid.*

[7] Radio Free Europe (Munich), Audience Analysis Section, *Assessment Memoran-*

Notes

dum *No. 23, Czechoslovakia: Audience Response to Western Broadcasts and Leaflets, September, 1954–August, 1955* (Dec. 1955); *Assessment Memorandum No. 24, Hungary: Audience Response to Western Broadcasts and Leaflets, April 1954–October 1955* (March 1956); *Assessment Memorandum No. 25, Poland: Audience Response to Western Broadcasts and Leaflets, May 1955–December 1955* (March 1956). Because the report on Poland covers a shorter period of time, certain additional material will be introduced from *Assessment Memorandum No. 17, Poland: Audience Response to RFE—Voice of Free Poland, April 1954–April 1955* (Oct. 1955). In the future references these sources will be cited only by number and country. These reports were the most recent available at the time this study was prepared.

[8] At regular intervals RFE's stations broadcast a list of cover addresses in various cities in western Europe to which listeners can write letters. These letters and the writers will be discussed in detail below.

[9] The geographical origin of the interviewee is that place where he either listened to western radio or heard about its existence. This is good evidence to indicate that word of RFE penetrated into the Soviet Union. For instance, a Pole recently repatriated from the Soviet Union who subsequently fled to the West reported that he heard of RFE's campaign to secure the release of Polish prisoners while in a forced labor camp near Karagenda (in Kazakstan). He even remembered passages from relevant programs, although it was not determined whether or not he heard these passages while still in the camp or picked them up after returning to Poland.

[10] All of the above information on interview sources was taken from *No. 25, Poland,* pp. i–ii.

[11] *Ibid.,* pp. iii–iv.

[12] *No. 23, Czechoslovakia,* pp. i–ii.

[13] *Ibid.,* p. iv.

[14] *Ibid.,* p. ii.

[15] It is of interest, however, that letters arrived from all parts of the country suggesting that RFE is received in all corners of the land. It might also be of passing interest that of the 93 letters, 35 were requests for medical advice or medicine, including one telegram direct from a hospital.

[16] *No. 24, Hungary,* pp. i, iv.

[17] *Ibid.,* p. ii.

[18] See, for example, Joseph T. Klapper and Leo Lowenthal, "Opinion Research and Psychological Warfare," *Public Opinion Quarterly,* vol. 15, no. 4 (Winter 1951–52), pp. 651–62.

[19] Richard C. Sheldon and John Dutkowski, "Are Soviet Satellite Refugee Interviews Projectable?" *Public Opinion Quarterly,* vol. 16, no. 4 (Winter 1952–53), pp. 579–94. See also Siegfried Kracauer and Paul. L. Berkman, *Satellite Mentality* (New York, 1956), Chapter I.

[20] Sheldon and Dutkowski, *op. cit.,* p. 593.

[21] *Ibid.,* p. 588.

[22] It is interesting and encouraging to note that in the few instances where RFE has received interview reports from VOA or the BBC they do not differ significantly from those RFE's own correspondents have written on the basis of interviews with the same individuals. See *No. 23, Czechoslovakia,* p. i.

[23] *No. 17, Poland,* p. vi. Although these statements were written specifically in regard to Poland, they are applicable to all of RFE's target countries.

[24] *Ibid.,* p. vi.

[25] *No. 23, Czechoslovakia,* pp. 4–5; *No. 24, Hungary,* p. 4; *No. 25, Poland,* pp. 4–7.

[26] *Ibid.*

[27] *No. 23, Czechoslovakia,* pp. 4–5; *No. 24, Hungary,* p. 4; *No. 25, Poland,* p. 5.

[28] *No. 24, Hungary,* p. 5.

[29] *No. 23, Czechoslovakia,* p. 5.

[30] *No. 23, Czechoslovakia*, p. 8; *No. 24, Hungary*, pp. 9–10; *No. 25, Poland*, pp. 5, 12–13.

[31] *No. 23, Czechoslovakia*, pp. 5–6; *No. 24, Hungary*, pp. 5–6; *No. 25, Poland*, p. 6.

[32] This is not to say that everyone who favors the BBC is critical of RFE. Nor is the BBC free from criticism. Some sources, even representatives of the intelligentsia, are annoyed by its "cold tone" and its refusal to "call a spade a spade." *Ibid.* Even its celebrated objectivity is sometimes questioned.

[33] *Ibid.* When RFE first went on the air, it was over-optimistic and might even have been labeled a "prophet of an early liberation." There is little doubt but that it has disappointed many of its early listeners. But this author feels that the days of easy optimism are past. See Appendix (How Long Will This Go On?) for a leaflet quite typical of RFE's general "propaganda line" in early 1956. That "line" can hardly be accused of raising false hopes for any "early liberation."

[34] See Raymond Bauer and Daniel Gleicher, "Word of Mouth Communication in the Soviet Union," *Research Memorandum No. 15*, Air Research and Development Command, Human Resources Research Institute (Maxwell Air Force Base, Alabama; Aug. 1953) for a discussion of the different roles word-of-mouth communication plays among different classes in a Communist state.

[35] *No. 23, Czechoslovakia*, p. 9; *No. 24, Hungary*, p. 12; *No. 25, Poland*, p. 15.

[36] *Ibid.* Many sources report that RFE's important news items and other information are rapidly disseminated around the countryside and are made known to those who have no radios. However, this may not be an altogether unmixed blessing. Inaccuracies creep rapidly into word-of-mouth disseminated information while the source may remain clearly identified. There is evidence that some of the complaints about RFE's inaccuracies came from people with no firsthand access to programs.

[37] *No. 23, Czechoslovakia*, p. 9; *No. 24, Hungary*, pp. 12–13; *No. 25, Poland*, p. 15.

[38] *No. 25, Poland*, p. 4. This, of course, was written before Gomulka came to power in October 1956.

[39] The Hungarian uprising in 1956 perhaps affected this kind of appeal. This point will be discussed in Chapter 11 below.

[40] *No. 23, Czechoslovakia*, p. 10; see also *No. 24, Hungary*, pp. 13–14, and *No. 25, Poland*, pp. 16–17.

[41] *No. 25, Poland*, pp. 17–18; see also *No. 23, Czechoslovakia*, p. 10, and *No. 24, Hungary*, p. 14.

[42] Radio Free Europe, "Effectiveness of Radio Free Europe" (New York, n.d.), p. 6.

[43] For example, "How many of us would be able, in open contest to overcome the arguments of our enemies who speak to a certain portion of our public over 'Free Europe'? We could only throw about such cheap slogans as 'slave of imperialism' and 'paid agent.'" *No. 19, Poland: Regime Press and Radio Response to Western Broadcasts, May–August 1955* (Oct. 1955), p. 2. (Quoted from the literary review *Zycie Literackie*, Jan. 23, 1955.)

[44] There are perhaps a number of reasons for this, but the most likely hypothesis is that the exile politician has played almost no role in the history of Hungarian politics in contrast to the situation in Czechoslovakia and Poland. The only two well-known Hungarian political emigrations, one in the nineteenth century led by Lajos Kossuth after the failure of the war for independence in 1848–49 and the other at the end of the seventeenth century led by Ferenc Rakoczi, never returned to the homeland. Contrast this with the recent history of Czechoslovakia and, to a lesser degree, with Poland. The Czech regime cannot ignore the political impact of the exile; historically he has been too prominent. The Hungarian people, on the other hand, are not aware of the positive role the exile can play, and therefore the regime does not have to be as concerned. It is interesting in this regard that a great number of the Czech attacks against RFE take the form of attacks against the exiles.

[45] *No. 16, Czechoslovakia: Regime Press and Radio Response to Western Broadcasts and Leaflets, January–April 1955* (Sept. 1955), pp. 3, 11, 13.

[46] Radio Free Europe, "Effectiveness of Radio Free Europe," p. 10. Continual attacks against RFE could be a dangerous course of action for the regime, for they certainly have increased RFE's reputation for power among the people.

[47] *Kronika* (Lodz), Jan. 16–31, 1956, p. 1. The author is indebted to Mr. Jan Novak, chief of the Polish desk, for bringing these two articles to his attention and for providing translations.

[48] *Tygodnik Powszechny*, Jan. 29, 1956.

[49] *Ibid.*

[50] Herman Field was arrested and subsequently imprisoned in 1949 while looking for his brother Noel Field behind the Iron Curtain.

[51] Quoted in *No. 9, Poland: Regime Press and Radio Response to Western Broadcasts, September–December 1954* (March 1955), p. 22.

[52] *Ibid.*

[53] *Ibid.*, pp. 23–24. A fifth hypothesis related directly to the question of how one interprets regime attacks on RFE. During the whole Swiatlo period RFE was attacked only six times on matters directly relating to Swiatlo. In only two of these was RFE mentioned by name. This would seem to indicate that the *number* of regime attacks on a given subject may bear little relationship to the degree to which the regime is hurt by western broadcasts. *Ibid.*, pp. 24–25. Regardless of whether or not RFE's broadcasts played any important role in the changes in Poland in late 1953 and 1954, the people of Poland apparently feel that RFE forced the regime to act. This, in the long run, could be the most significant result of the broadcasts. They increased tremendously RFE's reputation for power. Reorganization of the hated (and feared) UB, the reshuffle of the official staffs, the removal of officials, a general undermining of UB authority—all are attributed to the Swiatlo broadcasts. Many people who were released from prison at that time believe firmly that the action was primarily due to the Swiatlo broadcasts. A Polish source on vacation in the West reported that it was only because of the broadcasts that he was able to get a passport. The general opinion seems well summed up by two interview sources who said in effect, "The best argument for RFE is the changes that took place in Poland after the Swiatlo revelations. They convinced the people of the power of the free radio which successfully caused certain improvements in conditions in Poland." See *No. 25, Poland*, pp. 19–20. The important thing is not that those opinions are right or wrong, but that right or wrong the Poles themselves are strongly convinced the RFE forced the regime to act.

[54] See International Research Associates, Inc., *Hungary and the 1956 Uprising* (New York, Feb. 1957).

[55] *Ibid.*, p. iii. Emphasis in original.

[56] *Ibid.* See Marginal Tables, question 26. This section of the report is not paginated.

[57] *Ibid.*, questions 27 and 28.

[58] *Ibid.*, questions 33 and 33a.

[59] *Ibid.*, p. 8.

[60] *Ibid.*

[61] *Ibid.*, p. 8.

Chapter 9. Operations from the Berlin to the Poznan Riots

[1] "Czechoslovakia—Guidance No. 10," June 30, 1953.

[2] *Ibid.*, pp. 4, 8.

[3] *Ibid.*, p. 5.

[4] *Ibid.*, pp. 5–6.

[5] *Ibid.*, pp. 9–10.

[6] *Ibid.*, p. 10. This is one of the few instances in which RFE supports defection.

[7] *Ibid.*, pp. 6–7.

[8] Czechoslovak Guidance No. 13: The 1954 Czechoslovak Electoral Campaigns," Jan. 25, 1954, p. 4.

[9] *Ibid.*, pp. 4, 7.

[10] *Ibid.*

[11] One of the reasons why RFE felt it could assume the role of the voice of the opposition was that it was much better informed about events in Czechoslovakia than all but a handful of people inside Czechoslovakia.

[12] "Operation VETO (Phase One)," May 1954, pp. 2–3.

[13] "VETO: People's Opposition Campaign (Phase Two)," May 17, 1956, pp. 1, 3.

[14] *Ibid.*, p. 2.

[15] The author is indebted to the Czechoslovak desk at RFE-Munich for calling his attention to this regime response and for providing translations.

[16] "CS Target No. 17: For Our Campaign Re National Harvest of Self-Defense," June 30, 1954. For a more detailed discussion of this aspect of VETO, see also "Operation VETO," *News from behind the Iron Curtain*, vol. 3, no. 10 (Oct. 1954), pp. 16–22.

[17] "CS Target No. 18: Target for Our August Broadcasts," July 28, 1954.

[18] "Operation VETO," *News from behind the Iron Curtain*, vol. 3, no. 10 (Oct. 1954), p. 19. The Tesla quote is translated from *Prace*, July 3, 1954.

[19] *Ibid.* Quoted from *Prace*, July 6, 1954.

[20] "CS Guidance No. 14: Guidance and the Autumn Elections," Sept. 15, 1954, p. 8.

[21] *Ibid.*, p. 9.

[22] *Ibid.*, p. 3.

[23] *Ibid.*, p. 3.

[24] "Hungarian Guidance No. 15: Operation FOCUS," Sept. 8, 1954. See also Free Europe Committee, Inc., *President's Report for the Year 1954* (n.d.), pp. 14–15.

[25] *New York Times*, June 3, 1955, p. 3.

[26] The official position of the United States appears to be contained in a statement Secretary Dulles made to reporters at Brioni on November 6, 1955. The Secretary said that Marshal Tito and he had discussed the "problem of the States in Eastern Europe and were in common accord in recognizing the importance of the independence of those states, non-interference from outside in their internal affairs, and the right to settle the social and economic order in ways of their own choice." *New York Times*, Nov. 7, 1955, p. 7.

[27] *New York Times*, Aug. 25, 1955, p. 10.

[28] RFE Guidance, "Geneva, Belgrade and the Captive Nations," Aug. 15, 1955.

[29] Z. Jordan, "Debates on Culture during the 'Thaw'" (RFE-Munich working paper). Emphasis added.

[30] *Ibid.*, p. 8.

[31] Although these debates on culture went further and continued longer in Poland than in the other satellites, there was a "revolt" of writers in Hungary in late 1955 and early 1956 that revolved generally around similar issues and which RFE exploited in its broadcasts to that captive country.

[32] Special Guidance No. 26, "Twentieth Congress CPSU," March 27, 1956, pp. 9–10.

[33] See Special Guidance No. 26 (part 2), "Twentieth Congress CPSU," April 7, 1956, pp. 1–13.

Chapter 10. The Uprisings in Poland and Hungary

[1] See the *New York Times*, March 29, 1956, p. 10, for excerpts from this editorial on Stalinism and its abuses.

[2] It is interesting in this regard to point out that there had been rumors of Gomulka's release from prison almost a year before the Twentieth Party Congress, but

that even after the Rajk trial his name was not completely cleared. In fact, he was accused once more of having advocated "reformist moderation in collectivization and industrialization." See *News from behind the Iron Curtain*, vol. 5, no. 5 (May 1956), pp. 4, 11–12.

[3] *Ibid.*, p. 45.

[4] See *News from behind the Iron Curtain*, vol. 5, no. 6 (June 1956), p. 9, for a translation of an article from *Przealad Kulturalny*.

[5] *Ibid.*, pp. 5, 8.

[6] July 8, 1956, p. E-1.

[7] See New York *Herald Tribune*, Nov. 6, 1956, p. 18.

[8] Special Program, Nov. 9, 1956.

[9] "From Our Point of View," Nov. 4, 1956.

[10] At this time it was not certain whether or not Nagy was involved in the decision to call in Soviet troops. A later report over Radio Budapest on October 31 said that during this period Nagy was a virtual prisoner of the AVH and broadcast his appeals with a pistol at his head.

[11] Special Short: "Calling the Communist Party," Oct. 26, 1956.

[12] Special commentary G-4, Nov. 2, 1956.

[13] Apparently this service was desired by the Hungarians themselves. On October 27 RFE personnel in Austria were contacted by courier from one of the provincial freedom stations in Hungary, asking that RFE rebroadcast its programs because the station was too weak to be heard over a wide area, particularly in Budapest.

[14] An interesting account of the conferences between the Hungarians and Soviets is contained in Leslie Balogh, "Witness Tells How Soviet Dictated to Budapest Rebels," Washington *Evening Star*, Oct. 31, 1956, p. A-18. According to this account, which the writer reports was told him by a high Hungarian official present, Mikoyan and Suslov "flew into a rage" at Gero for panicking and calling in Russian troops. When they told him to resign his position as first secretary, he protested that he was needed to hold the party together and Mikoyan shouted, "The party already has fallen apart, thanks to your incredible blunders."

[15] However, there is some evidence to indicate that at the time it was made, the Russians had indeed decided to withdraw from Hungary. See Garthoff, cited below.

[16] Quoted in Raymond Garthoff, "The Tragedy of Hungary," *Problems of Communism*, vol. VI, no. 1 (Jan.–Feb. 1957), p. 8.

[17] Short Commentary H-5, Nov. 3, 1956.

[18] *Freies Wort*, Nov. 9, 1956.

[19] This charge was never as prominent in American papers as it was in German. See, for example, the *Passaurer Neue Presse* (Passau), Nov. 13, 1956, and the *Neue Rhein Zeitung* (Cologne), Nov. 8, 1956.

[20] Special Short: "World Press No. 1," Nov. 4, 1956. The quotes from the *Observer* are in the form they appear in RFE's translation of the Hungarian script. Obviously, the retranslation into English is not identical to the original English version.

[21] See the *New York Times*, Nov. 30, 1956. It is interesting that although this press conference was widely reported, a later interview in Copenhagen in which she retracted her strong words against RFE received almost no coverage. See *Die Zeit* (Hamburg), Dec. 6, 1956, which to this author's knowledge was the only German paper to carry an account of the second conference.

[22] "Our Propaganda in Hungary," *New Republic*, vol. 135, no. 25 (Dec. 1956).

[23] International Research Associates, *op. cit.*, questions 3–5, 8. However, indirectly, western radio did play its part. Forty per cent of the people in the IRA sample said that the example of Poland was the most important reason why the Hungarians were willing to attempt a revolution. If 84 per cent also relied most heavily on foreign radio for news of events outside Hungary, one can argue that western radio was a factor in supplying news about the event that was most responsible for the Hungarian uprising.

Chapter 11. A Nonofficial Instrument of American Foreign Policy

[1] This, of course, is looking at RFE from the American point of view. A democratic Pole or Czech or Hungarian in exile could evaluate the organization as an instrument of their people in exile in the West.

[2] Personal letter from Edward L. Bernays, Sept. 20, 1956.

[3] Lloyd Free in interview, Sept. 13, 1956, and Edward W. Barrett in interview, June 13, 1956.

[4] Lloyd Free in interview, Sept. 13, 1956.

[5] *Ibid.*

[6] Barrett, *Truth Is Our Weapon,* pp. 250–59.

[7] *Ibid.,* p. 114.

[8] *Ibid.,* pp. 234–56.

[9] *Ibid.,* p. 114.

[10] C. L. Sulzberger, "What's Wrong with American Propaganda," *New York Times,* May 14, 1956, p. 24.

[11] See for example, Audience Analysis Section, *Assessment Memorandum No. 27: Poland: Attitudes of Polish People Towards the Communist Regime, October 1954, September 1955* (April 1956). This memorandum analyzes in detail the major complaints the Poles have against their government as well as the government action that has received rather widespread support.

[12] Hugh Seton-Watson in interview, April 13, 1956.

[13] Sulzberger, *loc. cit.*

[14] International Research Associates, *op. cit.,* pp. 8–9.

[15] See Raymond Bauer and Daniel Gleicher, "Word of Mouth Communication in the Soviet Union," Research Memorandum No. 15, Air Research and Development Command, Human Resources Research Institute (Maxwell Air Force Base, Alabama; Aug. 1953).

[16] Harrison Salisbury, "Czech Youths Press Demands on Regime," *New York Times,* June 14, 1956.

[17] These interviews with men who must remain anonymous were conducted in June 1956.

[18] James A. Michener, *The Bridge at Andau* (New York, 1957), pp. 250–53.

[19] Raymond L. Garthoff, "The Tragedy of Hungary," *Problems of Communism,* vol. VI, no. 1, pp. 4–11.

[20] Personal letter dated Sept. 21, 1956. Among the momentary advantages that Doob recognizes are the following: (a) a private agency presumably does not have to clear all or any of its policies with government; (b) it is not dependent upon congressional committees for appropriations; (c) it can hire as technicians foreign nationals who could not clear our own security regulations; (d) in theory, at least, it can make statements, directly or otherwise, which have no connection with government; hence our officials can disown them or at least not be embarrassed by them; (e) it does not have to conform to civil service regulations regarding salaries, and hence *may* be able to attract more capable people.

[21] Personal letter dated Sept. 21, 1956. Doob goes on to say, "My suspicion—and I have called it just that—springs from impressions I got from government reports during the war. Then I spent some time in Germany in July of 1945. I talked informally with Germans about our broadcasts . . . they made no distinction between the VOA or BBC; for them both represented the enemy." Bernays raised a similar point: "There is one caveat, however. That is, it is generally known that Radio Free Europe is also supported by government funds. I do not know the extent to which this may be known in foreign countries or to what extent the people of foreign countries may have been made aware of this." (Personal letter dated Sept. 20, 1956.)

[22] International Research Associates, *op. cit.,* question 34 F/f.

Index

243

WHAT is Radio Free Europe? Where does it broadcast? Who runs it? What are its purposes? How good a job does it do? Although thousands of Americans are familiar with Radio Free Europe (many have contributed to its support through the Crusade for Freedom campaigns), few know enough about its background to answer these and similar questions. In this book a political scientist with first-hand knowledge gives a detailed account of the organization and development of this unique propaganda enterprise.

Radio Free Europe was established as a private broadcasting project in 1949 by the Free Europe Committee, headed by Joseph C. Grew, as part of the Committee's program of broad, long-range assistance to democratic exiles from totalitarian countries. The operational headquarters are located at